'Derek takes us through G
pausing at the significant po
to one or more of his peopl
God calls all sorts of people
the call from God is to every single one of Jesus followers. If you are still trying to work out your vocation this book is definitely for you.'

Linda Maslen, Leader, Fountains Church Bradford; New Wine Regional Director, North East and Yorkshire; Christians Together Calderdale Trustee

'With broad and insightful biblical reflection, coupled with fascinating anecdotes, Derek Walmsley's *God Calls Everyone* will help you think more deeply about your calling from God. This is a wise, helpful and lovely book.'

Matthew Porter, Vicar, St Michael le Belfrey, York, and author

'So many people are looking for something more from life, but often don't know how to hear the call of the One who made them. This book is so useful in helping us see how to find our story – our true and best life – within God's big story.'

Paul Harcourt, National Leader, New Wine England

'Are you considering God's purposes for your life? Then Derek Walmsley's readable, engaging and thoughtful book is for you. In short chapters he digs into the Bible, and offers insight after insight about what it means to walk with God and find your vocation. His searching questions chapter by chapter draw readers to reflect personally on their place in God's purposes. Top notch!'

Steve Walton, Associate Research Fellow, Trinity College, Bristol; Secretary, British New Testament Society, and author

'Often our vocation is spoken of in individualistic terms of "God's plan for my life". Derek Walmsley's excellent book, *God Calls Everyone*, helps us to see our vocation more in terms of what is my role in God's big plan, revealed in all of Scripture to transform the world through Jesus Christ. This is such a refreshing emphasis, and I therefore commend this book to you.'

David Devenish, Team Leader, Newfrontiers Together

God Calls Everyone

Finding our place in his great story

Derek Walmsley

Authentic

27 26 25 24 23 22 21 8 7 6 5 4 3 2

First published 2020 by Authentic Media Limited,
PO Box 6326, Bletchley, Milton Keynes MK1 9GG

British Library Cataloguing in Publication Data
A catalogue record for this book is available from the British Library.
ISBN: 978-1-78893-108-3
978-1-78893-109-0 (e-book)

Cover design by Warren Apit
https://sites.google.com/view/warrenport/home
Printed and bound by CPI Group (UK) Ltd, Croydon, CR0 4YY

Contents

THE NEW TESTAMENT

I've never done anything remarkable. I've never climbed a mountain or won a medal. I've never stood on a stage and been listened to, or crossed a finishing line before anyone else. When I look back, I have led quite an ordinary life. I sometimes wonder what the point of me was.

'Does God have a plan, and where does he see me fitting into it?' I asked the vicar once. He came to Cherry Tree with his leaflets, handing them around and trying to persuade us all into being religious.

'We each have a role to play, Miss Claybourne,' he said. 'Jesus loves everyone.'

'I'm sure he does,' I said. 'But love isn't enough, is it? You need to have some kind of purpose. I was wondering what mine might have been?'

Joanna Cannon, Three Things About Elsie
(The Borough Press, 2018, p. 69)

Foreword

We're used to books on ministry. We're even more used to books on the Bible. What we don't get so often is books that reflect on ministry through the discerning lens of the Bible.

But here we are with one book that does just that. Derek Walmsley has combined the good fruits of his ministry as an experienced Director of Ordinands and Vocations with his evident love of Scripture. He looks at ministry through the many biblical narratives of both Old and New Testaments and enables the reader to place his or her calling in the context of God's evolving, truth-telling word.

It's curious that most books on ministry float above the biblical story, touching down where appropriate to make a connection, but essentially starting from ministerial practice rather than biblical revelation. If the Bible is the core material on which the church bases its life, why would we not want to see our ministries shaped by its wisdom? Derek seeks to reset the balance.

Derek writes with a light touch, deftly combining ancient wisdom with new. His cultural antennae are as sharply attuned as his reading of Scripture. He is well acquainted with the messages, memes and madness swirling around in society today. It's all grist to the mill for Derek, just as it was for the men (mostly) who kept filling papyrus after papyrus in the Bible's formation, and just as it needs to be for those who want to serve Jesus today. We too need to hold the Bible in one hand and the electronic tablet in the other.

This book is for Christians of every denomination. Anglicans like me are shaped by Scripture, Tradition and Reason, mediated through experience. But the greatest of these (or the base) is Scripture, handled with intelligence and humility. The Bible is not safe; it changes us. But neither is the Bible safe from scrutiny. It's the most complex compendium of writing anywhere, but it's not without apparent contradiction and complexity. It's not God-dictated but God-breathed. It's not for us to tame or control the Bible, but rather it's for us to enter into a conversation with God. And ultimately it's for us to be invited into life in all its fullness.

All this is reflected beautifully in Derek's book. It's for anyone who's trying to listen to God's particular call in their lives, and to discern a ministry, lay or ordained. It's a gift to the whole church, one we receive with much gratitude.

John Pritchard
Former Bishop of Oxford

Preface

What are we supposed to do with our lives? What did you want to be when you grew up? What's the Christian perspective on this? Is our life's purpose something we sort out for ourselves? What does God want us to do? Does he have a plan? Does he call each of us to one specific purpose that is ours alone? Why am I bombarding you with questions?

It would be great if I could write a simple book that answers those questions, but the answers are not simple. This isn't another guide to vocation but a book that gets you to think about what you are doing with your life by exploring what the Bible has to say to all of us about these things. We are going to work our way through the key narratives and characters of the Old Testament through the lens of the New Testament and Jesus Christ, learning what implications this has for God's calling on our lives.

The chapters that follow will not all be the same length, because each merits a different amount of attention. It would be tidy to have fifty chapters that each contain three pages, but the Bible isn't like that and it makes for false divisions in a book like this. Each chapter will say what needs to be said, however short or long that may be.

Each chapter ends with some questions for further reflection, some ideas for additional reading, and other resources.

A passion for vocation

When I was a child, I dreamt of writing books. I would not have used the word then, but it was going to be my *vocation*. Now that I have grown up (stop sniggering please, friends) I have spent a good portion of my life as a church minister and more recently as someone whose job is encouraging vocations. It has become a passion, and it has provided me with many opportunities to speak to church gatherings and to walk with individuals while they share their lives with me as we discern together what God is calling them to do.

My passion to help others explore vocation is built on a much more important foundation – Jesus Christ himself. Although I went to church from my earliest years, I actually became a Christian aged 19 and began to grasp the extraordinary love of God in Christ. Among other things, this gave me a much greater self-confidence, although underlying this is my confidence in God. It also assured me that God's love would not change, whatever I did in the past, present or future, whatever I did or didn't achieve. God would love me even if I messed it all up.

My faith is also built on the foundation of Christian Scripture. I am utterly convinced that the Bible has so much more to tell us than we ever imagine. It contains our collective calling as the human race, as the church and as individuals. So this book is an attempt to bring these passions together and to help the reader to explore their own calling. I want to help us discover how *our story is part of God's story.*

I recently saw a tweet from an American pastor called Burk Parsons. I don't know anything about him but I like his name. He wrote: 'So many are looking for special revelation from God while it sits on their shelves gathering dust.'

I've read lots of books about vocation, often specifically about calling to the 'Anglican priesthood', because that's the focus of my job. I've found that many of them don't really begin with the Bible and can be a bit 'me' centred, although one notable exception is my friend Steve Walton's excellent little paperback *A Call to Live*. This is not to be critical of those other authors; some of those books are very good. But it seems to me that we should begin with the Bible and allow it to set the agenda, rather than jumping straight into our questions. There is a danger that we begin with our existing concepts of vocation and then use them as the lens through which we read Scripture, instead of the other way round.

There's a real risk when reading the Bible. We might read it like any other book and assume that we are meant to identify with the central characters – the heroes of the stories. But there are some problems with this approach. The chief problem is that the heroes are not heroes. Except for Jesus Christ (spoiler alert: he's the real hero), we are presented with a series of individuals, and a whole nation, who failed, but God used them anyway.

Superheroes for Jesus?

Nowadays the vast superhero movie/comic-book franchise is hugely influential. I hope we recognize that the universe it portrays is full of people with extraordinary but imaginary special powers that we can't ever expect to have. If you do, seek help immediately.

This superhero mentality is a particular risk for church leaders and perhaps even more for youth leaders. I cringe now at memories of youth events where the young people were told things like: 'You are a special generation. I believe God is going to use you to change the world.' Note for speakers: Jesus has already done that. In the Great Commission at the end of Matthew's gospel Jesus declares: 'All authority in heaven and earth has been given to me; go therefore . . .' So make it about him, not you.

What I'm saying is this: we must read the Bible as God's story, not as though it's our story. The Bible is not primarily about you. It's about God, the Father, Son and Holy Spirit. It's about God's extraordinary grace and his plan for his world. We need to read it to experience God's revelation to us and to discover how our story fits in with his story.

What this book is not

Unlike my friend Steve, I am not an academic and this book makes no claim to be definitive or to have all the answers. It is not a heavy work of theology, you may be pleased to hear.

What this book is

My prayer is that this book will be an enjoyable and readable aid for anyone who is hungry to understand God's call upon their life. I'm going to unfold the grand narrative of the Bible so that we can see God's story. As we do so, we'll discover that the various stories within the story are not really simple self-contained tales with a moral message to take away. Often they are stories of human success, but nearly always with human failure too – just like our lives. These stories are an account of God's work in history, his big plan for his world. As I've already said, the point is not to make the stories about us, but to see how we fit in with what God is already doing.

Along the way, I'll be using some illustrations from my own experiences and the lives of real people, some of them famous and some of them my friends. Rarely both, you understand. Sometimes I will change the names and some incidental details to protect the innocent – and the guilty! I'm also likely to quote Tim Keller. I play his sermons in the car on long journeys. I'm a bit odd that way, but he's a great preacher and I'm an auditory learner. As I enjoy music and visiting art galleries and museums, I've also thrown in some references for those who like that kind of thing.

You are not me and you will filter what I have to say through the lens of your own experience. I'm very aware that I'm writing as a charismatic evangelical Anglican white male living in Yorkshire, England, in the early twenty-first century, which will influence what I write. It's far from perfect but I hope it will point in the right direction and help everyone who reads it. That's my prayer. Why not make it your prayer too, as you begin?

A friend said once: 'Whenever we pick up the Bible and think "That's just what I thought", we are in trouble.' We all come to Scripture within our life context and with presuppositions, but if we accept that and try to be conscious of it, it might just help. Please forgive my prejudices and check the speck in your own eye.

I probably should warn you that we'll touch on some pretty heavy themes along the way such as suffering, sex, death, and the end of the world, and there won't be space to explore them in too much depth. It will be up to you to go away and do some more work – if you want to.

I'm also writing as a Diocesan Director of Ordinands and Vocations in the Church of England, and I hope this book will be useful for anyone exploring a vocation to ordained ministry. But it's emphatically not just for those who are possibly going to become vicars. The whole point is that God Calls Everyone (the clue is in the book title) and I want everyone to consider what that means for them.

FOR REFLECTION

- What prejudices or preconceptions might you be bringing to the way you read this book?
- Pray that you will be open to the possibility that God might want to speak to you in surprising ways.

FURTHER READING

Guinness, Os. *The Call: Finding and Fulfilling the Central Purpose of Your Life* (World, 1998).

Pritchard, John. *Living Faithfully: Following Christ in Everyday Life* (SPCK, 2013).

Introduction

Misunderstanding Vocation: Some Myths

For those who have only downloaded the electronic sample of this first section, is there a simple working definition of vocation that would save you reading the rest of this book? I'm going to get to some definitions of vocation in the second part of the introduction. I know you'll do the right thing and buy the full version of this book, but first we need to debunk a few myths.

Myth 1: 'It's what makes me fulfilled'

A little while ago, our daughter and her friend flew to Thailand and spent a relaxing week in the sun on the beaches. One day, the beach-bar owner suggested she could use his music equipment and be the DJ for the evening. She loved the experience, and on social media she posted: 'Dad, I think I've found my vocation!'

She was joking, but the story provides a hint of the way society sometimes sees vocation. It can be about 'what I enjoy', 'what makes me happy' or 'what gives me value'. For some, this can boil down to 'what makes me feel good about myself'. We might use the word 'fulfilment'. It doesn't take much thought to realize that there is the potential for something quite selfish about this on occasions.

I know this sounds harsh and I am not criticizing anyone who has made sacrifices to do such amazing things. I certainly don't claim that my own career choices have been perfectly motivated. I'm just trying to get us to begin to examine our purposes and ask ourselves some tough questions.

If you think I'm being unfair, then remember the prophet Isaiah's words: 'All of us have become like one who is unclean, and all our righteous acts are like filthy rags' (Isa. 64:6). And if you think he's a bit harsh, note that a literal translation of the second half of that quote is 'all our good deeds are like a menstrual cloth'. Ouch.

Also remember that one person fulfilled his purpose perfectly and it ended in death. On a cross.

While revising this book, I went to the Maundy Thursday Chrism Eucharist in Ripon Cathedral, where hundreds of clergy and a number of lay people from Leeds Diocese were renewing their ministerial vows. Our bishop, Nick Baines, was just back from a sabbatical and we wondered what he would have to say in his sermon. What had he learned?

He began: 'Never ever take your vocation – to lay or ordained discipleship and ministry – for granted. For when you do, it will have become a private possession, a personal commodity, an exercise in vanity. The call of God is and has always been very clear: it is not primarily *for* me/us; rather, it is *to* me/us, but for the sake of the world and the church through whom the world is to be reached.'

Myth 2: 'It will take away my freedom'

If we are not careful, we can all too easily forget that for there to be *calling* there must be a *caller*. Without God, the individual becomes *both* the called and the caller. But if we give ourselves over completely to God's will, what will happen to our freedom?

It's worth remembering that our freedom is actually more restricted than we might sometimes think. While many people in the richer nations do have greater freedom than previous generations, in the end people cannot choose what life deals them. Having education, money and living in a democracy all help, but we cannot select where we are born, who our parents are, what illnesses we might face and what other people's choices might do to us.

I also suspect the benefits of freedom are overrated. Søren Kierkegaard said that freedom can provoke 'dizzying' anxiety, describing the pressure that can come when we are answerable to no one. Others have recognized how we become trapped and answerable to our career, our possessions or our need to achieve everything on our 'bucket list'.

Instead, being answerable to *God's* call is actually highly liberating, although this feels counter-intuitive. Augustine prayed: 'Your service is perfect freedom', and his prayer was so good that it's still used, over a thousand years later.

The younger son in the parable known as 'The Prodigal Son' (Luke 15:11–32) enjoyed his freedom for a while, but it could never last. Fortunately, he 'came to his senses' and returned to the comfort and responsibilities of his father's house.

Myth 3: 'Vocation is for special Christians, chosen by God, for special tasks'

As my job includes interviewing people who sense they may have a calling to ordained ministry, one problem I sometimes face is meeting those who sense they have a call to *something* but their only role model is an often narrow concept of priesthood.

The church often seems to have a hierarchy of callings, where 'Ministers, Monks and Missionaries' (to quote my friend Steve Walton) are seen as holy people and anybody else is . . . well . . . not so holy. Despite the strong protests of Martin Luther, himself a monk, five hundred years ago, we still haven't nailed this (note the obscure pun for those who know their church history). We will hear more from Luther in later chapters.

Myth 4: 'My calling is my job'

We all need to face up to the fallen nature of the world. Our paid work is often hard and does not feel 'right' but may be the only option available. We can't always earn a living doing what ignites our passions. Paul wanted to devote his time to sharing the gospel around the world, but at times he had to earn his way as a tentmaker.

For many people throughout history and even today, work has been a necessary means to survival, involving no choice on the part of the worker, with no sense of a special message from God telling us to do it. On the other hand, unpaid activity can sometimes be something God has called us to do.

The two come together in the call to love God and our neighbour. We can do a paid job in a loving way, or as a means to have enough money to lovingly provide for our family, which is itself a vocation, and we can love those around us in any context. The word 'amateur' means someone who does something for the love of it, though unfortunately nowadays the word is generally used to describe someone who doesn't do a job as well as a professional.

Myth 5: 'I'm called to only one thing'

In the modern world, people are increasingly finding themselves with several careers. There are jobs now that didn't exist ten years ago. The question 'What do you want to be when you grow up?' no longer seems appropriate. Clergy have often had very different jobs before finding themselves called to their new role. But what they did before had value too. What did Jesus do until he was 30?

I recently met England footballer Peter Crouch and we discussed the book he had written, *How to Be a Footballer*, and the book I was writing – this one. I asked him what he planned to do with himself now his footballing career was drawing to a close. He became quite restless within seconds, scratching his head furiously and saying 'I really don't know'.

This from a multimillionaire sports star who is married to a lingerie model.

Myth 6: 'It all happens right away'

Not only do most people have several jobs in their lifetime, but anyone seeking a special, significant, 'spiritual' job will find that some of the Bible examples are not too helpful. As we will see, the call of characters such as Moses, Isaiah and Paul is unique to them. They seem to have instant work to do when called, but for most of us, revelation about a particular calling will be gradual and will involve the encouragement and discernment of others. And remember, Moses' special call didn't come until he'd had a bus pass for twenty years.

FOR REFLECTION

- Have you believed any of these myths?
- How might that have affected the way you think about your life?

OTHER

You can find Bishop Nick Baines' sermon for Maundy Thursday 2019 at:

- https://nickbaines.wordpress.com/2019/04/18/maundy-thursday-and-vocation/

A Brief Definition of Vocation

What is vocation? The problem is that it's a word that has been used and misused in different ways. For our purposes in this book, before we look at the Bible story and what that means for us, here's a quick guide to Christian vocation for everyone.

God calls *everyone*

If I am asked to speak about vocation but given very little time, I usually say that I believe *God calls everyone*, not just a holy few, and that there are three main things he calls us all to:

1. God calls us all to come to him in Christ, following him as a disciple (see for example Rom. 1:6). Nearly all uses of the word 'call' in the New Testament refer to this meaning of calling.
2. God calls us all to membership of his people the church.
3. God calls us all to serve the world.

If you need an even simpler summary, we are talking about a call to worship, community and mission. Churches or individuals that overemphasize or underemphasize one of these facets will usually find that their ministry is unbalanced.

This is God's general call to everyone everywhere. As we have already seen, vocation is mostly about a call that applies to everyone – a *common calling*. At a personal level we may have an *individual calling* to a specific role, but the common calling must have priority. Some people call these the *primary* and *particular* callings. For people working in dead-end jobs or unable to climb a career ladder, it would be condescending to describe their labours as a particular calling. All they can do is live out their common calling in that context, and there's nothing wrong with that. Much of this book will be about common calling, because without it we have no context for individual calling.

Many of us will have no sense of a special individual call but must serve the common call of God in whatever we do moment by moment. The special call is overemphasized, and that can make us feel a failure or inadequate, just because we are not doing something saintly or world-changing.

God calls everyone *together*

True vocation is not individualistic. We are called *together*. The church has a collective vocation and we need each other to fulfil it. Yes, the Bible does have lots of stories about individuals or families, but they are there to bring home the story of a nation and a world, just as Anne Frank's diary makes the death of six million Jews in the Holocaust so much more real and relevant to us. She didn't write the diary with that in mind, but moviemakers have recognized how that works – see *Saving Private Ryan* or *Schindler's List*.

Of course, it remains true that God does call individuals for particular roles (see Acts 13). But those callings have to be set in the wider context of our calling as a Christian community and God's big plan for his world (see Eph. 4). God calls the church, and the church's vocation is the context for any individual calling. Someone pointed out to me that Acts 13 is one of only four occasions in the New Testament when individuals are called to a task, and they mostly involve Paul who is a unique case. Otherwise, the callings are for everyone.

The immediate call

We should also note that there is sometimes an *immediate* call. By this I mean that we need to do something right now, in the moment, such as help the person who has fallen over to stand up again, or ring for an ambulance.

In his book *Visions of Vocation*, Steven Garber calls this 'the responsibility of knowing' but warns that in our modern world of instant communication we know about too many crises to be able to respond to them all. What would the Good Samaritan have done, for example, if he had come across fifty people in need of immediate help instead of just one? Nevertheless, we are still called to do something – helping one person at least, responding to one charity appeal, and so on.

The call is a response to God's 'vocation'

It's fundamental to realize that *our call is in response to what God has already done*. The Ten Commandments can appear to be a random set of demands to the casual reader, but they begin with 'I am the Lord your God who brought you out of Egypt . . . out of slavery'. God's people were being asked to trust the one who had already saved them, by being obedient to laws which would make their lives better. The gospel is essentially the same of course:

> For it is by grace you have been saved, through faith – and this is not from yourselves, it is the gift of God – not by works, so that no one can boast. For we are God's handiwork, created in Christ Jesus to do good works, which God prepared in advance for us to do.
>
> (Eph. 2:8–10)

> He has saved us and called us to a holy life – not because of anything we have done but because of his own purpose and grace.
>
> (2 Tim. 1:9)

A word of warning

To be called by God challenges two of the great idols of our time: comfort and freedom. When God asks us to do something, it might make us uncomfortable and it might take away our freedom. Just so you know.

So fasten your seat belts and come for the ride. Let's read God's story together.

FOR REFLECTION

- What do you want to get from reading this book? Are you open to the possibility that you might be called and this might involve sacrifice? Have you discussed this with anyone else?
- What do you consider to be your vocation now, before we begin?
- Pray that God will speak to you as you read.

FURTHER READING

Garber, Steven. *Visions of Vocation* (IVP, 2014).

Walton, Steve. *A Call to Live* (Triangle, 1994) (now out of print but often available second-hand).

OTHER

The Fuller Seminary De Pree Centre web page about vocation myths is at:

- https://depree.org/myths/

Ian Paul's excellent blog Psephizo has two really good posts about vocation in the Church of England and beyond:

- https://www.psephizo.com/biblical-studies/vocation-in-the-economy-of-god-i/
- https://www.psephizo.com/biblical-studies/vocation-in-the-economy-of-god-ii/

THE OLD TESTAMENT

Jesus was of course Jewish, as were his followers. For the Jews of Jesus' time the only Bible they had was the Old Testament. But the Scripture that Jesus and his contemporaries read is quoted extensively in the New Testament and is vital to our understanding of who he is and where he came from. And it's an amazing story with a lot to tell us, often in surprising ways.

1

God's Big Story: Overview

As I write this paragraph, I think back to just a few days ago, when I was called upon to explain the story of Genesis in two minutes to a couple of people as we bounced across the Jordanian desert in the back of a 4x4 jeep. As you do.

On several occasions in sermons or in one-to-one conversations, in churches or in pubs, I have given an outline of the whole Bible story in 5 minutes. I'm no longer surprised when people say 'That's amazing!' Not because I'm doing anything complicated or clever, but because people often have no idea of the big picture. They are used to hearing little bits of the whole, without any grasp of how it all fits together. Even in church, Christians often have a diet of two or three short readings followed by a 10-minute sermon.

The chapters that follow will be mostly chronological, though in most chapters about the Old Testament I will be jumping forward to show how the New Testament interprets or fulfils the Old, and I will be showing in particular how *Jesus* fulfils all of the Old Testament. Only in that context will we look at vocation. This means that the Old Testament will appear to be the subject of most of the book, with only a shorter section at the end concerning the New, but in fact we will have covered quite a bit of the New Testament as we have discussed how the Hebrew Scriptures are fulfilled.

The big story

So what's the big story? Apologies if you already know all this – feel free to move on to the next chapter.

The Bible begins with creation; in fact there are two accounts of this, in chapter 1 and 2 of Genesis. In chapter 3, everything goes wrong as sin enters the world, and this is quickly followed by the first murder. The next significant event is the flood and the story of Noah, followed by the tale of the Tower of Babel.

Then we begin the great story of Abraham and his descendants – his son Isaac and grandson Jacob. Jacob's twelve sons include Joseph, who becomes a ruler in Egypt and rescues the known world from famine, but then we move forward a few hundred years to when Jacob's descendants have become slaves to the Egyptians, and God calls Moses to lead his people out of Egypt. They are now called the Israelites, from the new name God gave Jacob.

Moses leads the Israelites across the Red Sea and through the desert towards the 'promised land' (in those days known as Canaan), but along the way they receive the law from God, including the Ten Commandments. They are also instructed to keep various festivals such as Passover, to remind them of these great moments in their history.

The journey takes forty years as God's people wander around the desert, and Moses dies just before they enter the land, so Joshua takes over. Once they have occupied the land, it is separated into areas for each tribe descended from the twelve sons of Jacob and there is a lawless period as the Israelites colonize what will become Israel, but in the meantime God raises up temporary leaders (known as 'judges') to lead the people when they are attacked.

Samuel is the last of the judges and first of the prophets. He appoints and anoints Israel's first king – Saul – but Saul proves a failure and David replaces him. David is followed by his son Solomon and the kingdom of Israel is at its height. David and Solomon are said to have written much of the 'Wisdom' literature, especially Proverbs, Psalms, Song of Songs, and Ecclesiastes.

But it goes downhill after that. There is civil war and the kingdom is divided into Israel in the north and Judah in the south. A succession of bad kings rule the two 'nations' until first Israel and then Judah is taken captive by the Assyrians and Babylonians. There are signs of recovery as Ezra and Nehemiah return to Jerusalem to rebuild the walls and the temple, but also stories of God's people surviving and keeping the flame going while in captivity, such as Esther and Daniel. Nevertheless, the Old Testament narrative ends here, only a third of the way through. What about the rest?

The books of Ezra, Nehemiah and Esther are followed in the Bible by the Wisdom books mentioned above. After that come the writings of the prophets, who are people who spoke or acted for God at key moments during the story we have just outlined. Here's where a simple Bible handbook comes in handy, with charts showing where the various prophets come in the historical timeline. The prophetic books are usually divided into the 'major' (the longer ones) and 'minor' (guess). Oddly, although the historical books end with Esther, the books of Daniel and Jonah, which are more narrative than prophecy, are included with the Minor Prophets.

The Old Testament ends with the book of the prophet Malachi, and several hundred years pass before the New Testament begins to tell us the story of the Jewish Messiah anticipated by the Old Testament. The Old Testament is the Jewish Bible and it was the Scripture that Jesus used. Jesus says that he has come to fulfil 'all the law and the prophets', which is a phrase sometimes used to mean the whole Old Testament. More about what he meant later.

The New Testament has four 'gospels' – Matthew, Mark, Luke and John – which are short biographies of Jesus, each majoring on his death and resurrection. They're followed by Acts – written by Luke as a sequel to his gospel – which tells us all about the beginning and spread of the church, guided by the Holy Spirit. In Acts we hear about Paul and his travels across the Mediterranean countries, planting churches everywhere. Most of the rest of the New Testament is made up of letters written by Paul and a few others, often sent to correct some particular difficulties in the churches he established, but not always.

The final book is Revelation, written by Jesus' friend John in his old age. It is often thought to be all about the end of the world, but that's to misunderstand it. Much of it had contemporary relevance and application, because John's vision was given to encourage Christians suffering persecution under Roman rule.

It's good that we end this introduction with Revelation, because that book in particular illustrates what can go wrong when we begin to interpret Scripture. People will often interpret Revelation as though it was all written about events today or in the near future, but it wasn't. They will also read meanings into the text that are fanciful at best. Once again, this is because they are reading it in isolation and not as part of the big story. We have to allow Scripture to interpret Scripture.

If we read the Bible carefully, we will discover an extraordinary richness as we spot numerous connections and insights. We have 66 little books written by over 40 authors over 2,000+ years that make one extraordinary volume with infinite connections, inspired by God's Holy Spirit. Some people have told me that seeing how it all fits together has been a strong encouragement to their Christian faith. It's complex, but it's a love-letter that asks for a response. That response will be our collective vocation.

FOR REFLECTION

- How well do you know the overall Bible story?

FURTHER READING

Clowney, Edmund P. *Preaching Christ in All of Scripture* (Crossway, 2003).

Fee, Gordon, and Douglas Stuart. *How to Read the Bible Book by Book* (Zondervan, 2002).

——. *How to Read the Bible for All Its Worth* (Zondervan, 4th edn, 2014).

Hacking, Stuart. *His Story: The Story of Why We Are Here* (Resource, 2014).

OTHER

There are lots of Bible resources on the web, some more accurate or helpful than others, but in the end there is no substitute for reading the book itself!

- The Bible in 5 minutes and 37 seconds (including about 37 seconds of intro and summary): https://www.youtube.com/watch?v=7_CGP-12AE0
- There's a simple text-based Bible timeline at: https://biblehub.com/timeline/
- The Bible Society has produced the Bible Course, an eight-session series that's great for groups. Details here: https://www.biblesociety.org.uk/explore-the-bible/the-bible-course/
- The Bible Project is a brilliant series of shortish movies uploaded to YouTube. It's a great way to get your head around the whole Bible story and the component books:
    - https://thebibleproject.com/
    - https://www.youtube.com/channel/UCVfwlh9XpX2Y_tQfjeln9QA

2

Adam and Eve's Story (Part 1): Stewards

Author's note: I have some great Christian friends who believe God made the world in six literal 24-hour days, and I have some great Christian friends who don't. For our purposes here, I'm only interested in what we can learn about *vocation* from the creation accounts in the Bible. OK?

In the beginning God created everything from nothing.

Along the way he created a man and woman whom we know as Adam and Eve. Before everything went wrong, there was work. And this work was *good* work, depending on what you enjoy, because there was some gardening involved. To be honest, I'm not Alan Titchmarsh and neither is my wife, thank goodness. Someone once gave us a cactus and we killed it by neglect. But the simple point is that before sin entered the world, work was good. As various writers have noted, work did not emerge after a golden age of leisure.

Although the second account of creation in Genesis 2 focuses primarily on Adam, in Genesis 1 we are told that man and woman were made 'in God's image'. Together they were called to do some things that will help us discover an important understanding of vocation. God tells them: 'Be fruitful and increase in number; fill the earth and subdue it. Rule over the fish in the sea and the birds in the sky and over every living creature that moves on the ground' (Gen. 1:28).

The first call

When speaking about vocation, I often ask: 'What is the first instruction given by God to humanity?' The answer, it seems to me, is 'Have sex', which is the best way we've ever found to 'be fruitful and increase in number'. As Benedick reflects when he changes his mind about marriage in Shakespeare's *Much Ado About Nothing*: 'the world must be peopled.'

But notice what follows in God's command: Eve and Adam are told to fill the earth, subdue it and rule over it. This can only be achieved if they multiply and pass on the instruction, so this must be a command to all people – a vocation for all of humanity.

Delegated responsibility

We're already being introduced to an important but neglected thread of Scripture: *stewardship*. A quick glance at several dictionaries shows that stewardship is about *delegated responsibility*.

Chapter 2 of Genesis tells us: 'The LORD God took the man and put him in the Garden of Eden to work it and take care of it' (Gen. 2:15). Afterwards, God brings the animals to Adam and gives him the responsibility of naming them. This is stewardship too.

In the New Testament, Jesus talks about stewardship quite a bit, including the strange parable of the Shrewd Manager (Luke 16). There is a lot we could say about the subject, but first we need to understand the way society worked in Jesus' day, and particularly the word often translated 'servant' but really meaning 'slave'.

Slavery in biblical times

The trouble with words is that they sometimes don't mean what we think they do, and they mean different things at different times in history. We also read words through our modern worldview. For some, 'servant' conjures images of Downton Abbey, but 'slave' perhaps brings to mind forced labour. In the first century AD, slavery was very different from the kind that immediately springs to the modern mind, where Africans were kidnapped and shipped overseas to undertake forced labour.

Slavery was common in the first-century Roman Empire. In the New Testament, the most commonly used word is usually translated 'servant', because that is a less loaded term for our modern ears. Slaves constituted up to a third of the empire and they had rights. They could buy themselves out of slavery and many were slaves for just a few years. Some were the slaves of kings after capture in warfare, but most were simply poor people in an agrarian society who had run out of money and who sold themselves into slavery. Their owners often gave them responsibilities, sometimes including the management of money. The story of Joseph illustrates this well: 'Potiphar put him in charge of his household, and he entrusted to his care everything he owned' (Gen. 39:4b). This verse sums up what I am trying to explain. God's call to the first humans and to us is about delegated responsibility.

Stewards of our world

In Genesis 1 and 2 Adam and Eve are commanded to be stewards – stewards with a master who has delegated responsibility to them. They are a prototype for the whole human race. We are all called to be stewards of our world.

This is an important concept to understand, especially in regard to vocation. It's well illustrated when we come to Paul's household code in Ephesians 6:

> Slaves, obey your earthly masters with respect and fear, and with sincerity of heart, just as you would obey Christ. Obey them not only to win their favour when their eye is on you, but as *slaves of Christ*, doing the will of God from your heart. Serve wholeheartedly, *as if you were serving the Lord*, not people, because you know that the Lord will reward each one for whatever good they do, whether they are slave or free.
>
> And masters, treat your slaves in the same way. Do not threaten them, since you know that *he who is both their Master and yours* is in heaven, and there is no favouritism with him.
>
> (Eph. 6:5–9, my emphasis)

Vocation for every Christian is to acknowledge that we all have a master and we are all responsible to him. We are to manage the resources he has entrusted to us – human or otherwise – as if we are serving him. In fact the word 'if' is not actually in the Greek text of Ephesians 6:7, because Paul is telling us that stewardship is the reality of what we are called to do, whether we know it or not. This is not a simile; it's how it actually is. Each of us is a steward with responsibilities. For the Christian, any job or unpaid task we do is to be done as if serving the Lord.

In the contemporary world, the word 'steward' appears in various contexts. The cabin crew on passenger jets are called stewards. In 2016 Monarch Airlines produced a great TV advertisement. The 30-second film shows various people being polite and helpful to others, and then we discover that they are all Monarch stewards and stewardesses – showing that kindness comes naturally to them. It's an ironic shame that Monarch ceased trading soon afterwards.

As we heard in a previous chapter, 'amateur' can be used nowadays as a term of derision, describing someone doing something badly, while 'professional' means doing a job well. But originally amateurs (from the Latin word for 'love') were those who did something for the love of it. Christian vocation is the work of true amateurs, paid or not, who do the job well because they love to serve God and neighbour.

The greatest steward

If the idea of the Christian life as being slaves to God and others seems a bit challenging, in this book we will discover that despite our weaknesses there is someone who has gone before us. In Philippians 2, we discover the perfect steward/slave: '[Jesus] made himself nothing, by taking the very nature [or form] of a servant, being made in human likeness' (Phil. 2:7). Paul begins that chapter by encouraging his readers to have the same attitude as Jesus, who washed his disciples' feet after the Last

Supper, and told them that if he, their Lord and master did this, then they should do the same for each other. We will return to this later when we look at Jesus' humanity.

The Christian gospel is not first and foremost about copying Jesus, as we will frequently note in this book. Nevertheless, Paul commends Jesus' servant attitude as an excellent example of Christian discipleship. As stewards who are called to serve our world, this is where our vocation begins.

FOR REFLECTION

- How hard is it to think of ourselves as slaves? Does it make a difference if we know that God is our master?
- How hard is it to wash someone else's feet? Does it make a difference to know that Jesus did this for his disciples as an example to them and us?

FURTHER READING

Cosden, Darrell. *The Heavenly Good of Earthly Work* (Paternoster, 2006).

Sherman, Amy L. *Kingdom Calling: Vocational Stewardship for the Common Good* (IVP, 2011).

LISTEN

- Bob Dylan, 'Gotta Serve Somebody', on the album *Slow Train Coming* (1989). Video at: https://www.youtube.com/watch?v=wC10VWDTzmU

OTHER

The Monarch Airlines video is at:

- https://www.youtube.com/watch?v=6IxOPBA8Grk

3

Adam and Eve's Story (Part 2): Rest

After six days of creating, God takes a rest.

'Surely God doesn't need a rest?' I hear you say. Good question. So, what's going on?

Notice that the text says he rested from his work, rather than saying he needed a rest. We're going to need to follow this thread through the whole Bible to understand this fully, but we should note for now that God rests after his work of creation and declares it 'very good'. The image is of completion, of someone sitting back with a satisfied feeling. Job done. Perfectly.

Later, in the Ten Commandments, God's people are commanded to keep the Sabbath, following God's example. Taking that day of rest is something which many commentators have agreed is a 'good thing', though we've never been very good at doing it – being either puritanically strict or insisting at the other extreme that we have the right do what we like on any day. But we all seem to agree on this: rest is good for us. We need a break.

Our obsession with work

I've read all the novels written by the popular Japanese author Haruki Murakami, but I was most fascinated by his non-fiction work *Underground.* The book is a study of the sarin terrorist attack on the Tokyo tube system. Murakami interviewed some of the bereaved but also some of those injured. Only twelve people died but thousands suffered long-term after-effects. He was particularly struck by the Japanese dedication to work; there were frequent tales of people who were struggling to breathe or see properly and they should have gone to hospital, but they insisted on finding a taxi to get to their office as soon as possible. Work was everything. This mindset is growing more pervasive in the western world too. Why this need to work? Who are we working for? Who are we trying to impress?

Lord of the Sabbath

When Jesus comes, he brings a new dimension to our understanding of rest. In the gospels, the religious teachers are desperately legalistic about Sabbath keeping. When Jesus' disciples pick heads of grain from the cornfields as they walk through on a Sabbath, they are accused of working, condemned for their actions, and Jesus is blamed. This incident is so important that it appears in all three synoptic gospels (Matt. 12:1–8; Mark 2:23–28; Luke 6:1–5). Why?

Jesus has three things to say in response to the Jewish leaders. First, he reminds them of a time when their national hero David did something unlawful because his men were hungry. This is similar to Jesus' argument elsewhere that practical needs can overrule the law – he heals on the Sabbath because someone is hurting.

Second, he tells them that 'The sabbath was made for humankind, and not humankind for the sabbath' (v. 27, NRSV). It was to give us appropriate rest, but not meant as something to legalistically enslave us.

But third, Jesus declares that he himself is 'Lord of the Sabbath'. 'The Son of Man is Lord of the Sabbath' (Matt. 12:8) are his words. What does he mean?

What are we looking for in life?

On the day I first drafted this section of this book, the BBC reported the sad story of one of the most successful athletes the world has ever known. His strivings achieved greatness, but his achievements were not quite enough to give that true peace and deep rest. Swimmer Michael Phelps was the most decorated Olympian of all time, with twenty-three gold medals. But after the 2004 Olympics he considered committing suicide. After each Olympics he sank into deep depression.

Phelps had an amazing vocation – to be the best swimmer, perhaps the greatest athlete the world has ever known. But even his staggering success wasn't sufficient. Winning each gold medal brought great pleasure, but it was not enough. After that, what is the purpose of life now? I've done what I set out to achieve . . . so now what?

The Deeper Rest

Tim Keller suggests that every one of us needs someone to affirm our work: 'That's very good', as God said of his creation. We all know that warm feeling when someone expresses appreciation for what we have achieved. Deep down, whether we recognize it or not, we all have that same need concerning our whole lives.

Who is there who could say 'Well done' to us? Who could say 'Well done, that's very good' without truly knowing us from beginning to end and in our most hidden moments? And let's face it, all of us have things we have said, done or thought that we know would not merit a 'well done' but just the opposite.

At Jesus' baptism, his Father declares: 'This is my Son, whom I love; with him I am well pleased' (Matt. 3:17). There it is! The declaration. 'That's very good!' But only Jesus has ever truly deserved it, which is why his work on the cross makes such a difference. What happened when Jesus cried 'It is finished'? The old Prayer Book says that Jesus' righteousness was 'imputed' to us. And now the Father can say about our lives: 'That's very good!'

Well done!

Do you see this? After the creation God could rest because his work was truly complete. Finished. It was very good.

The Old Testament story includes the rescue of the Israelites from slavery in Egypt, their many years of wandering through the desert, and the ultimate failure of a whole generation to 'enter God's rest' in the promised land. Read Hebrews 3 and 4 for a really good account of all this from the New Testament. When we get to Judges, we will see the Israelites struggling to enter into that rest, even though they are physically in the promised land.

Our works and our lives are never quite enough for anyone to say 'That's very good' – the final declaration that would make our hearts able to have the Deeper Rest. Only in Jesus Christ, the Lord of the Sabbath, do we truly discover that because of *his* work, God looks at us and says: 'That's very good.'

So here's the thing: vocation must begin with rest. Here's my advice: don't pursue a career, fame or fortune; pursue Jesus Christ and his kingdom.

FOR REFLECTION

- Do you get enough rest? Do you work too hard?
- Have you discovered the Deeper Rest? Do you understand that because of Jesus' work, God looks at you and says 'Well done'?
- Read Hebrews chapters 3 and 4.
- Rest in him.

FURTHER READING

Goldsworthy, Graeme. *Homeward Bound: A Sabbath Rest for the People of God* (Authentic, 2019)

Shulevitz, Judith. *The Sabbath World* (Ballantine, 2011).

OTHER

- Tim Keller sermon: 'Working and Resting' (1990): https://www.youtube.com/watch?v=ux0_5zctrsl

4

Adam and Eve's Story (Part 3): What Went Wrong?

For some people, Genesis 3 poses more questions than it answers. It tells the story of 'The Fall', when sin came into the world. Why did God allow this? Was this an accident? Who is the snake and did God create him too?

The text doesn't answer those questions, and we need to learn that the Bible always sets its own agenda, not ours. We must look at what we *can* learn, not what we can't. The story is very familiar, and if we read it carefully we see that it is exquisitely written and has much to teach us about human nature and our vocation as human beings.

But the story begins with the snake, who we assume is the devil, although we are not explicitly told this. He is 'crafty' and his approach to Eve reflects this. He does not urge her to disobey; he asks her a question that raises doubts in her mind about the only restrictive commandment that God seems to have given to the first people on earth.

Notice in passing how liberal God was before things went wrong. They can eat *anything at all*, except the fruit of one tree. At the time, it seems to be the only commandment. But the snake asks if this is really the case. Did God actually say that?

Eve takes and eats the fruit from the Tree of Knowledge and then gives some to Adam, who also eats. They got what they wanted but not what they needed. The man and woman are suddenly aware of their nakedness and shame, so they hide.

Sin and shame

I recently met the investigative journalist Jon Ronson, who had just published *So You've Been Publicly Shamed*, a book about people who have been caught doing something society disapproves of, and who now have the stigma for life. His book is about being stigmatized in the eyes of the public. But Adam and Eve only had each other to face up to, and they had committed the sin together. Their shame is their embarrassment before God for what they have done, and they hide from him. Modern society has grown uncomfortable with the idea of sin. We don't want to be accountable to God, but it's important that Christians retain this key understanding of why the world went wrong.

We must not get the idea that the entry of sin into the world was a surprise to Father God, after which he turns to Jesus and says 'What are we going to do now, Son?' Romans 8:20 says: 'For the creation was subjected to frustration, not by its own choice, but by the will of the one who subjected it'. If God foreknew (or indeed foreordained) each one of us, then the fall was no surprise to him, however strange this may seem.

Anyway, God comes looking for his people, as he always does, and his heart is broken. The original sin is a breaking of trust, and it infects everything. The man blames the woman and she blames the snake. When I speak about this passage, I sometimes risk the wrath of half the room by pointing out that God tells Adam that everything went wrong because he listened to his wife. But his real sin is disobeying God.

Norman and the Giant Apple

You've maybe heard of Roald Dahl's book *James and the Giant Peach*. Well, let me tell you the story of Norman and the Giant Apple.

Many years ago, I was leading a Sunday school group of 11-year-olds, with a friend called Norman. Norman made a papier-mâché apple the size of a football. He spent hours on his creation and it looked good enough to eat. The following Sunday morning, we put the 'apple' on a table in the meeting room, with a sign that said 'Do not touch'. Then we deliberately arrived a couple of minutes late so the children would be unsupervised for a short time.

When we walked in, the children were throwing the giant apple around the room to one another and laughing. When we pointed to the sign, each of them blamed the others for being the first to pick it up. At least they didn't try to eat it. The writer of Genesis understands human nature perfectly.

Grace: God's response to sin

When he has interviewed the guilty parties, God pronounces a 'curse', but the sense here is not that God is angry and taking revenge but describing the inevitable consequence of disobedience. They brought this on themselves. Men and women's relationships are damaged, and work becomes hard ('painful toil') and sweaty. And there will be enmity between Adam's 'seed' and the snake: 'he will crush your head, and you will strike his heel' (Gen. 3:15).

Writers have pointed out that although in the Genesis 1 creation story God simply made everything out of nothing by a word of his mouth, God now starts to 'work' too. The traditional pictures of Adam and Eve with a single pathetic fig leaf are not quite true to the text, which talks of them sewing leaves together, something we can assume was still rather inadequate as they are still hiding in the bushes when God turns up. While this was useful for artists throughout history because it allowed them to depict idealized naked people without including their genitals, it is not enough to cover their shame.

We often miss the bit afterwards, where God's extraordinary grace is glimpsed as he sits down and works. He makes proper outfits for the rebels – from animal skins. And note that for him to do that, there must have been a death – the death of the animal(s) – and therefore spilt blood too, a hint perhaps at how God will one day carry out the once-for-all act of redemption and remove our shame. Where forgiveness of sin is concerned, there's always a need for the shedding of blood. It always costs.

The second Adam

Adam and Eve are expelled from the garden into the wilderness. Many years later, first of all in the wilderness and then in another garden, the second Adam would face temptation from Satan, but unlike Adam and his wife Eve who wanted to be like God, Jesus would refuse to use his divine power for his own need to eat, and would declare 'Your will be done', recognizing his vocation to be fully human and suffer.

At the Last Supper, Jesus 'took . . . and ate', then he gave the food to his disciples, saying 'Take . . . eat'. And the next day, outside the city, he died on the cross of shame, naked and alone. Yet in that act, in which Satan strikes at the heel of a 'son of Adam', Christ crushes his head, as God had prophesied in the garden.

Paul explains it like this (but do read the whole chapter in Romans): 'For if, by the trespass of the one man, death reigned through that one man, how much more will those who receive God's abundant provision of grace and of the gift of righteousness reign in life through the one man, Jesus Christ!' (Rom. 5:17).

So what do we do?

What is our response? God clothed Adam and Eve and he offers clothes to us, and a fresh start where we don't need to take the fruit any more. Paul writes: 'clothe yourself with the Lord Jesus Christ, and do not think about how to gratify the desires of the flesh' (Rom. 13:14). Earlier in the same letter he says: 'Blessed are those whose transgressions are forgiven, whose sins are covered' (Rom. 4:7).

And when it comes to vocation and work, we must see that work was made good but damaged by the fall. It will often require sweat and hardship. Importantly, this means we can even be in the right vocation but still find it hard or frustrating. Karl Marx was right that work is spoilt by alienation – but not because we are alienated from the work itself but primarily from God. If we can restore our relationship with him, then we can begin to redeem work, see it in a new light and take satisfaction from it.

FOR REFLECTION

- Is there something that makes you feel ashamed? Is it stopping you fulfilling your vocation?
- Pray that God will open your eyes to see the wonderful truth of his forgiveness.

FURTHER READING

Blocher, Henri. *Original Sin* (Apollos, 1997).

5

Noah's Story: Saved through the Storm

The temptation when writing a book about vocation would be to take Noah's story and give it a provocative title like 'The Man Who Stood against the Tide', and encourage readers to stand out for God, even if they are the only ones to do so. That's all well and good, but such a challenge from a writer or preacher invariably leads to pride if we manage to succeed, or self-condemnation if we don't.

The story of Noah and the ark is one of the best-known and most loved of all Scripture passages. It invariably appears in those books of 'Bible Stories for Kids'. Which is a little bit odd, because although there seems to be a happy ending – the rainbow – the main thrust of the story is that the world was so bad that God had more or less decided to wipe *everyone* out and start again – the ultimate ethnic cleansing.

Noah (a 'blameless' man) is told to build a big boat and take not just his own family but also all the animal species of the earth. God will flood the whole earth and destroy every living thing, except the sea creatures presumably.

It's always good to look for literary structures in Bible texts. They can point to key words or phrases that the author wants us to notice. The flood story, which is spread over five chapters, is a highly complex structure, with a special literary shape. This involves the use of key words, phrases and in this case repeated numbers, to help us recognize that the crucial verse comes exactly in the middle. That verse says: 'But God remembered Noah and all the wild animals and the livestock that were with him in the ark, and he sent a wind over the earth, and the waters receded' (Gen. 8:1). Of course, God hadn't forgotten Noah. 'Remembering' means that he reliably kept his promise. The Psalms call on God to 'remember me' – and forget my sins.

The waters recede and dry land appears. Life starts once more and the rainbow appears as a sign that God will never flood the whole earth again. The mandate given to Adam and Eve is repeated: 'Be fruitful and increase in number and fill the earth' (Gen. 9:1).

But what happened afterwards?

Once the ark has rested on dry land, we have the weird end of Noah's story – the bit that never appears in the children's Bible stories. It's the subject of a great painting by the early Renaissance artist Giovanni Bellini, in which two figures are trying to hide the modesty of a naked old man while a third laughs at their attempts.

In the Bible story, Noah gets drunk and lies naked in his tent. His son Ham finds him and tells his brothers. The other two sons carry a garment into the tent backwards so they don't see anything, and drop it over their sleeping father.

What? Why is this odd tale in Scripture?

Some writers have speculated that this story condemns Ham, who is specifically described as the father of the Canaanites, who would later be notorious for drunken orgies. Drunkenness is condemned elsewhere in Scripture, but Ham didn't get drunk!

However, although the Ten Commandments don't come until later, we are instructed to 'honour your father and mother' and Ham has not done this.

But ultimately I think we are meant to see that even the drastic action taken by God has not reversed the 'nakedness' of Adam and Eve. There is still shame and things are not as they should be. The flood and the judgement that it demonstrates both point to something (and someone) more important.

Judgement

In the New Testament, the Noah account is usually mentioned when talking about judgement – more specifically the Last Judgement and our readiness for it. Jesus warns that before the flood came, people were doing the usual things like getting married, and like BBC weatherman Michael Fish in 1987, the stormy weather took them by complete surprise.

The water of the flood begins a biblical motif that will recur later, for example in the story of Moses leading the Israelites through the sea and the Egyptians drowning. Paul draws our attention to this in 1 Corinthians 10. His point is that coming through the waters does not guarantee that all will be well afterwards: 'Nevertheless, God was not pleased with most of them; their bodies were scattered in the wilderness' (1 Cor. 10:5).

Judgement is an important and much-neglected biblical theme that runs as a thread from the early chapters of Genesis right through to Revelation. It deserves to be taken a lot more seriously; a gospel with no room for judgement is not a complete gospel, however uncomfortable that might feel at first.

The prophet Habakkuk complains bitterly when God fails to enact judgement: 'Your eyes are too pure to look on evil; you cannot tolerate wrongdoing. Why then do you tolerate the treacherous? Why are you silent while the wicked swallow up those more righteous than themselves?' (Hab. 1:13).

When explaining the concept of sin and God's judgement to church groups, I often begin by helping people to recognize that we all actually *want* judgement. When we see news headlines about child killers and rapists, we want them to be caught and punished. We want justice, and justice means judgement. So we do want a God who will judge and punish.

Yale professor Miroslav Volf witnessed first-hand the terrible ethnic cleansing in the Balkan conflict. His book *Exclusion and Embrace* (Abingdon Press, 1996) was named one of the 100 most influential books of the twentieth century by *Christianity Today* magazine. He writes that non-violence must have its basis in the concept of divine judgement and vengeance. When a group of people have suffered terrible violence at the hands of others, they want to retaliate. They want revenge. They will take matters into their own hands – unless they believe in a God who is angry at injustice and wrong, and will do something about it. Volf gently but incisively challenges the notion of a lovely cuddly God. In chapter 7, he suggests that the idea of a God who refuses to judge is one of the 'pleasant captivities of the liberal mind', and such a God would not be worthy of worship.

The story of Noah is not about an example of a good man for us to copy. It is about a just and holy God who cannot ignore evil, just as a good surgeon cannot ignore cancer and must 'do violence' to his or her patient's body in order to save them.

But there is more.

Another 'blameless' man

At the risk of repeating myself, I'm going to constantly remind us that the Bible is not primarily about me or you. Centuries after Noah, there came another man who was truly 'blameless' before God. He was physically baptized in water to identify with sinners, and afterwards the dove that had disappeared from the flood story (Gen. 8:12) alighted upon him. He later was crucified naked with no one to cover him, which he described as a 'baptism' he had to undergo, and a cup of suffering he had to drink. Because of his death, our shame is covered, just as Noah's shame was covered and God covered the shame of Adam and Eve.

The Bible is *his story* and our common vocation must be seen in this light – in the light of Christ. The church community is to preach the good news, *including the warning of judgement*, make disciples, and baptize them in the name of the Father, Son and Holy Spirit. This is a vital part of our common calling.

FOR REFLECTION

- Why do we find it hard to talk about judgement? Is it because it makes us sound judgemental or intolerant? How do we deal with this?
- If God judges the earth, where should he draw the line? Should everyone be 'let off'?
- Do you believe that ultimately everyone will be 'saved'? If not, are you doing anything to ensure the people you love know about this?

FURTHER READING

Volf, Miroslav. *Exclusion and Embrace* (Abingdon Press, 1996).
——. *Free of Charge* (Zondervan, 2005).

OTHER

You can find a picture of Bellini's painting of Noah's drunkenness at:

- https://en.wikipedia.org/wiki/Drunkenness_of_Noah#/media/File:Drunkenness_of_Noah_bellini.jpg

6

The Tower of Babel Story: What Motivates Us?

I grew up in Blackpool, probably most famous for the 500-foot tower which dominates the town in a flat landscape. It was 5 miles away but I could see it from my bedroom as a child.

Near where I live now stands the tallest free-standing structure in the UK and the twenty-fourth tallest tower in the world, yet many readers will not have heard of it. It's the Emley Moor transmitting mast in West Yorkshire and it's nearly twice as tall as Blackpool's famous tourist attraction. You can see it from our local train station platform, even though it's 10 miles away and it really doesn't stand out in the distant landscape. Some towers are more famous than others and some people are more famous than others. They have made a name for themselves.

In the Bible, sandwiched between the well-known stories of Noah and Abraham comes the strange account of the Tower of Babel. It begins when the people say: 'Come, let us build ourselves a city, with a tower that reaches to the heavens, so that we may make a name for ourselves; otherwise we will be scattered over the face of the whole earth' (Gen. 11:4).

When I was first thinking about this story without checking the text, I pictured a Shard-like construction being built, or one of the 'ziggurats' that were built in ancient Mesopotamia, the land of the early chapters of Genesis. While refining this chapter, I saw a news item about an exhibition in Vienna dedicated to the paintings of Pieter Bruegel the Elder, including three quarters of all the paintings in the world attributed to him. It also included his two paintings of the Tower of Babel, brought together for the first time. Search for them online to get another way of thinking about what Babel's great tower looked like. Of course, we have no real idea.

But did you notice that the text I quoted above also mentions building a city? It's also mentioned again in verses 5 and 8, while there is only one mention of the tower, which suggests the important thing here is not that they want to literally 'reach to the heavens'. Rather, the key thought is that they want to make a name for themselves. They want to do something significant.

Many languages

The Brazilian artist Cildo Meireles has created an installation at the Tate Modern in London called 'Babel 2001'. It features hundreds of transistor radios all tuned to different stations. When you enter the room you see this tower, maybe 20 feet high, and then you hear a cacophony of voices and sounds in which it is virtually impossible to pick out a single phrase. Although I've said the tower is not the main point of the story, Meireles' installation does remind us of the way God dealt with the people's pride. He confused their languages.

There is a lot going on in the biblical story that we cannot cover – satire about other ancient myths and mockery of

Babylon, for example. But the main point is that God deals with human arrogance. Achieving anything without him is to achieve nothing.

I'm told that the Hebrew text of this section is highly complex with all sorts of literary devices, alliteration and puns. Notably, the key verse seems to be verse 5: 'But the LORD came down'. After this hinge verse, God confuses the language of the people so they can't communicate properly and the project fails. The people are scattered across the earth.

The name of the Lord

We should also note a rarely discussed biblical theme: the name of the Lord. God is concerned for his name. Modern readers are probably surprised to see that 'not taking the Lord's name in vain' is included in the Ten Commandments, and that Jesus seems unduly concerned about swearing oaths in God's name in the Sermon on the Mount. God's name signifies who he is. It represents him.

It's also interesting to see that Zephaniah 3:9 begins a section about the restoration of Israel with the words: 'Then I will purify the lips of the peoples, that all of them may call on the name of the LORD'. This verse connects people's speaking and their language with God's name. It is prophesying that God will one day sort out language, and his name will be praised. This prediction is fulfilled at Pentecost when people from nations across the world can understand the disciples as they praise God: 'we hear them declaring the wonders of God in our own tongues!' (Acts 2:11).

God come down

Pentecost follows Jesus' incarnation, death, resurrection and ascension. As with the Babel story, Jesus *came down*. And now that the Holy Spirit has *come down* on God's people, the judgement of Babel is being undone. Revelation paints a picture of the Age to Come as a great city, built by God, into which all the treasures of the nations will pour – as heaven *come down* to earth (more on this in the chapter on Revelation): 'Who will not fear you, Lord, and bring *glory to your name*? For you alone are holy. All nations will come and worship before you, for your righteous acts have been revealed' (Rev. 15:4, my emphasis).

Giving God a good name

It has been claimed that the famous preacher Billy Graham had a rule never to enter a hotel bedroom on his own or even be first to go in. He feared that inside there might be a naked woman and a photographer. He feared fake news, long before it was a thing. Even though he was committed to living a pure life, he was worried that bad publicity about him, even if untrue, would give God a bad name, and that his message would be tarnished.

A key motivation for all of us in our vocation must be to honour the name of the Lord. If you are asking 'What should I do with my life?' then this should be a key consideration. Will what I choose to do glorify the name of the Lord?

This is not because God is somehow insecure or gets upset, but because if he is dishonoured then other people might be turned off him and consequently miss out on their only source of help and salvation. He is worthy, as the Bible often says.

He is the only thing worth worshipping. 'The name of the LORD is a fortified tower; the righteous run to it and are safe' (Prov. 18:10).

Before we leave the story of Babel, we need to notice that it is immediately followed by the story of Abraham, which begins in Genesis chapter 12 with God promising to make him into a great nation, and *make his name great*. This is entirely God's initiative.

FOR REFLECTION

- Think about everything you have done today – or if it's early, everything from yesterday. Did you honour the Lord's name in your thoughts, words and actions?

OTHER

Breughel's painting of Babel is at:

- https://en.wikipedia.org/wiki/The_Tower_of_Babel_(Bruegel)#/media/File:Pieter_Bruegel_the_Elder_-_The_Tower_of_Babel_(Vienna)_-_Google_Art_Project.jpg

7

Abraham and Sarah's Story (Part 1): God's Big Plan

The remarkable story of Abraham runs from the second half of Genesis 11 to the first half of Genesis 25. It contains such a wealth of material that I wish I could write a whole book just on those chapters alone. Maybe one day . . .

The New Testament begins with Matthew tracing Jesus' family tree from Abraham. His call is where God's salvation plan for the world starts in earnest. Yet it actually begins at the very moment when the story of God's people was in danger of dying out. Why do I say this?

First of all, since the family line is an important factor in Israelite history, we have the devastating infertility of Abram's wife Sarai, who is now well past child-bearing age anyway. The 'Semite' family line (the descendants of Shem), through which God has been working, is about to end. By the way, in case you didn't already know this, God changes the names of Abram and Sarai to Abraham and Sarah later. Watch out for that. It might be important.

Second, in the ancient pagan world of many gods, the Semite line has been the budding monotheistic branch of the family tree since the days of Noah, but Abram's family is now mired in idolatry. How do we know this? At the end of the book of

Joshua, God reminds his people: 'Long ago your ancestors, including Terah the father of Abraham and Nahor, lived beyond the River Euphrates and worshipped other gods' (Josh. 24:2).

Genesis 12 tells us that God *had* said to Abram: 'Leave your country, your people and your father's household.' At the end of Genesis 11 we learn, however, that the whole family had set off – Abram had taken his father's household with him.

Sometimes when God calls, there are things we should be leaving behind but we take them along, and they become the reason why our calling may not be fulfilled. For some this may be family responsibilities, though let me stress that I do not want to condemn those who rightly take seriously their responsibilities for elderly relatives or other family members. Others might go when called, but take along the 'baggage' of their past, which could be psychological or emotional issues that they have never faced up to. Again, I am not condemning such people.

It seems that it was only when his dad Terah died that Abram finally set out to go where God called, which is why he is already old when our story gets going. Even then, he took his nephew Lot with him, which was to prove another hindrance to a smooth response to God's guidance. In fact, Genesis 12 tells us rather pointedly: 'He took his wife Sarai, his nephew Lot, all the possessions they had accumulated and the people they had acquired in Harran . . .' (Gen. 12:5).

In the New Testament, Jesus says something about what we take with us when doing mission: 'When Jesus had called the Twelve together, he gave them power and authority to drive out all demons and to cure diseases, and he sent them out to proclaim the kingdom of God and to heal the sick. He told them: "Take nothing for the journey – no staff, no bag, no bread, no money, no extra shirt"' (Luke 9:1–3).

Leaving home

I will tell my own story more fully later, but here's a taster: two days before my thirtieth birthday, I was wrestling with God regarding a growing call to ordination. We were enjoying Spring Harvest, a Christian holiday Bible week in Skegness. On the morning of that day, I had a pot of tea with Denise, a friend of my wife. She asked me bluntly but graciously if I was going to be a vicar. Although others had suggested it too, I played down my response. I was not keen.

The truth was, I was happy where I was. A combination of a small inheritance from my deceased parents, a decent job and a secure career meant I was very comfortable. By my mid-twenties we had a four-bedroomed house close to the sea with a double driveway that had two cars parked on it, and my job in information technology (IT) meant my wife didn't have to take paid work, so she could look after the two children we already had.

Later that day I was half-heartedly browsing the 'Opportunities for Service' wall that is displayed each year at Spring Harvest, when a stranger approached me.

She asked: 'Well? Are you going to do it?'

Caught on the hop, I found this a bit rude, to be honest. So I responded: 'I don't think so.'

'Why not?' she demanded.

'Well, I . . .' I looked for a suitable response. 'I have children. It would be unfair to move them when they're settled.'

'That's just an excuse,' she declared. '*You* are the problem. You should do what God calls you to do.'

With that, she walked away, leaving me a little shocked. Later that day I did respond to the call – more about that later. And by the way, two of our three children have lived overseas as adults so they are clearly not fazed by moving away from the familiar, unlike me.

But my story is too 'tidy' in some ways. It's like one of those stories you can read in Christian magazines that make it seem like being a Christian is all plain sailing and miraculous encounters. The Christian life is usually messy, and my story omits some of the challenges of my experience – leaving behind special friends and wider family for example, and giving up a secure well-paid job. If my father had still been alive, I suspect he would have disapproved and called me foolish. Maybe Terah did that, although it seems he didn't discourage Abram – he went with him, but only so far.

In Hebrews we are encouraged to focus on just one thing:

> Therefore, since we are surrounded by such a great cloud of witnesses, let us throw off everything that hinders and the sin that so easily entangles. And let us run with perseverance the race marked out for us, fixing our eyes on Jesus, the pioneer and perfecter of faith. For the joy that was set before him he endured the cross, scorning its shame, and sat down at the right hand of the throne of God.
>
> (Heb. 12:1–2)

Taking up our cross

Jesus made a profound statement that must be heard by anyone who desires to follow Christ and discover their vocation: 'Then Jesus said to his disciples, "Whoever wants to be my disciple must deny themselves and take up their cross and follow me"' (Matt. 16:24).

Throughout this book, we will often note that Jesus is not asking us to do something that he has not already done. Abram eventually left his family and answered God's call. Jesus left his 'family' in heaven, gave up the comfort and security of his Father's house, and became poor so that we might become rich. And of course his self-sacrifice did not end with his departure from heaven, but at the cross. He is the true and greater Abram.

The rich young ruler

In three of the gospels, we find the story of a rich young ruler. He comes to Jesus wanting to know what (else) he has to do to get eternal life. At first we might be disappointed that Jesus does not immediately say 'Follow me', but like all good evangelists, he deals with the person in front of him and asks questions. Has the man kept the commandments?

When the young man claims that he has been keeping the commandments, Jesus says there's only one thing more required (actually it's two things because they are interconnected). He must give up all his possessions, give the money away and then follow Jesus (actually that's three things, isn't it?).

We are told that the man went away sad because he was very wealthy. But, as Tim Keller has pointed out, there are two rich young rulers in this story. Jesus was around 30 years old when this happened and he was rich in heaven from all eternity, ruler of the universe, but he gave up everything for us.

From the perspective of vocation, here is a call to give up anything that might prevent us or distract us from doing God's will – money, power or anything else – and then come follow the true rich young ruler.

FOR REFLECTION

- What baggage are you carrying that might prevent you responding to God's call? Is there anything you might need to give up in order to fulfil your vocation?
- Have you grasped how much Christ gave up for you?

8

Abraham and Sarah's Story (Part 2): God Can Use Arguments?

In part 1 of Abram's story we saw how he was told to leave his family behind, but after many years' delay he eventually set off – and took his nephew Lot with him. It seems he still wasn't entirely leaving everything behind, but in Genesis 13 we see that despite Abram's disobedience, God is at work and he ends up exactly where he is supposed to be.

Abram has settled in Canaan and become very wealthy. Life is going well – so well in fact that there is not enough room for both Abram and Lot's possessions and flocks in the place where they have settled. Their herdsmen begin to quarrel and Abram must sort out the situation. He suggests that they separate and Lot agrees. Abram gives him the choice of where to live and Lot chooses the Jordan plain, which will prove to be not quite such a good idea in the next chapter when he will need to be rescued from trouble by his uncle.

But as a consequence, Abram is now in the 'right' place. In addition, God's long-term plan is for Abram to have an heir through whom his promises will be fulfilled. Until this point, Lot could be seen as the likely inheritor of all that Abram has, including the blessing of God, as he is the nearest male relative.

It's not spelled out in the text, but the separation now makes this much less likely.

In the book of Acts we read that Paul and Barnabas have a great ministry together. They are doing remarkable missionary work for the Lord. In chapter 15, Barnabas wants to take Mark on their next trip but Paul disagrees. They have a sharp argument and they part from each other; Barnabas takes Mark, but Paul takes Silas instead.

There are similarities between these stories, though it was not Abram and Lot who quarrelled but their herdsmen. But I simply want us to note how God often turns conflict into something positive. So many times in the Bible narrative, the Lord turns human failings into something for his glory. We will see this more fully later when we unpack the story of Abram's grandson Jacob and his great-grandson, Joseph. If you struggle with circumstances that seem to prevent you from responding to God's call, keep praying and see what he is doing. It might be part of the plan.

FOR REFLECTION

- Has there been conflict in your family? How was it/could it be resolved?
- Do you feel that your vocation is being held back because of a broken relationship? Does it make you feel unsuited for what God is calling you to do?
- Pray for recognition that God is bigger than human squabbles.

9

Abraham and Sarah's Story (Part 3): What's in It for Me?

Genesis 15 tells another story never told in Sunday school. The first half is fairly straightforward: God speaks to Abram in a vision and sets out in more detail how he will bless him, something the Lord had begun to tell him in chapter 12. He begins by reassuring Abram that he is God and he is Abram's 'shield and very great reward'. However, Abram is not entirely happy. As he and his wife are very old, who will inherit the great wealth that God has blessed him with?

Later God will teach Abram that having offspring is not everything. But now he reassures him that he will indeed father a child. And in fact from that child will come numerous descendants. God declares: 'I am the Lord.' He's always saying this and people generally don't realize the huge significance of this statement. To be fair, in a world where each nation had its own god (or usually gods, plural) it would be easy for Abram to think his god was just another one among the many. When Abram again expresses some uncertainty, God does something quite startling. We might find it a little weird.

Cutting a covenant

God tells Abram: 'Bring me a heifer, a goat and a ram, each three years old, along with a dove and a young pigeon' (Gen. 15:9). Abram cuts each animal, except the birds, into two and then falls into a deep sleep. What on earth is going on?

This is an ancient covenant ceremony. When two kings, wealthy men or tribal rulers made a treaty, they would kill animals and then walk together between them, declaring that if one of them breaks the treaty, they should be killed like the animals.

There is an example of this later in the Old Testament, describing an occasion when the leaders took it upon themselves to enact the same ritual:

> Those who have violated my covenant and have not fulfilled the terms of the covenant they made before me, I will treat like the calf they cut in two and then walked between its pieces. The leaders of Judah and Jerusalem, the court officials, the priests and all the people of the land who walked between the pieces of the calf, I will deliver into the hands of their enemies who want to kill them. Their dead bodies will become food for the birds and the wild animals.
>
> (Jer. 34:18–20)

Back in our Genesis story, as Abram sleeps, a thick darkness 'came over him', hiding God from him so that he will not die at the sight. So far, no one has walked between the halves of the animals. Then God speaks, and prophesies the whole story of Moses and the exodus.

If we thought the story was bizarre up to this point, it gets weirder. After sunset, in the literal darkness, a 'smoking fire pot and blazing torch' appear and pass between the animal carcasses.

Fire in the Bible is usually a sign of the judgement of God that comes with his holy presence. His fierce judgement (which we discussed above) is being declared against those who break his covenant with Abram. But here's the amazing thing: God passes between the animals *alone*. He is unilaterally declaring that if the covenant is broken, he will be the one to die. Because *he* is Abram's shield and very great reward. Tucked away in the longest psalm we find this: 'You are my refuge and my shield; I have put my hope in your word' (Ps. 119:114).

Our great reward

Abram was being taught to seek God for himself, not for what he offers. God himself is the 'great reward'; the reward is not some earthly blessing – not even of a son. Having God himself is a blessing, and any gifts he bestows are a bonus. And a time would come when God would demonstrate this even more powerfully.

Luke's gospel begins with an aged couple who can't have children, as with the story of Abram. Elizabeth and Zechariah's son John (the Baptist) will prepare the way for the Messiah. John will die as his reward for serving his Messiah, and the Messiah will die terribly too, as God himself takes the punishment for our rebellion. At the Last Supper Jesus broke the bread in two, as we do when we meet in remembrance of his death and passion. Perhaps we are meant to see an echo of the animals cut in two and think of the way God covenanted with Abram to die for our sake.

If we become Christians expecting health and wealth as part of the deal, we will almost certainly be disappointed. As we seek our vocation, we should expect no reward except God himself. Even if we should suffer or even die in the process, we already have our reward.

FOR REFLECTION

- What truly motivates everything you do?
- What final reward are you hoping for?

10

Abraham and Sarah's Story (Part 4): God's Plan My Way

In part 2 we heard God promise to Abram that 'a son who is your own flesh and blood will be your heir' (Gen. 15:4). Perhaps God did not make it clear enough where this child would come from, so maybe we should not blame Abram for what happens next. Or maybe we should blame Sarai, though that might be unfair, like blaming Eve for Adam's sin.

It's been ten years since Abram settled in Canaan and there is no sign that Sarai might produce a baby. So she has an idea. Sarai has a slave girl called Hagar, whom she probably picked up in Egypt ('Look what happens when you move out of God's will,' we might say). She suggests to Abram that he could produce a child by sleeping with Hagar. Unsurprisingly, he agrees. Surely this might be a way to bring about God's promise?

Men, what do you do when your wife encourages you to have sex with another woman? (Don't answer that.) We are told that Sarai 'gave' Hagar to Abram as his 'wife'. Note the similarity with Eve *giving* the fruit to Adam, and note that this sin will damage both Abram and Sarai.

Polygamy?

As an aside, it's worth noting here that the Bible does not teach or encourage polygamy. If a couple are struggling to conceive, this text is not a biblical example that you should follow.

In fact, although Genesis has several stories of men with more than one wife, we should remember that:

1. Bible stories are not always examples of good moral behaviour (to say the least).
2. Sometimes Bible stories are examples of bad behaviour so that we learn the consequences.
3. The patriarchs lived in an ancient world in which a woman had to be married or starve. Hence the instructions for men to marry their brother's widow. The arrangement was basically practical, not sexual.
4. Following on from point 3, we do not know how the relationships worked out in any detail, but this was a very different world from today.

Hagar conceives a child and the inevitable consequences follow. Sarai and Hagar do not get on at all, and in the end Hagar and her son Ishmael are expelled into the desert. But the God of grace hears her cries and he takes care of them. She too will be the mother of many descendants. How big is God?

Many years later, Jesus the Messiah declared: 'Before Abraham was, I am.' He is the true and greater heir of Abram, a flesh-and-blood son of his line. In Christ, God is bringing about his earlier promise to bless the nations of the world through Abram's family. God's plan was much bigger than Abram's.

This is a story of Abram trying to bring about God's plan by his own efforts. There is a lesson for our calling here. We risk seeing our vocation as 'helping God out' rather than joining in with what he is doing. We can try to do what seems to be the right thing but in the wrong way. We need to keep looking at the big picture of God's salvation plan and discover our place in it. We need to see what he is doing and join in.

FOR REFLECTION

- Are we getting ahead of God? Are we watching for what God is doing and offering ourselves as part of the outworking?
- Do we think our story is so significant that we forget that this is God's story and we only have a small part in it?

11

Abraham and Sarah's Story (Part 5): Walk Worthy

The concept of 'covenant' is complex and much debated. It may be that the problem comes from theologians trying too hard to standardize each biblical mention of the word in a variety of contexts into one simple meaning. In the ancient world treaties were made between people in a whole host of ways. Earlier in Abraham's story we saw the 'cutting' of a covenant. Now we see another covenant with a different kind of cutting. It's not for the squeamish.

God appears again to Abram and summarizes what he is about to say by declaring that he is 'God Almighty' (El-Shaddai) – affirming that he is the one true God. He immediately follows this by telling Abraham that this has implications: 'Walk before me faithfully and be blameless.'

This is important, although we may not realize it. Noah was described as 'blameless', but this is the first time in the Bible we have God telling someone to lead a good life. We won't reach the Ten Commandments for hundreds of years. This is the first recorded time God calls on a human being to live a moral life.

You can read the extended speech from God in Genesis 17. God changes Abram's name to Abraham (more later), then promises to make many nations from Abraham's children, including kings. He also promises that this land of Canaan will belong to Abraham's descendants for ever. And then he tells Abraham his part of the bargain: he and all his male descendants must be circumcised. Ouch.

Circumcision

Circumcision is not unique to the Jews and according to Wikipedia was practised in a number of ancient civilizations from the Egyptians to the Aztecs. About one third of all males in the world today are circumcised, mostly Muslims and Jews.

Paul, himself a Jew, was strongly opposed to any suggestion that Gentiles need be circumcised if they became Christians. Instead, he believed that 'circumcision of the heart' was required. The ancient ceremony signified being set apart for God, but now this would be something that believers did within, rather than with the outward sign. The outward sign of the new covenant was baptism. I find myself crossing my legs and feeling thankful for that.

Meanwhile, God changes Sarai's name too – she will be Sarah. Notice how both their names are changed to include 'ah' – a laugh. Abraham and Sarah's name change suggests a radical transformation. Not everyone who is called by God will have their name changed, but our common calling includes God's call to live radically changed lives – including the call to live a moral life. There's even a verse about calling that highlights this: 'For God did not call us to be impure, but to live a holy life' (1 Thess. 4:7).

As a young evangelical Christian I was brought up memorizing verses like 'For it is by grace you have been saved, through faith – and this is not from yourselves, it is the gift of God – not by works, so that no one can boast' (Eph. 2:8–9). We were constantly and rightly reminded that we are not saved by our good works but by our faith in God's grace. But the text continues in the next verse: 'For we are God's handiwork, created in Christ Jesus to do good works, which God prepared in advance for us to do' (Eph. 2:10). We are not simply saved from our sins to receive eternal life. There's work to do.

The book of Ephesians divides easily into two – chapters 1–3 and 4–6. The first half tells us how wonderful God is and what amazing things he's done. The second half is all about living that out. Chapter 4 begins: 'As a prisoner for the Lord, then, I urge you to live a life worthy of the calling you have received.' In the Greek text, Paul literally says 'walk worthy'. The whole direction of our lives should be a reflection of what God has done for us in Christ. What follows in Ephesians 4 is a series of examples of what this means, with instructions to stop doing something bad and do something good instead. Stop telling lies and speak truthfully; stop stealing and do something useful with your hands; don't say negative things but encouraging things; don't be angry, bitter and ready to fight, but be kind and compassionate to one another; don't get drunk but be filled with the Holy Spirit. He sums this up by saying we should put off the old self and put on the new self.

Taking off/putting on

Some years ago I was visiting a church in a notorious part of London and the speaker was preaching on this text (Eph. 4). He called forward an attractive young woman and asked her to put on a jacket, but she couldn't do it because she was already wearing a thick coat. A simple and memorable illustration, but it really came alive for me a few days later when I asked the pastor if the church had a ministry to the many prostitutes who worked in the local area. He said that they did and that some of them were now Christians and members of the church. 'In fact,' he said, 'do you remember the woman who helped with the sermon on Sunday? She's the preacher's wife, but she used to be a prostitute.' At that moment, the sermon illustration about 'taking off and putting on' became much more profound.

But what of us? We can see clearly that a prostitute needs to change and 'take off' her old life. But are there less obvious things about our own lives that need to be removed, and what things do we need to 'put on'?

Elsewhere, Paul also writes: 'Let us behave decently, as in the daytime, not in carousing and drunkenness, not in sexual immorality and debauchery, not in dissension and jealousy. Rather, clothe yourselves with the Lord Jesus Christ, and do not think about how to gratify the desires of the flesh' (Rom. 13:13–14).

The Bible gives a radical call to radical change, to live morally different lives. If we are no different from the culture around us, have we really given God our lives? Jesus talked about being faithful in small things. When talking to young people about guidance and God's will for their lives, I have sometimes asked them if they are willing to do the things he makes plain in his word.

Circumcision of the heart

And yet, we must be clear about this. A call to morality – a call to holiness – is a call in response to what God has done, not a call to behave well so that God will like us. This change comes not from gritting our teeth or escaping from the world in some way. In Galatians 3, Paul reminds his readers that this is a work of the Holy Spirit in us. As we have seen, his letters frequently call us to live out what God has *already done* in us.

Writing to Jews who believed that physical circumcision was vital, Paul explains it like this: 'A person is not a Jew who is one only outwardly, nor is circumcision merely outward and physical. No, a person is a Jew who is one inwardly; and circumcision is circumcision of the heart, by the Spirit, not by the written code. Such a person's praise is not from other people, but from God' (Rom. 2:28–29).

FOR REFLECTION

- Are you walking a life worthy of the grace you have received?
- What behaviours do you need to take off? What will you put on in their place?

12

Abraham and Sarah's Story (Part 6): Blessed

In Genesis 18, Abraham and Sarah are visited by three men. The text is initially ambiguous about their identity; Abraham offers food and drink to all three (vv. 4–5) but he has already addressed one of them as 'Lord' (v. 3). This is therefore considered to be what theologians call a 'theophany' – a human appearance of God himself in the Old Testament.

Hospitality

The text is remarkably detailed concerning the hospitality Abraham offers, although welcoming strangers is thought to have been normal in the ancient world. In several places in the New Testament we are encouraged to practise hospitality, notably in Hebrews, which probably has Abraham in mind: 'Do not forget to show hospitality to strangers, for by so doing some people have shown hospitality to angels without knowing it' (Heb. 13:2).

Paul also makes a similar point in Romans 12:13, saying simply: 'Practise hospitality.' The actual meaning of the Greek phrase here is 'Pursue love for strangers'.

We also get some quite specific detail about where everyone is during the different conversations in Genesis 18 – 'at the entrance to his tent'; 'under this tree'; 'in the tent' and notably 'at the entrance to the tent, which was behind him'. This appears to be because the writer wants us to know that at a key moment Sarah can hear the conversation. She hears the Lord declare that within a year she will have given birth to a son. Until now, we have only seen Abraham hearing from God, so this is possibly the first time Sarah has heard the voice of the Lord for herself.

Sarah laughs at the possibility of getting pregnant, which is understandable. Even though he has his back to her and she's in the tent, the Lord asks (his words are probably kind, not accusatory) why she laughed, and repeats his promise that she will indeed give birth.

Sodom

The chapter continues in a darker vein as God reveals to Abraham his plan to destroy Sodom. Although he must have Lot in mind, Abraham never mentions his nephew, who lives there, but he does intercede on behalf of the city, asking if God would really destroy the population if some 'righteous' people lived there – even if only a few. God agrees that he would not destroy the city if there were ten righteous people there.

Despite Abraham's prayer, Sodom is later destroyed and in the story of Lot's rescue we see just how bad a place it is. The two other men in chapter 18 are revealed to be angels at the beginning of chapter 19 when they visit Lot. Lot also offers them generous hospitality, including sheltering them at the risk of his own life. He is not saved because of this good deed, but because 'when God destroyed the cities of the plain, he remembered Abraham' (Gen. 19:29).

Wrath

We are welcomed to a heavenly banquet in the Age to Come, which may make us laugh like Sarah. Is that really possible? Yes, it is, but not because we deserve such a blessing. On the contrary, Paul says: 'Like the rest, we were by nature deserving of wrath' (Eph. 2:3) – see also Romans 3, and Psalms 14 and 53. He could have said: 'Like Sodom we were deserving of wrath.'

In Romans, Paul writes about the salvation of both Jews and Gentiles. He speculates: 'What if God, although choosing to show his wrath and make his power known, bore with great patience the objects of his wrath – prepared for destruction? What if he did this to make the riches of his glory known to the objects of his mercy, whom he prepared in advance for glory?' (Rom. 9:22–23). We are not destroyed like Sodom, although we deserve it. Instead, God found just one man who was righteous, and everyone was spared because that one man willingly took upon himself the fully justified wrath of God.

In the verse that precedes those verses I quoted from Romans 9, Paul writes: 'Does not the potter have the right to make out of the same lump of clay some pottery for special purposes and some for common use?' (v. 21). We must approach vocation with a sense of how 'lucky' we are – 'blessed' is a better word of course. We need an attitude of willingness to do whatever work God calls us to do, great or small. And that is enough.

FOR REFLECTION

- Count your blessings.

13

Abraham and Sarah's Story (Part 7): The Greatest Sacrifice

Genesis 22 is one of my favourite chapters in the whole Bible. In fact I fear that I might say too much here, because there is so much in the first nineteen verses alone, especially when it comes to calling. You could say that this one chapter manages to include many of the lessons we will learn again in later chapters of this book.

First of all, God takes the initiative. While it is important that we listen, so often God's personal call comes completely out of the blue. And when he calls, he calls Abraham by name – he is clearly meant to respond. Abraham's response is one word in Hebrew: '*Hineni*'. More of that below, but for now it is sufficient to say that this means 'Here I am' or 'I am ready!'

I believe that when God wants us to do something significant, he speaks louder. Most of the time we can get on with life without too much thought, but for life-changing decisions it is important that we hear clearly. When God calls Abraham in this chapter, he asks him to take someone to be sacrificed as a burnt offering. God tells Abraham who that is in four ways: 'your son, your only son, Isaac, whom you love'. In this way we know that God fully understands the shocking implications of what he is asking, and Abraham can have no doubt either. Isaac was the son God had promised for so long who had finally been born against all the odds. Now he is asking Abraham to sacrifice him.

If this seems horrific, remember three things:

1. God had told Abraham that he was his very great reward. The reward for Abraham's faith was therefore not a son but God himself.
2. In the end God would not actually let Abraham go through with the deed – it was a test through which he would learn a great deal.
3. Later, Jesus would say: 'If anyone comes to me and does not hate father and mother, wife and children, brothers and sisters – yes, even their own life – such a person cannot be my disciple' (Luke 14:26). Some commentators regard this as hyperbole, and it's probably true that Jesus is using classic rabbinic exaggeration to make his point. Nevertheless, he is insisting that he must always come first.

God tells Abraham to sacrifice Isaac 'on a mountain that I will show you' – a phrase similar to Abraham's original call in Genesis where he is told to leave his family and go to 'a land that I will show you'. Will he obey fully this time?

True worship

Early next morning Abraham saddles his donkey and sets off with Isaac and two servants. When they reach the place, Abraham tells the men to wait. 'We will worship and then we will come back to you,' he says. Scholars believe that the first time something is mentioned in the Bible, we should take note as it sets the tone for what follows. This is the first mention of 'worship' and it really puts a marker down, doesn't it? It shows how seriously we should take Paul's instruction in Romans: 'in view of God's mercy, offer your bodies as a living sacrifice, holy and pleasing to God – this is your true and proper worship' (Rom. 12:1).

It's also worth noting that Abraham says '*We* will come back'. The clause seems to be deliberately tantalizing. Does Abraham really believe that? Or is he lying to prevent the two servants from intervening? We had to wait many centuries until Hebrews was written for the answer: 'Abraham reasoned that God could even raise the dead' (Heb. 11:19).

As they climb the mountain, Isaac points out that they have everything they need for a sacrifice except the offering itself. Abraham's response is ambiguous again: 'God will provide the lamb.' Whatever Isaac thought this meant, he goes on and allows his father to bind him on the makeshift altar. Keep in mind that Isaac is probably a teenager now and his father is very old, so he could easily have fled, but he is a willing victim. The father and the son together are both willing participants here.

As the father raises the knife, God calls him again: 'Abraham! Abraham!' Presumably God calls twice to ensure he is heard. Abraham responds '*Hineni*' again. God tells him not to kill Isaac after all.

God has provided a sacrifice – Abraham sees a ram nearby caught by its horns – and Isaac is 'resurrected'. The writer adds a little note: Abraham called this place 'The LORD Will Provide', which suggests that this is no fable but something that really happened.

God says to Abraham: Because you have not withheld your son, you will have 'descendants as numerous as the stars in the sky' – something he had promised previously, but this time he adds: as many as the grains of 'sand on the seashore' (Gen. 22:17).

Hineni

I said we would return to *Hineni*. Although I am wary of making any incident too prescriptive, like Abraham we too can and should say '*Hineni*' – 'I am ready' – because this response is not unique. It repeats throughout the Bible, which means we can answer our test question: 'Is this text descriptive or prescriptive?' This time it's prescriptive.

When God called out to Moses from the burning bush, Moses replied '*Hineni*'. When Jacob asked Joseph to go to his brothers, Joseph said '*Hineni*'. When God called out to the young boy Samuel three times, Samuel finally responded '*Hineni*. I'm listening!' When God asked who would go for him, Isaiah cried '*Hineni!* Send me!'

The story of the offering of Isaac is an obvious prefiguring of Jesus' passion. The letter to the Hebrews, quoting Psalm 40, explains this profoundly:

> Therefore, when Christ came into the world, he said: 'Sacrifice and offering you did not desire, but a body you prepared for me; with burnt offerings and sin offerings you were not pleased. Then I said, "*Here I am* – it is written about me in the scroll – I have come to do your will, my God."'
>
> First he said, 'Sacrifices and offerings, burnt offerings and sin offerings you did not desire, nor were you pleased with them' – though they were offered in accordance with the law. Then he said, '*Here I am*, I have come to do your will.' He sets aside the

> first to establish the second. And by that will, we have been made holy through the sacrifice of the body of Jesus Christ once for all.
>
> (Heb. 10:5–10, my emphasis)

It's a bit odd that the writer tells us that sacrifices and burnt offerings are not required and God did not desire them. Didn't God ask for them in the Old Testament? But this Hebrews text is actually quoting the Old Testament. Did it contradict itself?

No. It's just as Hebrews says elsewhere – these things were given as means for forgiveness before Christ came. They served their purpose but had to be endlessly repeated. But now Christ has died 'once for all'. They were 'a shadow' of what was to come (Col. 2:17).

In fact, as we have already said, forgiveness always costs – it requires a payment, and for sin the payment is death, as Adam and Eve were warned. But God deals with this problem with the death of his Son once for all, the 'just for the unjust'. As Abraham told Isaac, God provided the sacrifice.

Meanwhile, how should we respond? With Abraham, every believer is called to say '*Hineni*' if and when a specific call comes. We must be ready and willing all the time, whatever God asks of us.

FOR REFLECTION

- Are you ready? If God calls, will you say '*Hineni!*'?

FURTHER READING

Levenson, Jon D. *The Death and Resurrection of the Beloved Son* (Yale University Press, new edn, 1995).

LISTEN

Find Leonard Cohen's song 'You Want it Darker' online and play it as you reflect. (Note: Do make sure to find the original version, not the Solomun (*sic*) remix, unless you are playing it in a night club.) There is a lyrics version here:

- https://www.youtube.com/watch?v=qzg1H520yJ4

14

Isaac's Story: Seeing What the Father Is Doing

What can you remember about Isaac? God reveals himself in the Old Testament as 'the God of Abraham, Isaac and Jacob', three individuals sometimes known as the patriarchs, but we hear very little about Isaac except as a character in the stories of his father Abraham and his sons Jacob and Esau. Isaac is the one who passively allows himself to be offered by Abraham as a sacrifice. Isaac is the one who is fooled by Jacob when he gets the blessing due to his brother Esau.

When things turn out well . . .

There's also another story about Isaac but he only appears at the end, almost as an afterthought. It's the story of how a wife was found for him. Abraham sees his own death approaching after the death of Sarah, so he insists to his servant that Isaac must not marry a local Canaanite girl, but someone from his own relatives must be found. In addition, the girl must come to Isaac, who must remain in the land promised by God to Abraham. The servant goes off to find the right fiancée.

I'm not a huge fan of cowboy films, but I know they often seem to include a scene in which two gunslingers meet in the middle of the street and see who is quickest to draw and shoot the other guy. In the Bible, stuff often happens at wells where people have come to draw water, and each time we come across such a scene, we should look for variations on that theme. Cutting a long story short, Abraham's servant finds a wife for Jacob at a well and she turns out to be ideal for him in every way, as requested by Abraham. She is Rebecca, the daughter of Abraham's relative Bethuel. She agrees to marry Isaac, who loves her very much and they live happily ever after, or at least until she gets pregnant with twins who are fighting in the womb even before they pop out.

The text here doesn't mention the name of Abraham's servant, but assuming it is the same servant that Abraham mentions in Genesis 15, this is Eliezer. So it is Eliezer who seeks and finds a bride for Isaac, which is fascinating since 'Eliezer' means 'God is helper' and in the New Testament it will be the Helper, the Holy Spirit, who reveals Christ to the believer and the church, and who is the seal of our 'marriage' to the Bridegroom.

'That turned out well . . .'

In John 4, Jesus comes to a place known as 'Jacob's Well' and there he meets a foreigner – a Samaritan woman. He offers her spiritual water and demonstrates supernatural insight about her difficulties finding a good man – she's had five marriages and is now in an unmarried relationship – and she is so impressed that she rushes off to town to say 'I may have found the Messiah'. As a result, many of the people there believe in him. Like Eliezer, she has gone away and brought back 'brides' for the Son, only this time they are foreigners and outsiders, because now the gospel is for everyone, not just one family.

Bringing people to Christ is the work of the whole church now, with the help of the Helper, or more accurately it is his work that he does through us. Like Eliezer we can pray for success and for circumstances to work in God's favour. Like the Samaritan woman talking to the townspeople, and like Philip talking to Nathanael (John 1), we can say 'Come and see!'

Not all are called to be evangelists. Let's face it, they are often extroverts with the gift of the gab, but as the church we are *collectively* called to call others to Christ. We may not like the idea of evangelism, but it is an aspect of our common vocation. Paul told Timothy to 'do the work of an evangelist', which suggests that Timothy wasn't especially gifted at it.

The good news is that it is something we do together. The even better news is that this is God's mission and all we have to do is join in. If only it was so simple. Well, sometimes it is . . .

'A funny thing happened . . .'

Just before Christmas 1986 I called round to my in-laws' after the church service on a Sunday evening, to pick up some presents. It was probably the first time I'd gone to the house without my wife. My father-in-law had been feeling low and was signed off work, but I was surprised when he asked 'Do you think God could heal me?' within moments of my arrival. He and his wife were not churchgoers at the time. I took off my coat and sat with him.

We talked and I explained that I could pray for him, though I could not guarantee healing. But I did say that all of us need the greater healing of our hearts that comes through the forgiveness offered by Christ though the cross. After about an hour, to my surprise, he said 'I want to do this', and quickly fell to his knees. I prayed with him and he asked Christ to be his Saviour and Lord, praying out loud for himself.

When I arrived home afterwards, my wife could scarcely believe the news. 'A funny thing happened . . .' I began. Remarkably, exactly twenty-five years later to the day, he died, and I conducted his funeral. God had been at work that evening and I have to say it had little to do with me except a willingness to recognize what God was already doing.

'Follow that chariot!'

In Acts, as the early church grows, we see God at work through the disciples, and how they pick up what he is doing and join in. Even though persecution has begun and the disciples are scattered, it becomes an opportunity for the Spirit to work through his people. Philip gets an angelic message and heads to the Gaza road from Jerusalem. He sees an important Ethiopian official in his chariot and the Holy Spirit prompts him to get alongside the entourage, where he hears the man reading from Isaiah. In those days most people read out loud rather than to themselves.

Philip asks if the man can understand the text. The man can't, but he invites Philip into his chariot to explain. The text is the 'suffering servant' passage, which is about Jesus, and Philip explains this. Further along the road they come to a place where there is water and the official asks to be baptized. As soon as Philip has performed the ritual, the Spirit takes him away – presumably on another mission.

Paul's encouragement to Timothy to do some evangelism suggests that our main vocation could be specific to one ministry, but also we should be encouraged not to limit ourselves and neglect other opportunities. Clergy who are natural evangelists need to ensure that pastoral work is done in their parish, even if that is achieved by freeing others to do it.

In Michael Green's excellent little paperback *Freed to Serve* he tells of times when people would turn up at the vicarage seeking counsel and he would refer them to his wife, or how he allowed capable businesspeople to chair the church council. Church leaders need to be identifying the gifts and strengths of their people and setting them free to serve.

Meanwhile, watch for the signs of God at work. And join in. But don't get in the way.

FOR REFLECTION

- Where are the 'wells' and 'chariots' in our lives now? In the kitchen at the office? On the bus? At the in-laws' house?
- Are you scared of sharing your faith? What's the worst that could happen? What's the best thing that might happen?
- Can you see God already at work in the life of anyone you know? Is he calling you to get involved in drawing them to himself?
- If you are a church leader, is any area of work being neglected because you lack the necessary gifting? Is there someone else who could do it?

FURTHER READING

Keller, Tim. *The Reason for God* (Viking, 2008).
——. *Making Sense of God* (Viking, 2016).
Lloyd, Michael. *Café Theology* (St Paul's, 3rd edn, 2012).
Pippert, Rebecca. *Out of the Saltshaker* (IVP, new edn, 2010).

15

Jacob's Story (Part 1): Mummy's Boy, Father's Son

Next time they make a movie about the story of Isaac's two sons, I have a suggestion for the casting team. Esau should be played by Sean Bean, and Jacob by Mr Bean. Esau was a big hairy bear of a man, and Jacob . . . wasn't. Isaac was proud of his oldest son and favoured him. Jacob was Mummy's boy.

Jacob learns early on that he can trick his way through life, or at least he thinks he can. He notes that although his older brother is bigger than he is, he isn't quite so clever or streetwise. So when Esau arrives home from a hard day being macho, Jacob is able to fool him into paying rather more than he should for a bowl of soup.

We also discover that Jacob may well have learned this manipulative behaviour from his mother, who helps him deceive his virtually blind father into giving him the family inheritance – which he never receives, we might note, because when his deception is discovered, he has to run for his life so big brother won't kill him. Note to self: you can't inherit anything if you are dead.

What follows is more humorous than we may have realized.

First of all, on his flight from his angry brother Jacob stops to sleep for the night at Bethel, although this is actually the name he gives it afterwards, as we will see. In the absence of a budget hotel, he sleeps out in the open with his head on a stone. In his dreams he sees a ladder up to heaven on which angels are ascending and descending. At the top of the ladder is God, who speaks to Jacob and tells him that he is the God of his father and grandfather. God adds: 'I am with you and will watch over you wherever you go, and I will bring you back to this land. I will not leave you until I have done what I have promised you' (Gen. 28:15). When he wakes up, Jacob declares: 'Surely the LORD is in this place, and I was not aware of it' (Gen. 28:16).

In the morning, Jacob sets up an altar in the spot where he has slept and without consulting the local council changes the name of the place from Luz ('light') to Bethel ('house of God'). His prayer that follows is both humorous and sad:

> Then Jacob made a vow, saying, 'If God will be with me and will watch over me on this journey I am taking and will give me food to eat and clothes to wear so that I return safely to my father's household, then the LORD will be my God and this stone that I have set up as a pillar will be God's house, and of all that you give me I will give you a tenth.'
>
> (Gen. 28:20–22)

Is this man serious? Did he not hear what God previously said? Jacob is trying to strike a deal with God – to manipulate him. Out of his extraordinary grace, God had already promised to be with Jacob and never leave him. But Jacob wants to renegotiate the terms: you can be my god, and I'll expect your protection, food, clothes and safety – and by the way, I'll give you back a tenth of what you give me. Generous.

Jacob has a lot to learn.

Every time our prayer is 'If you . . . then I . . .', we are negotiating with God. In fact, we need to always come to him saying 'Because you . . . I will . . .'

Meanwhile, was that place the 'house of God'? Was it the 'gate of heaven'? If we could find the exact spot today, would we discover a 'wormhole' to heaven, like something in a sci-fi movie? Or a wardrobe?

Nathanael

In John chapter 1, after the excitement of the prologue ('In the beginning was the Word . . .'), we meet John the Baptist, the one who will prepare the way for the Messiah by drawing people back to God. As well as baptizing, John has gathered some disciples but now begins to turn their attention towards Jesus, and we see brothers Andrew and Simon become followers of this man, whom John calls 'The Chosen One'. Andrew then calls Philip, who in turn tells Nathanael, saying: 'We've found the Messiah – it's Jesus from Nazareth.'

I like to say that Nathanael is obviously a Yorkshireman. He's a bit cynical but he calls a spade a spade. When he hears what Philip has to say, he declares: 'Can anything good come from Nazareth?' In Yorkshire the oft-quoted version is 'T'only thing good to come out o' Lancashire is t'road to Yorkshire.' (Note: I am from Lancashire myself and I once met Geoffrey Boycott. We didn't share many laughs.)

When Nathanael eventually meets Jesus, he has a surprise. Jesus says: 'Here truly is an Israelite in whom there is no deceit.' He knows that Nathanael is a straight-talker. Nathanael is caught off guard and asks how Jesus knows so much about him. Jesus responds that he had a vision and saw Philip talking to him 'under the fig-tree'. Jesus must be right because Nathanael is amazed and his cynicism is overturned: 'Rabbi, you are the Son of God; you are the king of Israel.'

I picture Jesus smiling at this point as he tells Nathanael: 'You believe because I told you I saw you under the fig-tree. You will see greater things than that . . . Very truly I tell you, you will see "heaven open, and the angels of God ascending and descending on" the Son of Man' (John 1:50–51). We should note here that 'you' becomes plural after 'very truly'. This is a message for everyone, not just Nathanael. Jesus is claiming that he himself is Jacob's ladder. What Jacob never realized is that Bethel was not the gate of heaven – after all, hadn't God promised to go with him wherever he went? But he wasn't listening properly.

God with us

At the end of Matthew's gospel, Jesus renews his call to his disciples. It's known as the Great Commission. The apostles are commissioned to go out into the whole world, to make disciples, to baptize them, thus joining them to the church in a sacramental ritual, and to teach them to do everything the apostles have been told. Then Jesus adds: 'And I will be with you always, to the end of the age.'

As Jesus' followers today, the commission has been passed down to us. With the apostles we are called to go out into the world and fulfil the rest of the Great Commission. We sometimes refer to our churches as 'the house of God', but while it's good that we have places set aside for worship and meeting together, Jesus, the ladder to God, goes with us wherever we go. Our faith is not just for special places on special days with special leaders (or ladders). Jesus sends us everywhere, and goes with us every time.

Of course it's useful to set aside a special day at a special time in a special place to focus on God. Unfortunately the unintended consequence is the risk of an unbiblical dualism that ends with us unconsciously thinking God is not interested, or at least less interested, in the other places and times. Your home, your workplace, the gym, the pub – Jesus is in all those places. Your vocation may be in what is unfortunately called a 'secular' place. But there's actually no such thing, no such place. God is everywhere you are.

Our vocation is not confined to special people (ministers, monks, missionaries) in special places (churches, chapels, cathedrals) and a special day (Sunday, Easter, Christmas). Christians are God's people at every moment. The simple command to love God and love neighbour can and should be implemented anywhere and everywhere at all times. This is God's call for everyone.

FOR REFLECTION

- Do we separate the sacred from the secular? Are there places where we subconsciously think that God is not there?
- If God is omnipresent, then what does it mean for Jesus to say 'I am with you'?
- Do you feel God with you in your place of work?
- How hard is it to feel that God is with you in the pub?

FURTHER READING

Stevens, R. Paul. *The Other Six Days: Vocation, Work, and Ministry in Biblical Perspective* (Eerdmans, 2000).

16

Jacob's Story (Part 2): Wrestling with God

In a previous chapter, I mentioned Leonard Cohen's amazing song 'You Want It Darker'. In the lyrics, Cohen refers to a 'dealer', who could be Jacob or it could be God.

Jacob wanted all his life to be the 'dealer' – to make contracts with God on his terms. As he arrives at the moment when he will have to face up to his past when he meets his brother Esau, he finds that he meets God first – in the darkness.

He has tried to soften up his brother by using all his cunning and craftiness. He's sent all his worldly goods and family ahead so that Esau receives them first. For all his wheeling and dealing he's got nothing at this moment. Now alone, he's confronted by a mysterious man who wrestles with him all night. Jacob will realize afterwards that the man wanted him to let go because 'no one shall see God and live', and daylight was coming. To get free, the man puts Jacob's hip out of joint, but Jacob still won't let go.

Jacob has a need to win and won't let go – literally unless this man blesses him. Remember, God had already told Jacob he was blessed many years ago when he was travelling in the other direction, fleeing from his brother, but Jacob still wanted to cut a deal.

The man changes Jacob's name to 'Israel', meaning 'he struggles with God', which sums up not only this moment but all of Jacob's previous life. He's been using deceit and trickery all along – even with his own brother, father and father-in-law. But now he's left alone and defenceless. All he can do now is lean on God and cling to him.

In Hebrews there is a brief but striking reflection on this incident: 'By faith Jacob, when he was dying, blessed each of Joseph's sons, and worshipped as he leaned on the top of his staff' (Heb. 11:21). At the end of his life, Jacob was a man at peace, settled in his faith, worshipping God and blessing his children and grandchildren, but leaning on his staff as he remembered how God had weakened him so he would have to lean on him.

The apostle Paul wrestled with God before his conversion, but also afterwards as he sought healing for a mysterious ailment – we don't know what it was despite much speculation: 'Three times I pleaded with the Lord to take it away from me. But he said to me, "My grace is sufficient for you, for my power is made perfect in weakness." Therefore I will boast all the more gladly about my weaknesses, so that Christ's power may rest on me' (2 Cor. 12:8–9). We'll expand on this in a later chapter, but note that Paul is definitely not suggesting here that the rather 'wet' and weak TV/movie caricature of Christians and particularly vicars (see: Rowan Atkinson, Derek Nimmo, Adam Smallbone – but not Geraldine Granger) is how it always should be. Those used by God in the Bible include Jacob and other 'weak' people but also some warriors, brave shepherds defending the sheep from lions, and tough fishermen. Remember the title of this book?

The point is, God uses our strengths but he also sometimes makes us weak to ensure that we don't rely on those strengths but upon him. Sometimes he has to take something away so that we can receive something better.

'My Way'?

Since I was ordained, I have conducted hundreds of funerals and, while I want each one to be as personal as possible, I have sometimes wondered about the wisdom of giving the grieving family too much control over the order of service. Is that music what they *really* want for the farewell of their loved one? There is sometimes black humour, such as the man who died of a coronary, whose family insisted we play the theme from *Titanic* at the crematorium. That's 'My Heart Will Go On' in case you didn't know.

Clergy discuss these things of course, swapping horror stories or funny incidents. We all share a collective dislike for 'My Way' by Frank Sinatra, although I do remind them that it could be worse. I once took the funeral of a young man who had known he was dying and insisted that his coffin should leave the church to a recording of 'My Way' . . . by Sid Vicious of The Sex Pistols. I spent several hours removing the swear words with some audio software I happened to have. Strangely, we were not taught audio editing at theological college.

We are emphatically *not* called to do it '*My* Way' and God will sometimes ensure that won't happen, even if it means giving us a limp. If God is calling you, better to let go than to wrestle with the one who is The Way.

FOR REFLECTION

- Has God weakened you to prepare you for something?
- Are you wrestling with him? Why?

OTHER

If you visit the Tate Britain gallery in London, look for Jacob Epstein's stunning sculpture *Jacob and the Angel*.

17

Joseph's Story: God Was with Him

As I said earlier, 'vocation' is a word that has fallen into misuse. Outside the church it now tends to mean self-fulfilment, with no reference to God at all, forgetting that there must be a caller for there to be a call – in grammatical terms there must be a subject as well as an object. Inside the church, though, we've over-spiritualized it and made it only about special callings – to priesthood, ministry, missionary work, and so on.

In one of Tim Keller's great talks that I heard some time ago – sadly I can't find it again – he paraphrases a sermon he heard Revd Dick Lucas preach many years earlier. I also have to paraphrase from memory what Keller said: 'If you were to go to a bookstall at a church and find a biography with the title *The Man God Uses*, you might immediately think it was the story of a missionary, teacher, church leader, or specialist in some sort of spiritual work. What you have in the story of Joseph is a highly successful *secular* official.' This is also true of some other biblical narratives, such as that of Daniel and his three friends.

Joseph's story is a long and remarkable tale. Although God later tells Moses he is 'the God of Abraham, Isaac and Jacob', it is Jacob's son Joseph who gets the most attention in the latter part of Genesis, as the main character in 13 of the last 14 chapters.

We first meet him as a teenager, the apple of his father's eye. He's often described as 'the dreamer', but he only has two dreams at the start of his story and after that he is always an interpreter of other people's dreams.

His brothers are jealous of his popularity with his dad – so jealous that they want to literally kill him. No one wants to actually be the one to do it, so they throw him in a pit. As 'chance' would have it, slave traders pass by and Joseph is sold to them instead, becoming chief steward for a man called Potiphar in Egypt. Joseph resists the sexual advances of Potiphar's wife – another bit we gloss over in Sunday school – but is unjustly accused of attempted rape and ends up in prison. But here's the thing: every time things get worse for Joseph, the Bible says 'God was with him'.

Finally Joseph's fortune changes, and after interpreting various dreams he becomes the prime minister, appointed by the king (pharaoh) of Egypt to prepare for a major ecological disaster: famine.

The whole of the known world comes to Joseph to be saved, including his brothers. Joseph strings them out for a while because they don't recognize him at first, but he eventually reveals who he is. His father Jacob is brought to Egypt and finally dies in the last chapter of Genesis.

Now Jacob is out of the way, Joseph's brothers are fearful that he will have them executed, but instead he says: 'Don't be afraid. Am I in the place of God? You intended to harm me, but God intended it for good to accomplish what is now being done, the saving of many lives' (Gen. 50:19–20). This is profound. What Joseph is saying suggests he believes that God's purposes were being worked out even in the evil actions of his brothers, even in his bad times. The Lord is in control, despite appearances to the contrary. Joseph never answered a 'call'.

Everything happens *to* him, often against his will and over a twenty-year period in which life just seemed to go downhill – one step forward, ten steps back, you might say. But he remains faithful, giving glory to God when he interprets dreams, which is the nearest he gets to having a vocation, it seems.

Being useful wherever we find ourselves

In the New Testament there is a short one-chapter letter from Paul to Philemon that primarily concerns a man called Onesimus. He had been a slave of Philemon and had fled from his master, but has run into Paul who has led him to faith. Paul sends him back and jokes about his name, which means 'useful', and suggests that while he was useless before, now he will live up to his name, because he has found Christ.

Joseph was a slave for many years and yet he always made himself useful. His faith is his motivation and eventually he gets his reward with his meteoric rise from the dungeon to the post of prime minister, like an early version of Nelson Mandela. In his new position, he effectively saves the world.

Another innocent man who suffered

Many years after Joseph, another man would be unjustly accused and hated by his 'brothers' when he had been sent to them by his father. Joseph survived death in the pit, but Jesus, though innocent and falsely accused, would actually die. But that death on 'Good Friday' would accomplish the saving of many lives, and his 'rising' from the prison of death was his vindication.

Vocation may sometimes simply be about staying faithful and looking for the signs that God is with us, even in evil times or trying circumstances, and making ourselves useful. In a later chapter I will tell the story of Hae Woo, a Christian in North Korea who planted a church in a labour camp. In her terrible circumstances, God was with her and working through her.

An old saying suggests: 'Blossom where you're planted.' Don't wait for a special call to come. It might never happen. Instead, wherever you find yourself, however bad it seems, remain faithful and look for the opportunities to serve God and others.

FOR REFLECTION

- Have you been through hard periods in your life? Were you able to see God at work at the time?
- Are you able to look back now and see God working things for good?

FURTHER READING

Yancey, Philip. *Where Is God When It Hurts*? (Zondervan, anniversary edn, 2002).

OTHER

For a great example of 'the man God uses', read the obituary of Richard Farnell in the *Church Times* at:

- https://www.churchtimes.co.uk/articles/2018/7-december/gazette/obituaries/obituary-professor-richard-farnell?fbclid=IwAR3tTP-8svBAk7LmmioXZa-y2c-jRApfX_oo5giZe2_zRMIm3tw4RDD3QE_E

18

Moses' Story (Part 1): Who Am I?

The story of Moses is another that is well known if you went to Sunday school or even heard it in school assembly, but once again there are plenty of not-so-child-friendly bits along the way that you may not have heard or remember.

Even his birth narrative is not for the squeamish. Moses' birth, four hundred years after Joseph, is at the time when the latest Egyptian king (Pharaoh) has decided that there are far too many of these Semites being born and orders the killing of all the Israelite baby boys. As most people know, Moses' mother hides him in a basket and pops it in the River Nile. Like you would.

It just happens (we get that a lot in the Bible, don't we?) that the basket is found by Pharaoh's daughter who falls for this cute kid and asks his real mother to nurse him for her. Imagine the conversation when she tells her dad about it: 'Yes, I know you want to kill all the Hebrew boys, but letting just one live wouldn't hurt, would it? For me, Daddy. Please.' So Moses grows up in the palace, treated as the 'Prince of Egypt' as the animated children's film describes him, which probably proved useful later when he would need access to Pharaoh.

We should remind ourselves occasionally that Bible narration often focuses on detailed action with long periods in between. After growing up in the palace, Moses is 40 years old when the next key event unfolds.

Moses sees an Egyptian mistreating an Israelite. His righteous anger is aroused against this injustice and he kills the Egyptian. Later he intervenes in a fight between two Israelites, but one of them (the one in the wrong of course) mocks him and asks: 'Who made you ruler and judge over us?' (Exod. 2:14). In simple terms, he is saying 'Who do you think you are?'

Joseph's brothers asked a similar question when he told them his dreams. Both Joseph and Moses eventually turn out to be rulers. Centuries later, the religious leaders in Jerusalem asked the same kind of question too: 'Jesus entered the temple courts, and, while he was teaching, the chief priests and the elders of the people came to him. "By what authority are you doing these things?" they asked. "And who gave you this authority?"' (Matt. 21:23).

Back in the Moses story, the man also adds: 'Are you thinking of killing me as you killed the Egyptian?' (Exod. 2:14). Moses realizes that word has got out about the murder, and he runs away.

Before we learn what happened next, pause to consider that Moses had acted as if he was the saviour of his people, but he would have to learn that God is the true saviour, before God could use him. All vocational thinking needs to take account of this.

Fleeing from Egypt, Moses arrives in Midian, where he meets and eventually marries Zipporah, daughter of Ruel, who is also known as Jethro. Moses is now the shepherd formerly known as Prince.

Another forty years pass.

Moses' big call comes when he is about 80 years old. No one is too old for God to use, and people do not have 'use by' dates, although to be realistic, in terms of church procedures it makes sense that we might think twice about sending someone to train for a paid post for several years if they are near to retirement from paid employment. Nevertheless, there is no retirement in the kingdom. Everyone has a part to play, paid or not, young or old. If vocation is ultimately about us loving God and our neighbour in whatever we are doing (and I believe it is), then we can all be on active service all the time.

Once again, we should be rather wary of making this story normative. Remember, when seeking to apply the Bible, we should always ask: 'Is this prescriptive or descriptive?' We can learn lessons, but just because Moses had to wait until he was 80 doesn't mean we should do the same. A vocation can come at 80 but need not wait until then. Like most of the Bible narrative, this is about God's unfolding plan of salvation, not some magic words that tell you personally and specifically what God wants to do with your life.

It's hard to say 'no' to God

And yet, the well-known story of Moses' call at the burning bush does resonate with many of us; perhaps we feel an affinity with Moses as he tries to squirm out of God's request. I sometimes meet ordination candidates who say: 'I've been trying to say *no* to God for several years now.' And then we both smile.

What can we learn from Moses' experiences? If you've not got this by now, we cannot treat this in a totally prescriptive way; if we do, then we all need to become shepherds in the Middle East and hang around waiting for bushes to catch fire. The story of Moses remains unique and descriptive. I don't remember meeting anyone else who was called by God out of a blazing hydrangea. Let's try to learn what this tells us about God before we consider what it might have to say about calling.

The first thing we should note, after God has got Moses' attention, is what God says before he asks Moses to get involved. He says: '*I* have seen the problem, so *I* have come down to rescue them. So now go – *I* am sending you.'

When God calls, it's often because he has seen the problem, he is going to do something about it, and by the way he'd like you to help him to do it, with his guidance and power.

A series of excuses by Moses follow. Here they are (see the table), with God's responses, and what he did later in Christ.

What Moses says	**What God says**	**What Jesus says/ does**
Who am I?	I will be with you	I will be with you always
Who are you?	I am who I am	Before Abraham was, I am
What about them?	Watch what I do	Believe because of my miracles
I can't speak very well!	I can open your mouth	Jesus is the Word
Send someone else!	OK, Aaron can go with you but you're still going	God did send someone else – Jesus

In summary, Moses says 'Who am I . . . that I . . . that I . . .?', and God responds 'I am'. It is not who *we are* that really matters; it's who *God is*.

Meanwhile, as the table shows, Jesus fulfils this Old Testament passage richly. The Word who is sent willingly by God, who performs miracles which John's gospel calls 'signs', and who declares 'Before Abraham was, I am', deals with our captivity to sin not by killing someone but by being killed himself.

After his resurrection, Jesus commissioned his disciples and us to go out into the world and make more disciples, promising that (like the pillar of fire and cloud in the desert) he will always be with us, whatever we are called to do. The church's vocation is to grow, to make disciples – an echo of God's first ever call: be fruitful and multiply. If we are seeking our vocation, this will be where we find it.

PS: On a very different note, when it comes to Moses and vocation, his real work did not begin until he was 80 years old. He spent forty years as a prince in a palace and forty years as a shepherd. Jesus spent thirty years as a carpenter. When it comes to vocation, these two examples (and there are many more) show that God values what we might wrongly call 'secular' work. Moses and Jesus spent more than half their adult lives doing something other than what we might wrongly call their 'spiritual' ministry.

Maybe sometimes the things we do that feel unimportant can be part of what prepares us for something later. I quote bestselling author Joanna Cannon on the front page of this book. Speaking at the Derby Book Festival in 2018, she was asked what she did before writing. She talked about the variety of jobs she had earlier in life, from working in a dog rescue centre, to barmaid, to delivering pizza, to perfume seller in a department store, to doctor. She recognized that each of these, in their own way, gave her an understanding of people and behaviour that makes her fiction so delightful in its observations of human interaction.

Nevertheless, we need to underline that while it may prepare us for something more, *whatever we are doing today* is an opportunity to serve God and others. Do not wait for the 'special' task. Serve him now.

FOR REFLECTION

- Moses' call is very unique and must not be considered a model for vocation. But if we think God might be speaking to us, it might be helpful to ponder Moses' responses and see if we are saying the same kind of things to God that he did. If so, might God be saying the same kind of things to us too?
- If you are in a job outside the church, do you recognize that God can use you there, and there is no division between the secular and the sacred?
- Moses' two roles as prince and shepherd prepared him for his role as Israel's leader. Is there something in your past life that has prepared you for your future?

FURTHER READING

Morse, Louise. *What's Age Got to Do with It?* (Monarch, 2017).
Stevens, R. Paul. *Aging Matters* (Eerdmans, 2016).

19

Moses' Story (Part 2): Fantastic Feasts and Where to Find Them

The story of the exodus from Egypt is reasonably well known. Some people have tried to demythologize it, as with other parts of the Bible, suggesting that the ten plagues might have happened through natural events, while others have tried to suggest that the whole thing is made up altogether.

Whatever our take on this, something significant occurred. It won't appear anywhere in the history books of Egypt because it was a national embarrassment and tragedy. Moses demanded that the pharaoh let God's people go and he continually refused, despite some powerful miracles, each of which caused mayhem in the country.

The plagues are not just an attack on the Egyptian king and/or his people. They're an attack on their belief in the Egyptian gods. Each of the ten plagues shows that God is in control and superior to the idol gods that the locals worshipped, from flies to frogs, from the sun to the Nile. Pharaoh's magicians frequently replicate Moses' miracles. This is like something out of a superhero movie where the hero with special powers fights an enemy who also has special powers. There is real spiritual warfare here. We see something similar in Elijah's contest with the prophets of Baal, although Baal's followers seem to be powerless. The Egyptian magicians are not.

In Acts 13 Saul and Barnabas come into conflict in Paphos with a false prophet named Bar-Jesus, also known as Elymas the Sorcerer, who tries to prevent them from converting the proconsul, Sergius Paulus. Paul, filled with the Holy Spirit, curses Elymas with temporary blindness. This is definitely a passage that is descriptive rather than prescriptive.

Screwtape and friends

When it comes to supernatural power, we should beware of glamorizing evil or suggesting that this sort of thing happens frequently. Church of England vicars are occasionally asked – usually by non-churchgoers – to exorcise rooms or places for various reasons.

I once spoke to the diocesan exorcist about this; he told me that when someone says a house is haunted, he turns up dressed all in black, perhaps looking like Neo in *The Matrix*, carrying a crucifix and black Bible, throws around some holy water while muttering a prayer, and the person is usually happy. He mostly deals with the felt needs and superstitions of those who call on his services, rather than real evil power.

Nevertheless, I have very occasionally had dealings with genuine demonic powers. This is not something to be sought out or sensationalized, but be assured that the power of the name of Jesus is infinitely stronger in these situations. Remember that this sort of thing is best left to those with the experience and wisdom to deal with it, and that there are real risks of psychological and spiritual damage. Do not try this at home.

The angel of death

Back to Exodus. Finally, after nine plagues have failed to convince Pharaoh to let the Hebrews leave, the angel of death comes for the sons of Egypt, including the son of Pharaoh himself, since he himself was worshipped as a god.

Jon Levenson's book *The Death and Resurrection of the Beloved Son: The Transformation of Child Sacrifice in Judaism and Christianity* is a challenging read and should probably only be attempted by those who have formally studied theology. Levenson is not a Christian, but his work has much to teach the followers of Christ. The book traces the development of child sacrifice, which was common in the ancient world, through the biblical material. He demonstrates that Yahweh demands that the firstborn son in each family should be offered to God as a sacrifice for sin. The troubling passage where Abraham offers Isaac seems shocking, but this is a thread throughout Scripture, not an isolated incident. In fact it is the beginning of God providing an alternative. As we said earlier, forgiveness is costly and blood is necessary for sin to be covered. Without the blood of the lamb on the Israelites' doorposts, the firstborn in their houses would have died too.

For more on this, search for *pidyon haben* on Wikipedia, which explains how even today in traditional Jewish families an offering must be made for the firstborn male a month after their birth. Instead of a literal sacrifice, money is given to the *kohen* instead, usually a token five shekels. Read the wiki article – I suspect you will find it fascinating.

The story of the lamb is also a captivating thread that runs throughout the Bible like the offering of the firstborn. The Israelites offered animals as sacrifices instead of children, but the writer of Hebrews says:

> The law is only a shadow of the good things that are coming – not the realities themselves. For this reason it can never, by the same sacrifices repeated endlessly year after year, make perfect those who draw near to worship. Otherwise, would they not have stopped being offered? For the worshippers would have been cleansed once for all, and would no longer have felt guilty for their sins. But those sacrifices are an annual reminder of sins. It is impossible for the blood of bulls and goats to take away sins.
>
> (Heb. 10:1–3)

The previous chapter ends like this: 'Christ was sacrificed once to take away the sins of many; and he will appear a second time, not to bear sin, but to bring salvation to those who are waiting for him' (Heb. 9:28).

Behold the Lamb

As John the Baptist said, Jesus is the Lamb of God who takes away the sin of the world, something we remember in the Church of England every time we share the Lord's Supper or Eucharist, which itself is a thanksgiving for Christ's passion, obeying his command to 'do this in remembrance of me'. Jesus instituted this sacrament at a Passover supper, where those present were remembering their deliverance from Egypt. Paul writes: 'Christ, our Passover lamb, has been sacrificed' (1 Cor. 5:7).

When we share the bread and wine, we also look forward to the marriage feast of the Lamb, when Jesus returns and the Age to Come begins. In communion, we remember, rejoice, receive and repent in readiness.

God told Moses that Passover should be celebrated every year to remind the Israelites of God's deliverance. Jesus instituted a more frequent feast to dynamically recall his work of deliverance for us. In Catholic and Anglo-Catholic circles there is nothing greater than the Eucharist and no greater responsibility than presiding at this great sacrament.

It is understandable that those from these traditions of the church who sense a call to this ministry see it as a very special vocation. We're sharing in a symbolic community meal with powerful significance, just as Passover was a family meal with significance. Receiving the elements of the Lord's Supper is something we celebrate together. But even if some traditions emphasize the role of the priest, this is still everyone's calling. Jesus' instruction 'Do this in remembrance of me' was and is a vocation for every Christian.

FOR REFLECTION

- What does the Lord's Supper mean for you? We are called by Jesus to celebrate it and yet many churches give it low priority.
- What do you think happens when we share the bread and wine?

FURTHER READING

Wright, Tom. *The Meal Jesus Gave Us* (SPCK, new edn, 2014).

OTHER

The Wikipedia article about the redemption of the firstborn son is at:

- https://en.wikipedia.org/wiki/Pidyon_haben

20

Moses' Story (Part 3): Now Can We Do What We Like?

Many years ago, at the Spring Harvest Christian holiday event, my wife and I were in a meeting and the speaker asked us to turn and introduce ourselves to our neighbours. Maybe you dread those moments, and I am not always keen myself. On this occasion the married couple we spoke to explained that they were there on the speaking team, and they had travelled from Switzerland, where they ran the L'Abri Fellowship founded by Francis Schaeffer. The woman was Schaeffer's daughter, Susan.

Schaeffer was one of the most influential evangelical Christians of the twentieth century. He came from the USA, and one of the things he insisted upon was that the USA was not a theocracy. A theocracy is where a nation and its laws are purely guided by their god. If such a thing has ever existed, it was the nation of Israel in the Old Testament. (The modern state of Israel is not the same; there are some influential orthodox Jews involved, but it is a modern democracy, of sorts.) Many laws in the UK are based on Christian principles, but we are not a theocracy and need to beware of how we apply the Old Testament laws to our modern world.

Schaeffer was clear that the Old Testament laws could not simply be applied to any nation, although the principles therein could be used. He was also worried about the mechanical application of laws, saying: 'Biblical orthodoxy without compassion is surely the ugliest thing in the world.' Some American evangelicals might do well to meditate on those words.

The Maker's instructions

Moses was given the law by God on Mount Sinai. We remember the Ten Commandments most of all, but there were lots more, including extensive instructions for the construction of the tabernacle or 'tent of meeting', and various ceremonial and hygiene laws. In their context, these instructions were very important. In a fairly primitive society, some of these laws were vital to survival and cohesion. Some of the instructions God gives to Moses were to prevent the people adapting the cultic practices of the nations around them, such as temple prostitution.

The little paperback *None of These Diseases*, written in the early 1960s by S.I. McMillen, examines the various laws given to Moses and highlights the great health benefits that would have resulted in the days long before anyone understood bacteriology, medicine, diet, and so on. But what do we do with this stuff now?

The early church had fierce debates about how much of the Jewish law the fledgling church should have to keep, especially over circumcision and dietary regulations. In Acts 15 the church leaders in Jerusalem meet to discuss the issue. Peter's contribution to the debate is startling: 'Why do you try to test God by putting on the necks of Gentiles a yoke that neither we nor our ancestors have been able to bear?' In other words, if you want Gentiles to keep the law of Moses, remember that we Jews never managed it.

The council decides to write a letter to the Gentile church leaders in Antioch. They write: 'It seemed good to the Holy Spirit and to us not to burden you with anything beyond the following requirements: You are to abstain from food sacrificed to idols, from blood, from the meat of strangled animals and from sexual immorality. You will do well to avoid these things' (Acts 15:28–29). So the leaders of the early church took the view that the requirements of the law given to Moses have passed. All they insisted upon came down to two things: don't eat meat that is being used in pagan ceremonies and only go to bed with your marriage partner. That's it.

What does the law require?

I'm rather glad that circumcision is not required of Christians, although we should note what happens in the following chapter of Acts. Paul is taking his new young assistant Timothy, a Greek Gentile, on his missionary travels so he has him circumcised so as not to create any possible barrier to the reception of the gospel among Jews. This is the same Paul who will get very angry in some of his letters with those who insist on circumcision. What is he playing at?

Here we see some guidance for our Christian lives – something also reflected in Paul's reflections on what food we are allowed to eat. Without going into all the detail, we might sum up his thoughts like this: Don't take offence and don't give offence except for the 'offence' of the gospel. If that offends, so be it, but don't let anything get in its way, especially your freedom as a Christian.

A couple of years after my ordination I was obliged to attend further training, which involved three days at a theological college in Oxford exploring the relationship between Christians and Jews. One of the speakers was a Christian minister from Texas and in his talk he insisted that Christians should actually keep the whole Old Testament law. To back up his argument, he quoted Jesus' words from Matthew: 'Do not think that I have come to abolish the Law or the Prophets' (Matt. 5:17). I quickly pointed out that there is a second half to this verse: 'I have not come to abolish them but to fulfil them.' He defended himself by saying: 'Of course there's no evidence that Jesus ever actually said those words.' We were a bit shocked and didn't respond at the time.

Some of us later cornered him and pointed out the dishonesty of quoting half a verse to make a point and dismissing the other half, at which point he told us bluntly that Jesus wasn't God and never claimed to be. We gave up.

The new covenant

But what did Jesus mean? The laws given to Moses were absolutely right for their time, but something has changed their significance. It's the reason we have an Old and New Testament. It's something to do with the words 'This is my blood of the new covenant' that Jesus said at the Last Supper.

After the resurrection when Jesus meets two disciples on the Emmaus road and they fail to recognize him, Luke says: 'And beginning with Moses and all the Prophets, he explained to them what was said in all the Scriptures concerning himself' (Luke 24:27). What would I give to hear that conversation? Always assuming I spoke the language of course . . .

The Bible is all about Jesus, even the Old Testament which never mentions him by name. This includes the law – even the dietary stuff, the strange rituals and the construction of the tabernacle, which according to Hebrews is a copy of the heavenly sanctuary. I would like to quote all of Hebrews chapters 6–10, but put this book down and read it if you like. For now, a verse we mentioned in the previous chapter will suffice: 'The law is only a shadow of the good things that are coming – not the realities themselves' (Heb. 10:1).

In the rest of the Sermon on the Mount, Jesus revisits the law and tells the crowds that if they expect to get salvation by their good works then they need to do more than the basic requirements of the law. They need not only to avoid adultery but also to check their whole lustful attitude. Anyone can love the people they like, but they have to love their enemies too. Eventually he sums it up: 'Be perfect, therefore, as your heavenly Father is perfect' (Matt. 5:48). Jesus seems to be saying: OK, by all means try to save yourself by keeping the law, but remember you must be absolutely sinless. Come and have a go, if you think you're holy enough.

Of course the gospel tells us that we all fall short and we need Jesus to fulfil the law on our behalf. Does this mean that we can do what we like? Paul dismisses this idea in Romans 6. The point is, in terms of salvation we can't earn it by good behaviour. Goodness has to be imputed to us by our incorporation into Christ and our sins atoned for by his death. But in terms of our ongoing behaviour, if we have been truly saved by grace, there will be fruit.

This is the whole argument of Galatians in which Paul insists that circumcision is no longer required because the Spirit is at work in us. In chapter 3 he calls the Galatians foolish for thinking that they were saved by faith and now need to keep laws. In chapter 5 he explains what it means to have the Spirit at work in us: 'But the fruit of the Spirit is love, joy, peace, forbearance, kindness, goodness, faithfulness, gentleness and self-control. Against such things there is no law. Those who belong to Christ Jesus have crucified the flesh with its passions and desires. Since we live by the Spirit, let us keep in step with the Spirit' (Gal. 5:22–25).

We must beware of any suggestion that vocation is a calling to keep rules. Everything begins and ends with what God has done. As we have already said, this is how the Ten Commandments begin: 'And God spoke all these words: "I am the LORD your God, who brought you out of Egypt, out of the land of slavery. You shall have no other gods before me"' (Exod. 20:1–3). These commandments don't begin with an instruction or law; they begin with a statement of what God has done. He's brought them out of slavery in Egypt. He loves them and can be trusted. These are good laws to live by. No other god is like this.

The summary of the law

Jesus was asked which laws were the most important. His response was to say: '"Love the Lord your God with all your heart and with all your soul and with all your mind." This is the first and greatest commandment. And the second is like it: "Love your neighbour as yourself." All the Law and the Prophets hang on these two commandments' (Matt. 22:37–40).

Any call to vocation can and must be seen as a call to love God and our neighbour. There is an Internet meme that has been falsely attributed to Martin Luther, though it's the sort of thing he might have said and sums up his thoughts. It says something like: 'The Christian cobbler does not accomplish his vocation by making shoes with little crosses on them; he does it by making good-quality shoes at a fair price and so fulfils the requirement to love his neighbour.'

Jesus' summary of the law is the great vocation of every believer: to love God and neighbour. Whatever we are individually called to do, it must include this; indeed this must be the guiding principle behind whatever specific calling we may have. As we have already said, this is something we can do wherever we are and whatever we are doing.

FOR REFLECTION

- How are you loving your neighbour in your work?
- In your home?

FURTHER READING

McMillen, S.I. *None of These Diseases* (Revell, 3rd edn, 2000).
Wingren, Gustaf. *Luther on Vocation* (Wipf & Stock, 2004).
Wright, Tom. *Virtue Reborn* (SPCK, 2010).

21

Moses' Story (Part 4): Leading the People

When my wife and I were on pilgrimage in Jordan recently, another group of travellers appeared at breakfast in our hotel. We learned that they were Druze believers, an ethnoreligious group who trace their ancestors back to Jethro, who was Moses' Midianite father-in-law. Apart from providing him with a job and a wife, Jethro also helped Moses with his leadership issues.

Successive kings, queens, presidents and prime ministers throughout history have discovered how difficult it is to lead a whole nation. Moses would probably want to say: 'Try doing it in a wilderness with scarce food and water while you travel across it.'

In Exodus 18, Jethro notices that Moses spends all day from sunrise to sunset 'judging' the people – acting as arbiter in their various disputes with one another. He has some wise words for Moses, telling him to appoint deputy 'judges' who will arbitrate in all but the most difficult cases. He adds: 'If you do this and God so commands, you will be able to stand the strain, and all these people will go home satisfied' (Exod. 18:23). It's interesting that delegation is often known as an 'art'. Jethro explains it in a beautifully simple way, but in practice many leaders find it hard. Letting go is not easy; trusting someone to do a job you have been doing is risky. They will not do it like you. They may fail and you get the blame. And if they do well, you might not look as good.

It seems to me that delegation is an important skill for Christian leaders to learn. God himself delegated when he gave responsibility to Adam and Eve, despite knowing they would fail. Jesus chose twelve apostles, knowing they would fail, one of them fatally. Paul told the Corinthians that the church is a body of many different parts, each with different gifts and a role to play, and should not be a one-man or one-woman band.

The gift of administration

In Acts, as the church expands rapidly, the apostles discover for themselves that leaders can't do it all. There are disputes to sort out and eventually they realize that they must delegate. Seven men are chosen as administrators, but they are not just pen-pushers. They have to be people who are known to be 'full of the Holy Spirit and wisdom'. We may not have noticed that they are set apart in a way we might have thought was reserved for clergy: 'They presented these men to the apostles, who prayed and laid their hands on them' (Acts 6:6). A short sentence follows that sums up the result of this decision: 'So the word of God spread' (Acts 6:7).

Here is clear scriptural warrant for the view that all work is sacred and there should not be a special class of work, done by ministers, monks and missionaries, as Steve Walton says. I have worked with the support of administrators all my life, even before I was ordained, and feel really blessed that every single one of them was excellent and liberated my work. Thank you, Philippa, Peggy, Margaret, Karl, Christine, Anji, Diane and Jenice. And apologies to anyone else I have been stupid enough to forget – I rely on administrators to remind me of these things.

We must value our administrators and others whose work is not up-front but vital and who would only be noticed by their absence. It is a noble and vital calling, and with the right person(s) the word of God will spread.

A gift of the Spirit

'Here is a trustworthy saying: whoever aspires to be an overseer desires a noble task' (1 Tim. 3:1). The same could be said of administrators. A couple of years ago I was preaching in a lively charismatic church and commented that I had been approached many times after services by people who wanted me to pray for them to be healed, or to speak in tongues, but no one had ever asked me to pray for the gift of administration. I had mentioned this in a number of sermons and talks over the years, but on this occasion a young woman came to me afterwards and ruined my illustration! She wanted me to pray for her because she had applied for the church administrator job.

As a postscript, remember what happened next in the Acts narrative. Stephen, one of the seven administrators just appointed, is working signs and wonders (this does not mean he understood spreadsheets or knew how to unjam the printer). His ministry and preaching upsets some people and he is arrested. After a magnificent speech that proves his wisdom and extensive Scripture knowledge, he is finally martyred. I have sometimes noted during church business meetings that the first Christian to die for their faith was the treasurer.

FOR REFLECTION

- Who are the people who work behind the scenes in your church's life? How do you show them your appreciation?
- Could God be calling you to a background helping role in your church – or outside it?

OTHER

The United Kingdom Church Administrators Network (UCAN) is an excellent not-for-profit organization set up in 2009 to 'support church administrators across the UK and to promote the Spiritual Gift of administration within the church'. Their website is here:

- https://www.churchadministrators.net/

22

Moses' Story (Part 5): 'Mustn't Grumble'

> It takes eleven days to go from Horeb to Kadesh Barnea by the Mount Seir road.
>
> (Deut. 1:2)

Though these words are at first obscure, when we work out what they signify they become poignant and sad. This is the journey that the exodus should have followed, but instead the Israelites wandered the desert for forty years. I've just checked on a maps app and it says that to walk from the Egyptian border to Jerusalem would take 137 hours if you could do it non-stop, but when you have toddlers and sheep and the treasures of the Egyptians to carry, it takes a little longer, I guess.

The Israelites rejected the advice of Joshua and Caleb, choosing to believe the report of the other ten spies about big scary giants inhabiting the land. As a result they found themselves wandering about in the desert for a whole generation. (For discussion: is democracy always the best way to run a country? Just asking for a friend.)

We haven't the space to review all those years, but one story will suffice. In Numbers 20 the Israelites arrive and camp at

Kadesh in the desert of Zin. The people complain, as they often do during the wanderings. They whinge that they would have been better remaining slaves.

God tells Moses to gather the people in front of a nearby rock. Moses is to speak to the rock and it will gush out all the water they need. But when the people gather, Moses speaks angrily to the people before he speaks to the rock, saying 'Listen, you rebels, must we bring you water out of this rock?' (Num. 20:10). He seems to be implying that he is the one supplying their needs, but he also goes on to strike the rock twice.

God is angry with Moses for this, so angry that he warns that Moses will now not be going into the promised land. Instead of speaking to the rock, he had hit it twice. So what? This seems tough until we learn more about the rock.

In 1 Corinthians 10, Paul is warning the Corinthians against presumption. He writes about the Moses story: 'They all ate the same spiritual food and drank the same spiritual drink; for they drank from the spiritual rock that accompanied them, and *that rock was Christ*' (1 Cor. 10:3–4, my emphasis). The rock was Christ! Paul says that the rock 'accompanied them', as though this same rock somehow went wherever they did and supplied water when needed. And Moses hit the rock twice instead of speaking to it. God says: 'You didn't believe in me, Moses.'

Since the days of Moses, the Jewish people have remembered God's provision during their wilderness wanderings by celebrating the Feast of Tabernacles. For a week they build temporary shelters and live in them instead of their homes. It is this festival that is being celebrated in John 7 when Jesus makes a startling claim: 'Let anyone who is thirsty come to me and drink. Whoever believes in me, as Scripture has said, rivers of living water will flow from within them' (John 7:37–38). Great news! But our lesson here is not to presume upon God, as we noted above.

In 1 Corinthians 10, Paul continues, condemning the Israelites' idolatry, revelry, sexual immorality, testing of God and . . . grumbling: 'And do not grumble, as some of them did – and were killed by the destroying angel' (1 Cor. 10:10). It's almost amusing to see that alongside these other evils, we find 'grumbling' worthy of God's severe judgement. There is a reason for this. In *The Great Divorce* C.S. Lewis famously suggested that this is where hell begins.

The lesson is about attitude. When discussing vocation we tend to think about what we are called to do, but here we are reminded about the *manner* in which we obey God. 'Mustn't grumble' is a popular expression, but sadly, churches seem to always have at least one person whose vocation is to let the minister know how good it used to be and why this new idea will never work.

In one church we belonged to, there was a woman whose reaction to any suggestion of change was to declare: 'Oh, we tried that in my church years ago and the church emptied.' We wondered how many times her church had emptied. Nowadays of course we can grumble any time of day or night via the wonders of the Internet.

In Philippians Paul writes: 'Do everything without grumbling or arguing, so that you may become blameless and pure, "children of God without fault in a warped and crooked generation." Then you will shine among them like stars in the sky as you hold firmly to the word of life' (Phil. 2:14–16).

Just a thought: wouldn't it be sad if we were to find our true purpose, our great vocation, and then spend our days grumbling about it?

FOR REFLECTION

- Do you recognize yourself in any of the above comments about church grumblers? Do you justify it with comments about needing to be realistic?

FURTHER READING

Lewis, C.S. *The Great Divorce* (Collins, 2012).

23

Moses' Story (Part 6): Lifting Hands in Prayer

In Exodus 17 the Israelites are attacked by the Amalekites. Moses tells Joshua to choose some men and go and fight them. Moses, his brother Aaron and a man called Hur stand on a hillside and watch the battle.

Moses holds out his staff over the valley and the Israelites start winning, but whenever he lowers his hand the Amalekites are in the ascendancy. So Aaron and Hur find him a stone to sit on, and then they hold up his hands until sunset, when Israel has won.

I suspect that when all has been revealed in the Age to Come, we will discover that throughout history when the church was triumphing it was because there were those who were praying, unseen, metaphorically holding out their staff, or holding up the hands of someone else's staff.

Praying together or alone?

I was reflecting on the story of Moses having his hands lifted up and it occurred to me that I pray best when I pray with others. Our church used to hold monthly prayer meetings. We had strict rules about starting and ending: 8 p.m. start even if some people are late, 9 p.m. end, and doors locked by 9.05 p.m. I was always amazed by how quickly the time passed and how much praying I managed to do. An hour on my own was much harder work. Similarly, praying with the church staff team each morning was easier than on my own.

There are many examples of people praying together in the Bible, but Jesus talks about praying on our own too in Matthew 6. At first we might think that he is saying we should only ever pray alone, but that's not his point. The context is a warning against being too showy and public with our prayers, fasting and giving. He's challenging the motives of some people who like to impress others with their piety. Praying alone is important, but there is nothing wrong with praying together, especially if it helps us.

Prayer support

When I was running a busy parish church I was tremendously blessed by the prayer support of others. Every Tuesday at 4 p.m. my phone would ring and Dudley would ask me what was in my diary for the week ahead. I knew that he and his wife Moira would faithfully pray every day. He would pass on the details to Robert, Barbara, Josephine and Duncan, who would also all be praying devotedly. This work was unseen and unknown by many people in the church. It was all organized by Jane, who had set up similar support for other key people and ministries. I am glad to include their names in this book in appreciation for all their prayers over many years.

'When you pray . . .'

Jesus does not tell his disciples to pray. He assumes they will ('When you pray . . .'). Paul sometimes asks the readers of his letters to pray for him.

Prayer is the vocation of every Christian, but some will discover a particular calling to pray for leaders and others. Many churches and missionary organizations send out regular prayer bulletins. It saddens me that I have not always been very faithful in praying for others as much as others have prayed for me.

If you don't know how or what to pray for others, picture them in your mind and use Aaron's blessing: 'The LORD bless you and keep you; the LORD make his face shine on you and be gracious to you; the LORD turn his face towards you and give you peace' (Num. 6:24–26).

When we find it hard

Prayer is so hard, isn't it? It rarely comes naturally, except in a crisis, and then it can feel as though we are asking for help from a friend we haven't spoken to for months.

But always remember that God's grace is bigger than our feeble attempts to live out our religion. He always stretches out his hand to us. 'Who then is the one who condemns? No one. Christ Jesus who died – more than that, who was raised to life – is at the right hand of God and *is also interceding for us*' (Rom. 8:34, my emphasis).

When we are not praying, Jesus is still praying, and we are welcome to join him any time.

FOR REFLECTION

- Is God calling you to pray regularly for someone or an organization?

FURTHER READING

Duncan, Bruce. *Pray Your Way* (Darton, Longman & Todd, 1993) (a guide to how your Myers-Briggs type finds a particular style of prayer more helpful than others).
Greig, Pete. *How to Pray: A Simple Guide for Normal People* (Hodder & Stoughton, 2019).
Hallesby, O. *Prayer* (Augsburg, 53rd edn, 1963) (out of print).
Keller, Tim. *Prayer: Experiencing Awe and Intimacy with God* (Hodder & Stoughton, 2016).
Pritchard, John. *How to Pray: A Practical Handbook* (SPCK, 2nd edn, 2011).
——. *How Do I Pray? A Little Book of Guidance* (SPCK, 2015).
Wilkinson, David. *When I Pray, What Does God Do?* (Monarch, 2015).
Wright, N.T. *The Lord and His Prayer* (Eerdmans, 1997).

24

Moses' Story (Part 7): Knowing God

In Exodus 33, we have a glimpse of Moses 'at prayer' as he goes to the tent of meeting:

> As Moses went into the tent, the pillar of cloud would come down and stay at the entrance, while the LORD spoke with Moses. Whenever the people saw the pillar of cloud standing at the entrance to the tent, they all stood and worshipped, each at the entrance to their tent. The LORD would speak to Moses face to face, as one speaks to a friend.
>
> (Exod. 33:9–11)

Moses was never elected leader of his people. He didn't seize power by a military coup. This private prayer-life is where Moses' real authority came from.

I don't think I have ever heard a sermon about 'authority'. In the gospels, Jesus' authority is frequently questioned by those in . . . er . . . authority. The context is usually a miracle he has performed – someone who has been sick all their life gets wonderfully healed and the religious leaders question who gave Jesus permission to do this. By contrast, in Luke 7, the centurion (not a religious leader, obviously) is commended by Jesus for his faith in Jesus' authority over his servant's illness. The centurion describes himself as 'a man under authority' and he recognizes that Jesus has similar authority over sickness.

The subject of authority also comes up in the context of Jesus' teaching. For example: 'When Jesus had finished saying these things, the crowds were amazed at his teaching, because he taught as one who had authority, and not as their teachers of the law' (Matt. 7:28–29).

Before Jesus was eventually betrayed in the darkness, temple guards had been sent earlier to arrest him in the daylight, but they returned saying: 'No one ever spoke the way this man does' (John 7:46).

A leading authority

In TV news or newspapers we are sometimes given a quote from an expert in their field, who is described as a 'leading authority' or even 'worldwide authority'. I'm always amazed that there are these people who have devoted their lives to a deeper understanding of a rare Amazonian spider, Ming vases or toenails. I searched for 'leading authority' online, and the second autocompleted search suggestion was 'leading authority on chimpanzees'. (It was a link to Jane Goodall, for those who really want to know. Do get out more.)

There are clearly different types of authority. There are those in official positions of power and those whose expertise makes them 'an authority' – someone we trust because they have specialized knowledge. Jesus' authority falls more into the latter category, but there's something more.

Knowing the Father

Listening to Jesus, the crowds instinctively knew that here was someone who was a leading authority on God and who spoke meaningful truth into their lives. But this was more than just knowing the information. Jesus knew his facts, but he also knew the Father and had come to introduce him to the people who should have known him better.

When Jesus prayed, the disciples listened. This man was intimate with God his Father and they yearned for that kind of relationship with God too. The night before his death he prayed an especially intimate prayer and the disciples heard it. It's recorded for us in John 17 and it underlines our point here. He talks (prays) in the third person about himself: 'For you granted him [Jesus] authority over all people that he might give eternal life to all those you have given him. Now this is eternal life: that they know you, the only true God, and Jesus Christ, whom you have sent' (John 17:2–3).

We are all called to know God personally. I remember hearing a Christian singer called Gus Eyre explaining this many years ago. He told us about a time when he was in a crowd of people outside a concert venue where Sir Cliff Richard was performing later. Cliff's luxury car pulled up and he walked into the building while security guards held back the army of fans. But as he did so, he looked up and nodded 'Hi Gus!' with a smile, much to the rest of the crowd's amazement. Gus and his band had toured the UK with Cliff a couple of years earlier, so he knew him personally.

But this illustration does not come close to giving us a sense of God's deep love for us, the depth of relationship he seeks from us. Paul writes: 'I pray that you, being rooted and established in love, may have power, together with all the Lord's holy people, to grasp how wide and long and high and deep is the love of Christ, and to know this love that surpasses knowledge – that you may be filled to the measure of all the fullness of God' (Eph. 3:17–19). This is not just knowing about God, but knowing him more than we know our closest friend. Notice that Paul calls it 'a love that surpasses knowledge'.

In Matthew 7, Jesus says that some people will do amazing miracles but on the Last Day we will discover that they did not know God. The evidence of this will be that they did not do the will of his Father. As James will say later in the Bible, real faith will result in fruit. What should we do with our lives? Knowing God will cause us to desire to do God's will.

Don't try too hard!

Recently I was praying and reflecting on the importance of truly knowing God, and growing in my personal relationship with him. This may be obvious to everyone else, but it occurred to me that much of the time I try hard to make this happen and I fail. It's because (once again) I make it all about me and not about him. It's the usual trap – we try too hard instead of letting him reveal himself to us. Obviously we have a part to play, but that will usually mean simply praying and watching for the signs of him at work, then joining in. Jesus prayed in Gethsemane: 'Not my will but your will be done.' That's how he encouraged us to pray in the Lord's Prayer, isn't it?

FOR REFLECTION

- Do you know about God more than you know God? Consider what it means to know God himself.
- Pray to the Father, asking that he will take you deeper into relationship with him.

FURTHER READING

Packer, J.I. *Knowing God* (Hodder & Stoughton, 3rd edn, 2005).

25

Bezalel's Story: Gifted by the Spirit

Have you done the Alpha Course yet? I hope that anyone who reads this book who hasn't already been on one will get there soon. If you have one at your church, invite me to speak! One thing I especially enjoy is when I'm invited to lead the talks about the Holy Spirit on the Alpha Course.

In the introductory talk, we are introduced to the first person mentioned in the Bible who was filled with the Holy Spirit. He's called Bezalel:

> Then the LORD said to Moses, 'See I have chosen Bezalel son of Uri, the son of Hur, of the tribe of Judah, and I have filled him with the Spirit of God, with wisdom, with understanding, with knowledge and with all kinds of skills – to make artistic designs for work in gold, silver and bronze, to cut and set stones, to work in wood, and to engage in all kinds of crafts.'
>
> (Exod. 31:1–5)

The Holy Spirit is always involved when the Bible talks about the place where we meet God – the tabernacle, the temple, or the living stones of the church. We'll return to this later in the chapter about Ezra and Nehemiah (Chapter 56).

One of the sad things about church history is that when 'corrective' movements of the Holy Spirit emerge, Christians sometimes manage to take them too far. The pendulum swings beyond what is reasonable. With the Pentecostal movement it became almost compulsory to speak in tongues, despite Paul's challenge to the Corinthians to see the rich variety of things the Spirit might do in each church.

Similarly, when the Reformers got upset about the worship of Mary and the saints, the selling of indulgences and general superstition, they decided that the best way to deal with this was to smash up anything decorative. This mindset had some support in the Ten Commandments where the making of images was forbidden. Some also rejected the gifts of the Holy Spirit, saying they had ended after the apostolic era.

Even now, images are not part of any mosque you might care to visit, but the decoration is frequently stunning, made of amazingly complex coloured patterns. By contrast, some more conservative Reformed churches can be deliberately plain and dull. The walls of the church where I was vicar for many years were painted a simple salmon colour, although there was an impressive stained-glass window. On one occasion a visiting vicar friend commented: 'It looks like a pink crematorium!'

Bezalel was given artistic abilities by the Spirit of God to make the place where he would be worshipped beautiful. All great art has its origins in God himself, whether designed for churches or not, and can move our spirits in worship.

Certainly many artists see their creativity as a vocation: 'So Bezalel, Oholiab and every skilled person to whom the LORD has given skill and ability to know how to carry out all the work of constructing the sanctuary are to do the work just as the LORD has commanded' (Exod. 36:1).

We only need to see a sunset to recognize that God is the great artist, but there is something of the image of God in each of us, and in some people the creative spark is especially bright. Only God can create out of nothing, but the rest of us can have a go at glorifying him by arranging bits of his creation into something beautiful. It may be our vocation.

FOR REFLECTION

- Does the church value the work of artists as much as in the past when church buildings were less utilitarian and built skilfully to the glory of God, and stained glass was a stunning creation in the days before photographs, let alone moving images?
- Since 'beauty is in the eye of the beholder', have you sometimes felt your artistic works are poor because others don't appreciate them? Done to the glory of God, could simple artistic creations actually be part of your prayer life – painting, gardening, writing, singing, or many other things?

26

Joshua's Story: 'Moses My Servant Is Dead'

Bible characters sometimes appear from nowhere. They seem to be called by God without any history or back story. However, there are a few of them who slip into centre stage having been around for a while and step into a role that they have been groomed for, by accident or design.

Apprenticeship was something believers were doing long before the TV series. Learning a 'trade' has a long tradition outside the church, but we can see that Joshua was being prepared for his future ministry as he watched and helped Moses.

According to Numbers 11:28, Joshua had been Moses' helper since he was a boy. One of the twelve spies who scouted out the promised land, he and Caleb gave a 'Minority Report' and urged the Israelites to enter the land, but the views of the other ten prevailed. As a consequence the Israelites wandered around the desert for forty years and a whole generation missed out on what God had been promising. Indeed Joshua and Caleb are the only survivors from Egypt to enter Canaan.

After Moses' death, Joshua is the obvious choice to take over as leader, because despite being ignored when he gave his report, and despite allowing the Israelites to get away with serious idolatry while Moses was up Mount Sinai, he has grown into his role as Moses' right-hand man.

Be bold!

There is a well-known Christian chorus based on words from the book of Joshua. It's called 'Be Bold!' and proclaims that the singer is not afraid or dismayed (neat but obvious rhyme) and we, too, can be victorious because God is with us.

God tells Joshua not to fear because he is with him. Is this prescriptive for us? The context in Joshua 1 is the scary moment for Joshua when Moses has died and God calls him to take over and lead the people into the promised land. It's appropriate that Joshua is reassured that Yahweh is with him as he had been with Moses. Later it says: 'That day the LORD exalted Joshua in the sight of all Israel; and they stood in awe of him all the days of his life, just as they had stood in awe of Moses' (Josh. 4:14). Joshua is not unique in being encouraged like this. In Psalm 31 King David writes: 'Be strong and take heart, all you who hope in the LORD' (Ps. 31:24).

But is it as simple as that? In chapter 5, just before the glorious victory over Jericho, a mysterious stranger with a sword meets with Joshua. Joshua asks whose side he's on, thinking him to be a soldier, but the man replies that he is on neither side because he's the angelic commander of the Lord's army.

This is an important reminder for Joshua and us that God is with us in a very specific way. He is not going to automatically give us victory over everything we face. It will not really be Joshua who wins the battle at Jericho, but God. Joshua must do what he's told. We see this unfold throughout the book and it will be a pattern repeated in other Old Testament stories, particularly Gideon's tale, for example.

Don't mess with God

In the story about the conquest of Jericho, Joshua is given very specific instructions which the Israelites obey, and victory is smooth. However, when it comes to the next challenge, the city of Ai, things go wrong. Israel suffers defeat. God explains to Joshua that a man called Achan has pocketed some of the spoils won at Jericho for himself, instead of dedicating them to God.

The Israelites take drastic action and put Achan to death, and soon afterwards put right their earlier defeat. The action they took seems drastic, but God is laying down a marker for the future, so that they understand the seriousness of Achan's deception.

In the book of Acts, after the joys of Pentecost and the initial exciting, rapid growth of the church, we are metaphorically slapped in the face with the story of Ananias and Sapphira, who are believers who give to the work of the church but hide the fact that they have a little more money than they are letting on. When Peter confronts each of them in turn with their deception, they drop down dead. Their demise parallels the punishment of Achan. God puts down a marker as if to say 'Don't mess with me'.

At the end of Joshua's book, he prepares to die and reflects on Israel's amazing history up to this point. He himself had been born in Egypt, but he looks even further back to Abraham's call and the miracles and guidance of God. He asks the people whose side *they* are on and declares: 'as for me and my household, we will serve the LORD' (Josh. 24:15).

The people respond: 'We too will serve the LORD, because he is our God', but to their surprise perhaps, Joshua is not so sure: 'You are not able to serve the LORD.' He goes on to add that they will never live up to such a promise. The reality is that God would be well within his rights to deal with all of us as he dealt with Achan, Ananias and Sapphira. We cannot presume upon him.

And yet, we must not be too negative about all this. Paul famously declares: 'If God is for us, who can be against us?' (Rom. 8:31). He can say this, not because of our failings but because of Jesus' finished work. 'Jesus' is the same word as 'Joshua' in Hebrew, and now a greater Joshua has come. Now we can be bold and strong, not because we are special but because the Lord our God *is* with us. He is on our side as we serve him. Jesus commissioned his followers, not to conquer the land of Israel with weapons, but to conquer the whole world with his message, and added: 'And surely I am with you always, to the very end of the age' (Matt. 28:20).

FOR REFLECTION

- In what ways have you experienced God being with you?
- If he seems far away, ask him to reveal himself to you right now. Don't expect instant answers but look for his touch in the days ahead.

27

The Judges' Story: 'Are You Coming In or Going Out?'

After Joshua has led the Israelites into the promised land, the land of Canaan is divided into territories for each of the twelve tribes of Israel, named after the twelve sons of Jacob. (Actually it's slightly more complicated: the Levite tribe don't get any land because they are the priests and instead of farming they have a religious duty and so receive income from the tithe. But there are still twelve territories because there are separate bits of land for the descendants of Joseph's two sons Ephraim and Manasseh, sometimes called the 'half tribes'.) I hope you're following this . . .

A phrase I remember hearing many times during my childhood is: 'Are you coming in, or going out?' In the days before central heating was common, poorer families such as ours only heated one room and so standing in the doorway letting in cold air while you made up your mind about something was certain to make you unpopular. Hurry up!

The book of Judges is a liminal experience (from the Latin *limen*, 'a threshold') for a whole nation. Initially, 'liminal' was used to describe individuals on the threshold of adulthood and the rites of passage that different cultures have for those in their teens, but it has come to be used more generally to describe testing times of transition for groups of people, during which they grow. We might call them 'make up your mind in the doorway' moments.

Staring down a lion

I recently enjoyed lunch with a fellow minister, who told me his extraordinary life story. Born in Harare, Zimbabwe, he was the son of an Anglican priest, but as far as he was aware there was no expectation that he might follow in his father's footsteps. As a teenager his sense of vocation was instead moving towards working with big game animals on the huge nature reserves.

One day, he was helping to guide a party of tourists when they suddenly came upon a lioness who was very unhappy that her cubs were under threat. Roaring loudly, she charged at them. The tourists did the 'wrong' thing and ran for their lives; fortunately the lioness ignored them but instead came within a few feet of my friend and his colleague, who had a gun. Unfortunately, he hadn't had time to load it. They remained still, staring down the lioness, and eventually she just walked away.

For my friend, that was a very quick liminal experience. You might imagine that the fear he felt was what put him off his intended career. Initially it didn't, but in time, God used it to bring him to the place where he saw in himself the kind of inner strength that might be needed in Christian ministry. We reflected that sometimes the resolve required to enable individuals or communities to overcome a difficulty is akin to staring down a lion.

The question for God's people at the centre of their liminal experience is: 'Are you coming in or going out?' After the death of Joshua, as the Israelites settle into the promised land, the question is whether they will truly enter in and possess the land that God has provided. In the book of Judges several things happen in doorways or tent entrances until they climax in a very gory tale at the end of the book in which a concubine is gang-raped and left for dead – on a doorstep. Another Bible story that your nice Sunday school teacher never mentioned. We'll come to it shortly.

It's by no means certain, but it appears that there are twelve judges in the book. As you asked, they are Othniel, Ehud, Shamgar, Deborah, Gideon, Tola, Jair, Jephthah, Ibzan, Elon, Abdon and Samson. It also seems that there is one judge per tribe. Some are well-known names, and we will get to them in a minute. Others have only brief mentions, but their stories fall into a basic pattern. The people forget God and rebel; they are attacked by other nations; they pray for deliverance; God raises up a 'judge' who leads them to victory over the enemy. Repeat. And again.

So, let's have a quick look at the some of the better-known judges in the chapters that follow.

28

Deborah's Story: God Uses . . . a Woman

It might not be politically correct today, but it has been suggested that in its time, the story of Deborah is meant to tell us that there were no suitable men to lead the nation, so God raised up a woman to shame them. Indeed the climax comes when another woman, Jael, kills the enemy leader Sisera, who had told her to 'stand in the doorway of the tent' and guard him. Like many of the stories in Judges, it's a bit gory and involves the first use of a tent peg to pin something down *inside* the tent.

There's a question I'm reluctant to answer here: is killing ever right? It merits a lot more discussion, with consideration of the 'just war' and a 'lesser evil', but here are some brief thoughts.

For our ethics module at theological college, students had to prepare short talks on moral issues and then defend them. One of my fellow students spoke about war and took a strong pacifist anti-war stance. Emotionally I was drawn to her arguments, but I found myself asking 'What if?'

What if . . . you could prevent your child from being killed by shooting the killer? She would kill, the student said. What if . . . you could save a friend in the same situation? She would kill. What if . . . it was a stranger you could rescue? She reluctantly admitted she would kill. What if you could save a whole village where you lived but it involved killing a few people who were attacking you? She didn't want to answer that. She could see where I was headed.

Throughout this exchange, we were being watched silently by another student. He was training to be a vicar, like me. Previously he had been in the SAS, and when they stormed the Iranian embassy in London in 1980, he was the first in, abseiling from the roof into the centre of a hostage situation where there were six fanatical terrorists. His book *Baptism of Fire* tells his story, and recounts not only his brave exploits but also his powerful conversion.

War is a messy business and there are no easy answers to the moral and ethical questions involved. Chaplains operate within the armed forces – I know some of them and they tell me how they have gone with soldiers into combat unarmed themselves, requiring great bravery.

Is fighting for your country a vocation? Many people would say 'yes', but at the same time question the need for the conflict itself, as evidenced by the reaction to Tony Blair's darkest hour when he joined in the 2003 invasion of Iraq. I remember standing outside Parliament when the vote was taken, praying for the right decision and feeling they made the wrong one. Critics of the 'just war' claim there has never been a war that was justified. Judges makes no comment on Jael's actions, but the implication is that she did the right thing and that God approved. Discuss.

FOR REFLECTION

- Can killing ever be justified for Christians? Would you do it to save a loved one?
- Could you see yourself as an armed forces chaplain?
- Have a look at the arguments for 'just war': https://en.wikipedia.org/wiki/Just_war_theory

FURTHER READING

Collins, Frank. *Baptism of Fire* (Corgi, new edn, 1998).

29

Gideon's Story: God Uses . . . Insignificant People

Kevin DeYoung has written a little book with a title so long that it could be the whole text of the book. It's called *Just Do Something: A Liberating Approach to Finding God's Will, or How to Make a Decision without Dreams, Visions, Fleeces, Impressions, Open Doors, Random Bible Verses, Casting Lots, Liver Shivers, Writing in the Sky etc*. His fellow conservative American theologian, Bruce K. Waltke, has written a similar but more in-depth book, called *Finding the Will of God: A Pagan Notion?*

Apart from giving his name to an international ministry which puts Bibles in hotels and schools, the most memorable thing about Gideon is that he 'put out a fleece' to check that what God had already told him to do was correct. On a number of occasions I've heard Christian friends say they are going to do that too, because they have a difficult decision to make and are seeking God's guidance.

The thing is, I suspect none of my friends ever actually got a lamb fleece and put it outdoors, awaiting the test results from the lab next morning. In fact, Gideon already had clear guidance from God. The story does not demonstrate how to discern God's will; it shows God's extraordinary grace, even in our doubts. We do not need to 'put out a fleece' literally or metaphorically.

In Acts 1, after Jesus ascends into heaven, the disciples wait as instructed for the Holy Spirit to come and empower them. While they are waiting, they decide it would be good to replace Judas, and they propose two names with certain criteria before drawing lots. This is the last time this way of deciding things is mentioned. After the Spirit comes, they pray and fast and decide. See Acts 13:1–3 for a good example of this, and 1 Corinthians 2 for some of Paul's reflections about 'having the mind of Christ'.

Paul also has something to say about discerning God's will:

> Therefore, I urge you, brothers and sisters, in view of God's mercy, to offer your bodies as a living sacrifice, holy and pleasing to God – this is your true and proper worship. Do not conform to the pattern of this world, but be transformed by the renewing of your mind. Then you will be able to test and approve what God's will is – his good, pleasing and perfect will.
>
> (Rom. 12:1–2)

In David Wilkinson's excellent little book *When I Pray, What Does God Do?* he describes agonizing in his youth over God's guidance in every decision. While this is commendable in many ways, he realized that most things had already been revealed in the Bible, and mostly that involved loving God and loving his neighbour. He adds that once he realized this, somehow decisions about the other stuff became easier and more natural.

Nevertheless, despite some excellent points in Waltke's and DeYoung's books, there is much biblical support for miraculous guidance. Although he's a scientist, Wilkinson does not throw the whole supernatural baby out with the bathwater. Sometimes God does speak into our individual lives.

I remember debating with a theological college friend who insisted that God does not speak today and all spiritual gifts have ended. I asked him if he would listen if another Christian brought him a message he felt was from the Lord. He said a firm 'no'. So I asked: 'What if five friends, all unaware of each other, brought exactly the same message?' He still insisted he would ignore this completely.

Actually the Bible contains a vast number of supernatural interventions by God. Unless we take a very conservative view, like my friend, surely we learn that God speaks, and he speaks through individuals and circumstances to bring guidance. This has been my own experience.

However, remember that the initiative is always God's. We can be hopeful or expectant, we can pray for wisdom, but in the end God is sovereign and will reveal what he chooses in his time and his way. If we are seeking guidance, we must leave it to him to decide how and when to communicate it. Jesus himself warned against looking for signs.

In the wider context, the story of Gideon is all about who is actually bringing salvation and who should therefore get the glory. Gideon's story can be told as a tale of heroism as he trusted in God, but we must not make him a hero. He took a lot of persuading – probably too much – before trusting God, but God's grace and patience were bigger. The hardly-ever-preached postscript to his story is that he falls into idolatry. Remember that a key theme of the books of Judges and then of 1 Samuel is a demonstration that the true king of Israel is God himself, and no one else.

FOR REFLECTION

- Do you feel too insignificant to serve God? Pray for a greater sense of your worth in his eyes.
- Have you ever 'put out a fleece'? Is this a good way to discern God's will when facing an important decision?

FURTHER READING

DeYoung, Kevin. *Just Do Something* (Moody, 2014).
Harvey, Dave. *Am I Called?* (Crossway, 2012).
Huffman, Douglas S., ed. *How Then Should We Choose?* (Kregel, 2009).
Waltke, Bruce K. *Finding the Will of God: A Pagan Notion?* (Eerdmans, 2nd edn, 2016).

30

Abimelek's Story: Not Chosen by God at All

Abimelek (or Abimalek) is Gideon's son and his name means 'my dad is the king'. He is not one of the judges, even though his story appears in the book. He is included as an example of someone who was not called by God but presumes that he has been, or at least claims authority he has not been given. In later years the kings will often be heirs in a family line of succession, but the judges were not like that.

Abimelek's story is a short and violent episode that acts as a warning to others who would seek power for their own ends rather than godly obedience. He meets his end when a woman pushes a large stone from a tower which crushes him. To avoid the ignominy of being killed by a woman, he asks his armour-bearer to thrust his sword into him.

It really isn't worth pretending for your own ends that God has called you. Hopefully this is rare, but I do worry when I come across 'career clergy' who are evidently working their way up the hierarchical ladder. I suspect some of them don't even realize it themselves. Paul writes: 'Do nothing out of selfish ambition or vain conceit. Rather, in humility value others above yourselves, not looking to your own interests but each of you to the interests of the others' (Phil. 2:3–4).

We have been noting throughout this book that the Bible is God's story and it is God's initiative that matters. Abimelek took matters into his own hands without reference to God. Although his father had been a much-admired judge, there was no expectation of a family succession when it came to authority in Israel. But as for us, we are children of the king, who calls us to serve the one who has been given 'all authority'.

FOR REFLECTION

- In the previous chapter, we saw how Gideon felt unworthy of the task to which he was called. In this chapter we have seen the opposite. Do you look at yourself with overconfidence or arrogance sometimes?
- Pray for an honest heart and mind.

31

Jephthah's Story: 'Will I Really Be Your Lord?'

Jephthah from Gilead is something of an antihero – a scoundrel who does something good. In contrast to Abimelek, he is one of the true judges, but like all the others, he is far from perfect. He's the son of a prostitute and his half-brothers throw him out of the house, so he flees to the wilderness and gathers a band of outlaws around him. Maybe that's where Robin Hood got the idea.

But then when the people of Israel are crying out to God once again for deliverance, this time from the Ammonites, they come to him humbly asking for help. His response is interesting: 'Suppose you take me back to fight the Ammonites and the LORD gives them to me – will I really be your head?' (Judg. 11:9). After the Ammonites reject peace negotiations, we are told: 'Then the Spirit of the LORD came on Jephthah' (Judg. 11:29). Then he goes out and wins the battle.

As we have seen, throughout the Old Testament we continually discover that characters in each story are in some way 'types' of Christ, prefiguring what he will do. Jephthah is another example. He is rejected by his brothers but he nevertheless wins the victory on their behalf. And his question mentioned above is the question Jesus asks us: 'Suppose I win the battle on your behalf, will I really be your head?'

It's a very different setting, but there are echoes of this in the Anglican services of baptism and confirmation, where the candidates or the baby's parents are asked if they turn to Christ as Saviour, and then immediately afterwards, if they accept Jesus Christ as Lord.

However, like all the other characters that prefigure Christ, Jephthah is flawed and in this case he is very reminiscent of Jacob. Note particularly his attempt to strike a deal with God. He promises something strangely foolish: 'And Jephthah made a vow to the LORD: "If you give the Ammonites into my hands, whatever comes out of the door of my house to meet me when I return in triumph from the Ammonites will be the LORD's, and I will sacrifice it as a burnt offering"' (Judg. 11:30–31). It's a rash promise and one that will devastate him. The first thing out of the house is his daughter, an only child. Although commentators have sought to find a hint in the text that he didn't fulfil his vow, they have never really detected any.

Our Lord did not make any rash promises, but he is the sacrifice that won the victory. Do not make rash promises about serving God and vocation. Rest on what God has already done.

FOR REFLECTION

- Does God's call upon your life feel like a 'deal', or a natural response to his love?

32

Samson's Story: The Strongest Man Who Ever Lived?

On the face of it, Samson is an unlikely hero. An impetuous, short-tempered womanizer, Samson is nevertheless used by God. We are told that the Spirit of the Lord 'stirred him' as he grew, and that the Spirit 'came upon him', making him supernaturally strong on at least three occasions. In fact, it is not his hair that makes him strong at all, although he has been dedicated to God from the womb, and the sign of this was that he never troubled the local barber, so his hair does symbolize God's anointing. But his strength comes from God, not his hippie locks.

His impulsive behaviour continues to get him into trouble, and eventually he is captured, blinded (again not for Sunday school, folks) and paraded before all the followers and priests of the heathen god Dagon. There he pushes on the pillars of the pagan temple, using his returning strength, and brings down the whole building, dying in the process, killing all the idolatrous worshippers of Dagon and achieving his greatest victory over the Lord's enemies.

Later another child, who was dedicated to the Lord from birth in remarkably similar ways to Samson, prepared the way for the Messiah. John the Baptist said he was not worthy to 'even untie the sandals' of the man who came after him. The Messiah himself did not defeat his enemies by violence, even though he was filled with the Holy Spirit without measure. But he did defeat his enemies at the moment of his death, even though he forgave them. You could say he was the strongest man who ever lived, because he chose to do that, facing the powerless agony of his crucifixion with his eyes open. Jesus is the true and greater Samson whose greatest victory is in his death, not by violence but by love.

When it comes to vocation, we must never discount the rebels in our society with short tempers and an eye for pleasure. God can still use them for his glory, though it is right that church leaders should usually meet certain criteria. For example, Paul tells Timothy: 'Now the overseer is to be above reproach, faithful to his wife, temperate, self-controlled, respectable, hospitable, able to teach, not given to drunkenness, not violent but gentle, not quarrelsome, not a lover of money' (1 Tim. 3:2–3). So I am not suggesting that we ignore the behaviour of Christians in positions of responsibility. Nevertheless, Samson's story shows us that God can always make use of the 'rough diamonds' around us. Maybe even you.

FOR REFLECTION

- Do you know someone who sometimes behaves badly and yet could be used by God with a little encouragement? Pray for them and consider speaking with them.

33

The End of the Judges' Story: X-Rated

We've noted several times that there's a surprising amount of gory stuff in the Old Testament that probably wasn't mentioned in Sunday school. Even if you've heard some of the bloodthirsty stories elsewhere in the Old Testament, I don't think you've heard this one. This time I won't retell the whole story – read it for yourself in Judges 19. Let's just say it involves gang rape and ends up with a dead woman . . . on a doorstep (see Chapter 27). She didn't make it into the house, and Israel has not truly made it into the land. To add to the horror, her 'master' takes her body and chops it into twelve parts, which he sends to each of the twelve tribes, as if to say 'Look how bad things have got'. Imagine the postman arriving with that parcel. And leaving it with a neighbour.

The novel *Blindness* by the brilliant and quirky Nobel prize-winning Portuguese writer Jose Saramago tells of the breakdown of society when nearly everyone goes blind. Only one woman, unnamed in the book and played by Julianne Moore in the movie, is unaffected by the mystery virus. So she sees the absolute collapse of human morality as everyone, including her own husband, fights for themselves. Saramago is an atheist, but the book echoes Judges and even includes a gang rape, which in the film takes place completely in the dark but is more disconcerting as a consequence.

There is a sort of happy ending to the novel/film as people recover from the virus, but the book of Judges does not end positively. The last line of the book sums up the sorry state of God's people: 'In those days Israel had no king; everyone did as they saw fit' (Judg. 21:25).

Like everyone in Saramago's book, we can be blind to just how bad society is. Julianne Moore's character is a Christ-like figure who literally sees the brutal selfishness unfolding around her. Remember him weeping over Jerusalem? Can we learn to see with his eyes?

FOR REFLECTION

- Have you been raised up by God for a time of crisis?
- Is there something troubling you that could mean God might be asking you to be the one to respond?

34

Ruth's Story: Family Loyalty, a Love Story or Something More?

Ruth is a lovely little story from the period of the judges. It's only four chapters so why not put this book down and read it for yourself first?

The book begins with a family from Bethlehem who become refugees in Moab (today this is in Jordan) when there is a famine. The couple are called Elimelek and Naomi and they have two sons, Mahlon and Kilion, who marry local Moabite girls called Ruth and Orpah after their father dies. Later the two sons also die and the three women are left – at a time when to be a woman without a husband was likely to endanger your survival. Naomi decides it's time to return to Bethlehem, where she might find relatives to care for her, and the daughters-in-law want to come too. Ruth insists they should stay in their own country and remarry within their ethnic group, but although Orpah agrees, Ruth insists on going with Naomi. She utters the well-known line: 'Where you go I will go, and where you stay I will stay. Your people will be my people and your God my God. Where you die I will die, and there I will be buried' (Ruth 1:16–17).

This is much more significant than we might think at first glance. Nations were much more ethnically divided from one another than today. Each nation had its own god or gods. Ruth was choosing to put loyalty to her mother-in-law before some challenging considerations. We will shortly hear that in Israel Ruth went out to work, but not Naomi, because she was now quite old. When Naomi died, Ruth would soon be on her own, a foreigner in a strange land.

Arriving in Bethlehem, Naomi and Ruth are destitute, but the law of Moses makes provision for 'gleaning' – farmers were to leave some of their crops unharvested for the poor to pick up in order that they could survive. They have arrived at the time of the barley harvest and Ruth goes to the fields, which happen to belong to a relative of Naomi called Boaz.

Another provision of the law of Moses is that near relatives of widows and orphans should ensure they are cared for. Such a person was known as the 'kinsman redeemer'. Boaz learns who Ruth is and ensures that she is safe, although we learn that in the town there is another, closer relative to Naomi. Naomi and Ruth don't know this, but Boaz is a kind man anyway and he is generous to Ruth.

The next part of the story is a little questionable, we might say. Naomi instructs Ruth to wait until the evening when Boaz has fed well and got a little drunk, and has lain down to sleep. She should uncover his feet, and lie next to them. She is also told to wash, dress well and put on perfume. She's trying to seduce him. There are sexual overtones to this that are only increased when we know that 'feet' is sometimes a euphemism for genitals, although there is no explicit suggestion of physical intimacy.

Anyway, when he awakes, probably because his feet are cold, Boaz is keen to do the right thing. He explains that he is not the nearest relative but he will sort things out in the morning. He lets Ruth spend the night at his feet – again there is no suggestion of impropriety – but she slips away early, avoiding the walk of shame.

Next morning, Boaz does as he promised and acquires from the nearer relative the right to Naomi's land and marries Ruth. The book ends with a reminder via a brief family tree that Boaz and Ruth are the grandparents of Jesse and thus the great-grandparents of the future king, David. Incidentally, in 1 Samuel 22 when David is being pursued by Saul he asks the king of Moab to care for his parents. He's using his Moabite ancestry to win a favour, although later when he is king, he will annex Moab under Israelite rule.

There is a lot more going on here than a simple love story. Here's a tweet I saw recently from someone called Sam Ward: 'My only issue with our reading of the book of Ruth is that we make romance the motive for redemption. Boaz provided for the poor, welcomed the widow and served the hungry at his table. Boaz followed God's concern before his own.'

Ruth is not really a romantic tale, although it ends happily. Boaz obeys the law of Moses and is to be commended. Naomi's advice and Ruth's behaviour may be a bit naughty, but Boaz is sinless despite the temptation.

The story is important in God's big story as he works through history. Ruth is not just part of the family line of David but also of someone 'born in David's town', and in the genealogy of Jesus that begins Matthew and the whole New Testament, we see Ruth mentioned, along with three other women. The others are Tamar, Judah's wife, who seduced him even though she was his daughter-in-law; Rahab, a Gentile prostitute; and Bathsheba, the woman taken in adultery by King David. They're all women who initially seem to have questionable backgrounds, though there is a strong case to be made that they are all victims of men's sins. But they are there in God's plan.

Jesus is not just the end of a family tree that demonstrates God's providence. He is also the true and better Boaz, a kinsman redeemer who keeps the law of Moses. And he marries his bride, the church. A saviour who is uncovered as he dies naked on the cross, but covers up the sins of his bride. A redeemer who pays the price for his bride and whose wealth becomes shared with her. In case you missed the point, that bride is us, the church. And in case you missed another significant thing about this story, Ruth is a Gentile – an outsider.

We can take the story as a lesson in keeping God's commands, or a lesson in family loyalty, but we must see it first and foremost as a story of God's providence and grace, even to Gentiles, a story which prefigures the story of Christ himself. This limits its usefulness as a specific guide to vocation, of course, but it does have something to say.

Boaz, like Jesus of course, keeps the law. He ensures his workers follow the guidelines about gleaning. He is following the prophet Micah's words even though they are not yet written, because they sum up the justice demanded by the law of Moses: 'He has shown you, O mortal, what is good. And what does the LORD require of you? To act justly and to love mercy and to walk humbly with your God' (Mic. 6:8).

In the New Testament, James writes: 'Religion that God our Father accepts as pure and faultless is this: to look after orphans and widows in their distress and to keep oneself from being polluted by the world' (Jas 1:27). This is another item to add to our list of the things God calls everyone to do, and it's a significant theme in the Bible. It's a call to be selfless on behalf of those who cannot help themselves, to welcome and love the outsider, the widow, the poor, following the example of our Saviour and Lord.

FOR REFLECTION

- Why not sit down and read Ruth again? It's only four chapters, after all. You might glean something.

35

Samuel's Story: 'I'm Listening'

The call of Samuel is a natural 'go to' story for vocation, but as you might expect in this book, it's more complicated than that. Once again, we must consider if this is prescriptive or descriptive for us today.

The wider context is important here. In the Old Testament there are eventually three leadership roles when the kingdom of Israel is established: prophet, priest, and king. The priests are appointed by virtue of their family line, descendants of Aaron/ Levi. The prophets are just the opposite in many ways, charismatic mavericks inspired by the Spirit of God. In the next chapter we will learn about kings.

Samuel bridges the gap between the lawless period of the judges and the slightly more ordered period of the monarchy. He is the last of the judges and the first of the prophets. The judges are raised up by God to lead for short periods during a crisis, but the kings will normally reign until their death. Samuel will anoint the first king, ending the time of the judges. Anointing will be an expected role of the prophets in the future – see for example the way David arranges for Solomon to be anointed king by Nathan the prophet and Zadok the priest (1 Kgs 1:38–39).

Samuel's story does not begin with his calling but with his mother, desperate to have a child and praying at the tabernacle each year when she goes there with her husband. When she gives birth she brings Samuel to serve the Lord there, even though he is a young child. Her song of praise is remarkably like Mary's song when the angel has visited her with news about the saviour that she will carry.

When the boy Samuel's call comes in the middle of the night, God speaks to him three times, but he does not recognize the voice and it requires the old priest Eli to realize what is happening and instruct Samuel in how to respond. When it comes to a specific calling from God (as opposed to the general calling to all of us) it will invariably be necessary for others to be involved, perhaps encouraging us or even recognizing what God is doing before we do.

'Have you considered . . .?'

I had been attending my local Anglican church for several years when a new curate-in-charge arrived. His name was Peter and he was much younger than the previous chap, who sincerely loved the Lord but was a little old-fashioned. I wondered what the new man would bring.

I was to be surprised. In his first sermon he spoke about God's call and then when I met him for the first time afterwards he said: 'I think that message was for you, Derek.' So began the process where God pursued me and I wrestled with him.

There is an amusing postscript to this. Many years later when I was now a curate myself, I sat next to a stranger at a wedding reception. We started talking and he asked me where

I was from. When I mentioned where I used to live, he asked if I knew a vicar called Peter.

'Yes,' I replied, 'he persuaded me to explore ordination.'

The man smiled and said: 'I'm actually a vicar myself . . . and I persuaded Peter to consider ordination.'

Small world.

Eli was an old man and he was not in the best place with God, yet he had the wisdom to recognize that God was speaking to Samuel. Sometimes we need to be watching for the signs of God's Spirit at work and be the ones who tap someone on the shoulder and gently ask: 'Have you considered . . .?' We don't have to be the vicar or church leader to do this. Sometimes it may even be better that we are not.

God's specific call rarely, if ever, comes as a literal voice from God to the individual, despite the story of Paul's experience on the road to Damascus in Acts 9. That story is so unique and significant that it is told again in Acts chapters 22 and 26. Luke wanted the church to know that Paul's unusual experience really happened because if someone says 'God told me' without any other evidence, it causes doubts to rise up in our minds. But Paul's calling is not prescriptive and for most of us the discernment must come from within a Christian community. In fact, even in Paul's case there was a lot more to it, and other people were involved. We discern God's will *together*.

Churches as diverse as the Roman Catholics and the Salvation Army have formalized the discernment process, and leaders are under a chain of command, basically obedient to those 'above' them. But even in those strongly hierarchical contexts there is much to be said for members of the Christian community informally talking to one another and for individuals to consult wise friends regarding God's guidance. It doesn't always have to come from the 'top'.

Barnabas

'Barnabas' means 'son of encouragement' – it was his nickname. His real name was Joseph. I have sometimes heard sermons that encourage us to 'be a Barnabas', and there's nothing much wrong with that except to say that I would prefer to just say 'be an encourager'. It's only a matter of words, but it's worth remembering that in Acts 15 the same Barnabas who got that nickname, and who looked after Paul in his early days, also fell out with him so badly that they parted company. More honesty from the Bible about real people.

Nevertheless, encouragement is an important habit. We've just heard how I met the vicar who encouraged my vicar to explore ordination, who in turn encouraged me. I believe there is an overemphasis upon the 'inner voice' in Christian circles, and that we should learn as Christian churches to 'encourage one another' (1 Thess. 5:11). Vocational discernment is a matter for the whole Christian community – locally for most roles and sometimes nationally, especially for those who will be appointed leaders and ministers.

In some translations, the references to ordination in Paul's letters to Timothy are actually described as the 'laying on of hands'. We may have imported meaning back into these texts, thinking they are about the formal ordination of priests, whereas the context suggests a more informal and charismatic event, with the local church commissioning individuals for specific roles.

Meanwhile, as in the earlier story of Abimelek, we should always beware of the individual who claims to have a solo commission from God, but more positively watch for signs of God at work in others and take opportunities to encourage them.

FOR REFLECTION

- Who could you encourage today? What would becoming an encourager look like?
- Take a moment to give thanks for anyone who encouraged you at key moments in your life.
- Think of the people you know well. Is there anyone who you think might have a particular calling from God? Pray first, and then approach them. Pray for them.
- If you think you may be being called to do something significant, ensure you discuss it with Christians you trust.

36

Saul's Story: Did God Make a Mistake?

We can learn a lot from the story of Israel's first king, but it also raises a few questions, especially: 'Does God make mistakes?', 'Does God really order genocide?' and: 'What's all this about donkeys?'

The story begins when Samuel, the last of the 'judges', is getting old and his sons look like the worst possible candidates to take over, and anyway there is no family line of succession, as we learned earlier. There is no line of succession for judges. But he appoints them anyway – a bit of the story that is usually forgotten. Once more, like all Bible characters except Jesus, Samuel is not perfect.

This prompts the elders of Israel to propose a different solution. The other nations around them have kings, but Israel has never had a king since its people arrived in the promised land, only those individuals whom God has raised up in times of crisis – the judges.

God tells Samuel: 'It's not you they have rejected, but me. However, listen to their request but warn them of the consequences. Your sons will become soldiers in the king's army. Your daughters will become the king's attendants. And then there's the tax. And VAT. And the exorbitant cost of royal weddings.' But they insist: they must have a king. So Samuel agrees to their demands – but who will he anoint as king? (We'll think about anointing in the next chapter.)

Donkeys?

A few years ago Scripture Union made an excellent video series called *Blood and Honey* featuring Tony Robinson – yes, that Tony Robinson: Baldrick in *Blackadder*. He brilliantly retold the stories of the Old Testament. His version of the story of the first king of Israel begins with Saul wandering around shouting 'Donkey! Donkey!'

And this really is how we first meet Saul. His dad's donkeys have wandered off and he's been sent to look for them with his servant. After several days searching, Saul wryly remarks that they should give up and go home or they will be the lost ones being searched for. The story is already a comedy and it is descending into farce.

But the unnamed servant has a better idea. He suggests that they consult a local 'seer' and helpfully he has a bit of loose change in his pocket to offer for information concerning the whereabouts of the donkeys. When they run into the seer, it turns out by God's providence to be Samuel, and the prophet has already been told by God that he will meet the future king. He tells Saul not to worry – the donkeys have already been found – and also suggests that they have a meal together tomorrow to celebrate, up on a nearby hill. When Saul turns up for the party, he finds himself being anointed king by the prophet.

Samuel gathers the people of Israel for a big announcement, like the tense climactic final of a TV talent show. He builds the tension by announcing that the first king of Israel is someone from the tribe of Benjamin. Then he says it is someone from the clan of Matri. Then he announces the man is from the family of Kish. Finally, he tells everyone that the new king is . . . dramatic pause . . .

A reluctant king

As I mentioned earlier, I recently met England footballer Peter Crouch, who is several inches north of 6 feet tall. I have photos of our meeting, and I'm glad he was seated and I was standing up as I'm more than a foot shorter than him. He's also quite lanky and not the typical strong, muscled striker. On social media he's been a figure of fun, sometimes portrayed as a giraffe.

Saul was a bit like this, it seems. I'm told that the word for 'king' in many languages is similar to the word for 'tall', probably because it helps if the leader of any army is the big guy. Saul is very tall and so perhaps well suited to his royal role, but there's something comical here when Saul is eventually found vainly trying to hide among the suitcases that everyone brought when they gathered. According to the text, when they finally bring him out, he walks through the crowd 'a head taller than any of the others' (1 Sam. 10:23).

In an anticlimax, Samuel simply announces that Saul is the new king, explains the new constitution and sends everyone home. Only a couple of chapters later do they hold a party.

Called and anointed but a failure

Sadly, one lesson we need to recognize here is that those chosen and anointed by God can fail. Saul proves to be a poor king, often plagued by depression and insecurity. God soon tells Samuel that he regrets appointing Saul: 'Then the word of the LORD came to Samuel: "I regret that I have made Saul king, because he has turned away from me and has not carried out my instructions." Samuel was angry, and he cried out to the LORD all that night' (1 Sam. 15:10–11).

We should not doubt that God knows what he is doing. When the Bible talks like this, or even of God 'repenting', it is using human language. This is rather like a parent allowing a child to make a mistake and then saying loudly: 'I wonder what went wrong there?'

What were the instructions that Saul failed to carry out? Saul had been told to wipe out the Amalekites – man, woman, child, babies and animals. But he didn't do it.

The shocking instruction to commit genocide is a subject for another whole book, and there is no book that has ever truly solved this issue, but here let us just say that God is commanding radical surgery in the way a doctor might cut off a whole leg or arm or part of a brain, in order to remove serious cancer. A surgeon did some horrible things to my wife but we are grateful for his actions because they saved her life. Later, Jesus would say rhetorically that if our hand or eye causes us to sin we should cut it off or pluck it out. We should get serious about dealing with the things that take us away from God. Many of the nations that surrounded Israel practised unspeakable evil, and drastic action was required to prevent Israel being perverted to their ways.

This argument is complex and my comments are simplistic because, as I say elsewhere, there is no easy explanation for suffering, although it's worth remembering that when facing terrible news the atheist has no one to blame or to turn to for help. Life without God really is meaningless. Give up on God when times are hard and you give up on the one thing that might give hope. (See the chapter about Job for more about this subject.)

Meanwhile, the action is now becoming a black comedy. Samuel comes to Saul to ask if he has followed the Lord's instructions in full, but when he arrives, he doesn't need to ask. Saul is so guilty that he greets Samuel like a naughty child, saying: 'The Lord bless you! I have carried out the Lord's instructions!'

Samuel responds: 'So . . . er . . . why can I hear the sheep bleating and the cows mooing?'

Saul blames his men, and then attempts a pious excuse: 'We were going to offer them as a sacrifice.'

Suddenly the comedy ends as Samuel shouts 'Stop!' and goes on to tell Saul that he has been rejected by God. Soon, as we will see in David's story, Samuel will anoint a new king, but Saul will grimly hold on to power until his bloody death several chapters later. Ironically, news of Saul's death is given by an Amalekite, who claims that he killed Saul at his request. If Saul had obeyed God and killed all the Amalekites, this man would not exist.

The true king

Many centuries later, a man would die on a cross with the words 'the king of the Jews' nailed above him. Unlike tall Saul, according to Isaiah's prophecy about him, this man 'had no beauty or majesty to attract us to him, nothing in his appearance that we should desire him' (Isa. 53:2).

In the week before his death, this man knows exactly where the donkeys are. He rides one into Jerusalem, and is anointed, not as a king but for burial. He shares a final meal with his friends and then the next morning the crowd cries: 'We have no king but Caesar!' The people of Israel, having rejected God as king once in favour of a human monarch, now reject him again in favour of a pagan despot.

In the very end, Saul gave up his life so he wouldn't suffer torture and shame. The true king gave up his life accepting torture and shame. A recent Internet meme says: 'Throughout history kings sent out their people to die for them, but there's one king who died for his people.'

Saul clung to power, but according to Philippians 2:6–7, Jesus, 'being in very nature God, did not consider equality with God something to be used to his own advantage; rather, he made himself nothing by taking the very nature of a servant'. This is the true king, who takes up his vocation willingly, not reluctantly, and on behalf of others, not himself. Jesus is the true king, not just of Israel, but of the whole world.

Vocation means sacrifice

When it comes to our vocation, we are called to recognize that it involves humility and sacrifice. Vocation begins with Christ as king. The Philippians quote above is an illustration of the attitude that Jesus had, which Paul says should be our attitude too. The King of Kings and Lord of Lords becomes a willing servant and a sacrifice. Whatever our vocation involves, it should include putting God first and looking out for the needs of others. Without that, we're just looking for donkeys on our own.

FOR REFLECTION

- What does it mean to make Jesus our king? Is this an old-fashioned way of illustrating what our relationship with him should be like? Can you think of any more contemporary way of describing the need to give him control over our lives?
- Consider: are you hanging on to a job or role that you should have left by now? Are you still called to the place where you are?

FURTHER READING

Wright, Chris. *The God I Don't Understand* (Zondervan, 2008) (includes a long section about how we might explain God's command to kill the Canaanites).

Wright, Tom. *How God Became King* (SPCK, 2012).

WATCH

Tony Robinson's *Blood and Honey* videos can be found at:

- https://www.youtube.com/watch?v=_9ggITRvh4I

37

David's Story (Part 1): Anointing

Long before Saul's death, David was chosen by God to be his replacement as king. Samuel had been told by God that one of Jesse's sons was the one, but he did not know any of them before he arrived at Jesse's house in Bethlehem. The older sons were paraded before him but not one of them was suitable, according to the voice of God whispering in Samuel's ear. It would appear even David's own father didn't think he was the one, but eventually, after seven sons of Jesse have been rejected, David is sent for.

Before writing this, I went back to the text to check the detail. You may know the famous words from this passage: 'People look at the outward appearance, but the Lord looks at the heart.' In my memory they were said about David, but in fact they were said about the oldest son, Eliab. When David arrives, God says: 'Rise and anoint him; this is the one.'

Saul had been anointed the first king, but many years before him the priests from Aaron's family line were anointed for their particular role. The practice was symbolic of someone or something being set apart for God's purpose. Isaiah the prophet later said that 'the Lord has anointed me to proclaim good news to the poor' (Isa. 61:1).

The anointed one

The term 'messiah' translates the Hebrew term *masiah*, which is derived from the verb *masah*, meaning to smear or anoint. One of David's descendants, a 'son of David', would later be called the Messiah, or in Greek the 'Christ'. The anointed one. Jesus fulfils the typology of the Old Testament in every way – as the true priest, king and prophet – the chosen one of Israel. For further details, check the book of Hebrews.

Because of Christ's saving work, all Christians are now set apart by God for his purpose: '*He anointed us*, set his seal of ownership on us, and put his Spirit in our hearts as a deposit, guaranteeing what is to come' (2 Cor. 1:21–22, my emphasis). I have seen glossy adverts for Christian events that talk about the speakers as 'anointed preachers'. But *all* Christians are anointed to serve God and fulfil their calling. Just occasionally, however, some individuals are set apart for particular tasks:

> Now in the church at Antioch there were prophets and teachers: Barnabas, Simeon called Niger, Lucius of Cyrene, Manaen (who had been brought up with Herod the tetrarch) and Saul. While they were worshipping the Lord and fasting, the Holy Spirit said, 'Set apart for me Barnabas and Saul for the work to which I have called them.' So after they had fasted and prayed, they placed their hands on them and sent them off.
>
> (Acts 13:1–3)

This is an important passage that demonstrates something of how God's guidance works. When I first read this, I pictured a brief charismatic prayer-meeting at which someone stood up and gave a 'word' to Barnabas and Saul. But note that the context is worship *and fasting*.

Now, I'm pretty good at fasting between meals, but find it a bit tough beyond that. If these people were fasting, then we are talking about something that lasted at least 24 hours and possibly longer. I'm not suggesting this was a worship marathon either. People could have come and gone freely for a few days, and at some point during this time the group recognized that Barnabas and Saul should go on a mission trip. Note, too, that they follow this up by praying for the mission team, laying hands on them. And fasting is mentioned again, so this was not a quick prayer of blessing.

Some people can't understand why the Church of England takes so long over the discernment process for those offering themselves for ordination. But the church is not just sending people on a mission trip; it's giving them a 'title' for life, setting them apart for a whole life of service.

It's probably clear by now that I'm not a big fan of the unfortunate over-separation of clergy and lay people in my denomination. Everyone is called. Any progress towards changing the imbalance should consider the Acts 13 text, not by ending the ordination of clergy but by praying for and affirming the calling of all lay people. Including you.

FOR REFLECTION

- Use a Bible concordance to find references to anointing.
- What might God have anointed you to do?

FURTHER READING

Kendall, R.T. *The Anointing* (Hodder & Stoughton, 1998).

38

David's Story (Part 2): Goliath

The story of David and Goliath is one of the best-known stories in the Bible. Even if you didn't go to Sunday school, it's likely you first heard it in school assembly. Sadly, you may not have heard the full story, but more seriously, it was probably explained wrongly.

Israel is at war with the Philistines, one of whom is Goliath, whose name nowadays is something synonymous with 'quite big'. He challenges the Israelites that he will fight their best man, and whoever wins means his whole nation has won. Understandably none of the Israelites wants to give it a go, even with an offer from King Saul that they can marry his daughter. You won't look good on the wedding photos if you've been beaten to a pulp.

The Israelite soldiers include David's brothers, and David is sent by his father to take food to them. On arriving, he can't understand why no one has taken the challenge, so he tells them *he* will fight Goliath and goes to the king to offer his services. Despite everyone's doubts – he's only a boy – Saul agrees to this. Saul must be either desperate or impressed – because remember, if David loses then Israel loses.

The fight itself is the bit we remember most. David picks up five stones and goes out to face Goliath, who is amused of course. But David takes his sling and fires a perfect shot into Goliath's forehead. The giant crashes to the ground – but he's not dead. Oh, no, he's not dead until David chops off his head with his own sword – another juicy bit they didn't mention in Sunday school. They also didn't mention the Israelite army chasing the Philistines to kill them afterwards.

What can we learn?

So when it comes to the significance of this passage, especially for understanding vocation, you may well have heard the teacher/preacher encourage you to follow David's example of trusting God for victory. Right?

Wrong. Let's be honest. How many times in life does David beat Goliath? On the very rare occasions a lowly football team beats a glamorous club, we call it a 'giant-killing' or even 'David beats Goliath' and it's big news because it's so rare. It's exceptional, even if/when we trust in God. And if that's what the preacher said, then they set you up for disappointment. Normally you lose to the big guy, and a preacher who tells you that you just need enough faith is setting you up to feel bad about yourself for not believing enough.

So what *can* we learn? The answer depends on who you identify with in the story. If you identify with David, that's not surprising as we've been brought up to identify with the hero of every story. We project ourselves onto the hero and think we can or should do the same.

The problem is, if you take that approach to Scripture, then (as one Internet meme points out) you are going to struggle when David later commits adultery with Bathsheba. If you identify with him in the Goliath story, you have to identify with him there too, so if you are being encouraged to follow David's example then you have to consider if you should spy on women taking baths and arrange the death of their husbands.

What we need to do instead is identify with the soldiers who were too scared to fight Goliath. Someone comes to fight on their behalf, despite their derision. An anointed one.

David's brothers derided him. When the Son of David came into the world, John says: 'He came to that which was his own, but his own did not receive him' (John 1:11). Like David, Jesus is the one who fights on behalf of his brothers and wins the battle as our representative man. We are called to respond to that by living in the light of his victory – not by chasing and killing our enemies but by loving them just as Christ loved us.

We are all anointed by God to serve him, but when it comes to vocation, we are not all Davids. We are mostly foot soldiers, although there is some clearing up after the battle to be done – some smaller victories that come as a follow-up to Christ's amazing victory over the big guy. But let's not inflate our own importance. We are never the hero, only his followers.

FOR REFLECTION

- Does it disappoint you that you are probably not meant to be a David, but a soldier? Does that demotivate you?
- Can you see that this story is about God's extraordinary grace as he fights for his people through his anointed one? Praise him!

39

David's Story (Part 3): King of Israel, Improved Version

The story of Saul highlighted all the negative issues arising from kingship. God is meant to be the true king of Israel, and in our lives as Christians. But Saul's 'replacement', David, highlights many of the positive aspects of kingship, though it does this by pointing towards a greater king. By now I suspect I don't need to tell you who I'm talking about.

David is by no means perfect, as we shall see in the next chapter. We remember once again that Old Testament figures prefigure and point towards Jesus Christ, but we also always see their failings.

We have already seen that like the Christ, David is anointed, and like Jesus he wins the victory on behalf of his people. We hear that he is 'a man after God's own heart' (1 Sam. 13:14), which evidently Saul was not. It's interesting that David was not totally rejected by God when he committed physical adultery but Saul was rejected for spiritual adultery. For all his failings, David's heart was for God whereas Saul's was not. We need to examine ourselves and ask if we are a Saul or a David in this respect.

The famous Christmas carol, 'While Shepherds Watched . . .', quotes from the message given to the shepherds by the angel: 'Today in the town of David a Saviour has been born to you; he is the Messiah, the Lord' (Luke 2:11). Jesus was born in Bethlehem because Joseph was a descendant of King David and he had gone there to register in the census. It was his home town. So this baby will be the Messiah (Christ) and the Lord. Meanwhile in Matthew's gospel the visitors to the nativity are the magi, who want to worship the baby born to be king of the Jews.

Can you grasp how staggering this is? This baby is:

1. a descendant of David
2. the king of the Jews (Israel)
3. the Messiah/Christ – the anointed one
4. worthy of worship – therefore God.

This means that all the expectations and prophecies of the Old Testament are now being fulfilled in Jesus. This is the one. He's a human being and a king, but not just a king and a special chosen one; he's actually God himself!

The magi brought extraordinary gifts to this king. As you may have heard, gold is a gift for a king, frankincense is for a priest in a temple, and myrrh is anointing for burial. Jesus will be a king, but he will also be a priest offering himself in death as a sacrifice for all of us.

As such a king he is worthy of all our worship. Our common vocation is to proclaim him as Lord and King and bring him all our gifts.

FOR REFLECTION

- If you were one of the magi, what would you bring to Jesus?

40

David's Story (Part 4): Bathsheba – Let's Talk about . . . Intimacy

This is a long chapter, but it needs to be. And it's for Adults Only.

The BBC programme *Question Time* is noted for heated debate, featuring a panel of politicians and celebrities and a studio audience whose members ask them questions. I never watch it normally, because it raises my blood pressure just before bedtime, but I applied to attend the filming in February 2001 and to my surprise I was selected to be in the audience. I was then further shocked and amused when I was chosen to put a question to the panel. In the end, mine was the 'warm-up' question just before the programme went live, so it was not shown on TV. My question was: 'Archbishop George Carey said this week that the private morality of our political leaders matters. Do you agree?'

In the debate that followed I found myself exchanging banter with former health minister Edwina Curry. She claimed that what a politician got up to in their private life had no bearing on how well they ran the country. It was not long afterwards that she admitted in her published diaries that she had had an affair with John Major when he was the prime minister.

Money, sex and power

Richard Foster is well known for his book *A Celebration of Discipline* which helped a generation of evangelicals to discover deeper prayer and fasting, but he also wrote a rather different book called *Money, Sex and Power*, in which he said that the downfall of Christian and secular leaders is usually due to one of these three temptations. It is often the case that some people already have plenty of all three, but still want more.

In the case of David, after many years as king he had everything he wanted. But as Paul would warn centuries later: 'if you think you are standing firm, be careful that you don't fall!' (1 Cor. 10:12).

An Internet meme gives a lovely one-line summary of what happened next: 'A man after God's own heart turned into a man after the woman next door.'

It's tempting to explain David's moral failure in the words that begin this part of his story: 'In the spring, at the time when kings go off to war . . .' (2 Sam. 11:1). Did David slip into sexual sin because he was idle instead of going into battle with his men? The text does not say this, though it seems possible. We are simply told that from his palace he could see a young woman bathing. She's called Bathsheba.

Enjoying the view?

Many years ago, I spent a week decorating a bedroom. While painting the window frames, I noticed that the young woman next door had decided that the weather was good enough to spend that summer tanning her shapely body wearing just her bikini bottom. The painting was taking me a lot longer than I expected until I confessed the problem to my wife, who was very understanding. I was moved on to wallpapering.

When David casually looked out from his palace he wasn't looking for sex, but once he found the opportunity, he took it. We could say something here about David's actions not only being a sin of lust but also being an abuse of power, something very much in the news in recent years. Was Bathsheba willing or was she unable to say 'no' to the king? And it's not just royalty or politicians. Church leaders are particularly in a position of power, sometimes without realizing it, and using that power to manipulate vulnerable people is a truly appalling sin.

But it gets worse. Check 1 Chronicles 11:10–47 and you'll see that Uriah was one of David's 'mighty men' – his closest friends before he became king, when he was on the run from Saul. Uriah was someone who had stayed loyal to David and risked his life for him. David has not only committed adultery; he's done it with the wife of someone who would die for him.

There's even worse to come. Bathsheba becomes pregnant, so David arranges for her husband, Uriah, to come home from battle and sleep with her too, so he'll think the child is his. But the plan fails because Uriah feels he cannot indulge himself while his fellow soldiers are out fighting. When Uriah returns to the battle, David instructs the commander of his army to ensure he is placed where the fighting is fierce, so he will be killed. After this inevitably happens, David takes Bathsheba as his wife and all seems well for him, even though murder has been added to the earlier sin of adultery. He's got away with it.

'You are the man!'

But the prophet Nathan comes and tells David a little parable about a man with one lamb and a rich man with many animals who forcibly takes the poor man's lamb to feed to some party guests. David is outraged and declares that the man should die.

In a dramatic moment, Nathan declares the point of his story: 'You are the man!'

Convicted of his sin, David is genuinely repentant – you can read his words in Psalm 51. But Nathan declares a punishment upon David that will come upon the whole nation, and many people will suffer as a result of his misdeed.

Many years later, Jesus would be tempted 'in every way as we are' – which must include sexually – but remained sinless. And because of his suffering, many people no longer are condemned for their misdeeds. He is the lamb that was slain so we could have a banquet.

'Lead me not into temptation'

As a young man training residentially at a theological college in a nice part of north London, I felt shielded from the temptations others face. When you are surrounded 24/7 by a committed group of Christians, some of this world's distractions are less obvious. I was away from the battle.

One day, I woke early and before going to chapel I had a walk in the woods with my camera, hoping to catch a glimpse of one of the foxes that roamed the grounds. Instead, in some undergrowth I spotted a single page torn from a glossy magazine. It was pornographic – a photo of a naked woman with her legs apart. I was aware that children often played in those woods, so I quickly put it in my pocket and took it back to my room to throw it away safely. But then I thought: what will the cleaner think if they find it? The bursar's daughter often cleaned the students' studies. So I put it in a drawer and locked it.

As the morning passed, the picture seemed to burn a hole in my brain. There was a part of me that wanted to keep it and enjoy looking at it. I found myself trying to justify 'looking after it' so no one else would be tempted by it. In my lectures I thought somehow everyone knew about that picture. I knew that God did.

After morning break, we had a guest speaker, an evangelist called Daniel Cousins. During his talk, he recalled his student years at our college, and remembered how one day he had been walking in the woods and came across . . . a page from a pornographic magazine. For the next few minutes, Daniel described all my thoughts and emotions perfectly. Finally, he said: 'I knew I had to get rid of it or it would eat me and destroy my ministry.'

As you might imagine, God had my attention and when I got back to my study I did what Daniel had done. In fact I burned it. I still wonder what I would have done if Daniel had not told us honestly about his struggles. If we do not deal drastically with sexual temptation, it will indeed destroy our ministry.

Radical holiness

In the Sermon on the Mount, in Matthew 5, Jesus challenges those who think that because they haven't actually had sex outside marriage, they are safe and pure. He says: 'You have heard that it was said, "You shall not commit adultery." But I tell you that anyone who looks at a woman lustfully has already committed adultery with her in his heart' (Matt. 5:27–28).

What should we do about lust? It's true that in 1 Timothy 2:9 Paul encourages women to dress modestly, but this is not prudishness about skimpy dresses. He's talking about prayer and saying that jewellery, hair and make-up are not needed to look beautiful before God.

But back in Matthew 5, Jesus places the responsibility firmly upon the one doing the lusting and says drastic action is necessary:

> If your right eye causes you to stumble, gouge it out and throw it away. It is better for you to lose one part of your body than for your whole body to be thrown into hell. And if your right hand causes you to stumble, cut it off and throw it away. It is better for you to lose one part of your body than for your whole body to go into hell.
>
> (Matt. 5:29–30)

If you struggle with the woman next door sunbathing topless, don't ask her to cover up. *You* take action to deal with your desires. Move house if necessary.

It's striking that religious men of all faiths are often keen to tell women to cover up, as though it's their fault that men lust after them. In rape court cases, the defendants often claim 'she was asking for it'. But Jesus' words say nothing about how the woman is dressed, only the attitude of the one looking.

Sexual desire is one of the strongest forces in the universe. It is manifest today in the vast numbers addicted to Internet pornography. It is also one of the greatest risks to fulfilling our vocation. As a vicar, I have had several conversations with men who have come to me to confess their porn addiction and masturbation. They all want to know the secret of how to stop. If only it was that simple.

The anatomy of lust

In the 1980s, a Christian magazine in the UK featured a controversial article, 'The War Within: An Anatomy of Lust', taken from an American publication. An anonymous Christian leader recounts with brutal honesty his struggle with sexual temptation. He tells the story of his visits to strip clubs across the USA when travelling to preach. When he finally confesses his sin to another Christian leader he admires, his friend breaks down and admits to even greater depravity.

Eventually the author begins to turn his life around. After many prayers he is able to begin to conquer his temptations. How? By coming to the place where he realizes that his behaviour prevents him enjoying a greater intimacy – intimacy with Jesus Christ.

But here is the essence of the problem: we *know* that pornography is not good for us. We *know* that time praying would be of much greater benefit. But sexual pleasure drives us, and the rewards are quicker than a long, disciplined life of praying. To truly pray demands effort and concentration. The brain is lazy and this means that 'instant reward' decisions are very tempting. And it's why watching porn is very much easier than praying or reading our Bibles, even though we know that porn is not good for us.

'I'm not worthy'

Money, sex and power will be the downfall of many vocations, and a problem for those who are called into leadership. At the same time, previous failures can make us feel unworthy of Christian vocation.

In Michael Faber's extraordinary Victorian period novel, *The Crimson Petal and the White*, made into a drama by the BBC, one of the main characters is William Rackham, heir to a perfume company, who happily sleeps with a prostitute with little conscience. His brother Henry is a devout Christian but harbours desires for Emmeline Fox, a widow who rescues prostitutes. He keeps his desires under control, but Henry is absolutely convinced that if he offers to become a priest, as he feels God is calling him, somehow everyone will know that he has lustful thoughts, and so he considers himself unworthy to apply for the priesthood.

There is of course some truth in this. It's right for the church to expect holiness from our priests and preachers, but at the same time we should expect them to be human and fallible. When Jesus talks about lust in the Sermon on the Mount, the wider theme of his message is to show that we cannot be perfect law-keepers, despite the Pharisees' belief that that was the way of salvation. It's not simply about keeping within the rules; it's about the attitude we have and what's wrong with our hearts.

This is not to suggest that we give up and do not need to aspire to a holy life; far from it. But many Christians today (mostly men) live a double life in which they are secretly William Rackham in private and Henry Rackham in public, scared to allow the Holy Spirit to shine a light into their dark inner world. We all need to let him begin to clean us up.

Christian vocation for everyone includes a call to radical holiness. We are swimming against the tide in the modern world, but I don't think God wants us to lower our standards. On the other hand, we need to recover a more positive image of holiness – and of sex. It has had a 'thou shalt not' tag for too long.

A positive attitude to sex

Sex was God's idea. In the right context it is a beautiful thing. Like the rest of creation it has been marred by sin, and at its worst it's about my selfish pleasure. At its best it's about how I can please someone else. Some writers have even suggested that it acts as a covenant renewal ceremony within marriage.

I heard about a vicar speaking to a group of young people many years ago who told them: 'Sex is dirty and disgusting, so save it for the one you love.' The Song of Songs, tucked away among the Wisdom literature of the Old Testament, is a glorious celebration of sexual love. It's a God-given gift so let's follow the Maker's instructions. Don't let it destroy our vocation, or more importantly our relationship with God.

FOR REFLECTION

- Which would you prefer: a life of porn or a life of prayer?
- What are you going to do about it?
- Why are you waiting? The sooner we deal with sin, the easier it is. It can be too late.
- Some Christian men have set up accountability groups where they tell each other honestly about their struggles. Others have installed software that emails their wife a list of all the websites they have visited. What radical action do you need to take?

FURTHER READING

Chester, Tim. *You Can Change: God's Transforming Power for Our Sinful Behaviour and Negative Emotions* (IVP, 2008).

Foster, Richard. *Money, Sex and Power* (Hodder & Stoughton, 2009).

Gerali, Steve. *The Struggle* (NavPress, 2003).

Roberts, Vaughan. *Battles Christians Face* (Authentic, 2013).

——. *Talking Points: The Porn Problem* (The Good Book Company, 2018).

OTHER

The article referred to in this chapter is here:

- https://www.christianitytoday.com/pastors/1982/fall/warwithinanatomylust.html

41

Solomon's Story: Building a House for God

One of the people who encouraged me on my journey to ordination was my old headmistress, who happened to see me preach and took the time and trouble to write me a letter praising my sermon. She had taught me English at A level and ignited an interest in the poet Gerard Manley Hopkins, especially his long poem 'The Wreck of the *Deutschland*'. The poem is quite depressing because it concerns the death of a group of nuns in a shipwreck and the eternal question of the meaning of life.

Another fond memory of her was that she insisted that in school assembly, at the beginning and end of every term, we would have a Bible reading. It was the fairly well-known passage about there being a time or 'season' for everything. In the 1960s Pete Seeger wrote a song based upon it called 'Turn, Turn, Turn', which was a big hit when The Byrds covered it. It's an encouraging passage in the midst of the sometimes depressing book of Ecclesiastes. We rarely read the verses that follow:

> What do workers gain from their toil? I have seen the burden God has laid on the human race. He has made everything beautiful in its time. He has also set eternity in the human heart; yet no one

can fathom what God has done from beginning to end. I know that there is nothing better for people than to be happy and to do good while they live.

(Eccl. 3:9–12)

What's the point of life?

Ecclesiastes is quite depressing because it seems to be about the pointlessness of life. We live and we die, like the nuns in the shipwreck, and everything in between will be forgotten. So we might as well enjoy each day and do good while we're here.

The book was attributed to King Solomon, either as the writer or being quoted extensively by whoever did write it. If this is the case, then we have an example of someone who has everything – in this case not just wealth but also women, status, achievements and even great wisdom – but feels empty. That's certainly what the writer says, whoever it was.

Solomon, David's son, was the king when the united nation of Israel was at its greatest height. He was the one who built the great temple and who garnered the admiration of the surrounding nations. He had hundreds of wives, great wealth and great power. He is commended by God for seeking wisdom when asked how he wishes to be blessed.

Something greater than Solomon

Later another king of a different sort would be admired for his wisdom and be known as 'the teacher', although he chose to forego the greater wealth of his heavenly glory to come and build a living temple on earth, his people. He would point out that not even King Solomon in all his glory was as beautiful as a simple flower of the field which has an even shorter life than human beings. He also challenged his generation to repent because 'something greater than Solomon is here' (Matt. 12:42).

We Christians today are that living temple that Jesus was building. Paul says that we are 'built on the foundation of the apostles and prophets, with Christ Jesus himself as the chief cornerstone. In him the whole building is joined together and rises to become a holy temple in the Lord. And in him you too are being built together to become a dwelling in which God lives by his Spirit' (Eph. 2:20–22).

Peter also writes: 'you also, like living stones, are being built into a spiritual house [or temple of the Spirit] to be a holy priesthood, offering spiritual sacrifices acceptable to God through Jesus Christ' (1 Pet. 2:5). Every Christian is a priest. There is no longer a need for any sacrifice to be made for sin, but our lives should be a living sacrifice of ourselves, our true worship (Rom. 12:1). Nor is there any need for a temple because all believers together are a living temple indwelt by God's Spirit. Together we grow as we support one another in love.

Later in Ephesians, Paul changes the metaphor from a building to a body and tells us what we should all be aiming for: 'Instead, speaking the truth in love, we will grow to become in every respect the mature body of him who is the head, that is, Christ. From him the whole body, joined and held together by every supporting ligament, grows and builds itself up in love, as each part does its work' (Eph. 4:15–16).

This is what should give our lives meaning and purpose: giving ourselves wholeheartedly to God for his service, and doing it *together* as God's holy people, a living temple where God is worshipped. This is the church's great vocation. We're not meant to do this stuff on our own.

FOR REFLECTION

- What is your view of priesthood?
- How are you contributing to the 'priesthood of all believers' and building up the body of Christ?

42

Job's Story: Suffering as Vocation?

The book of Job is seldom read in church or at home but, in my experience, Christians are nevertheless usually aware of its contents. Job is a good man who seems unknowingly to be the subject of a wager between God and Satan. That's one of the reasons it's thought that the book may not be literally true, but rather a story with a simple purpose: to dismiss the idea that we suffer because of our bad behaviour, as suggested in the book by Job's 'comforters'.

Apart from the prologue and epilogue, it's written as an extensive poem. We don't know who wrote it, or when it was written. Some of the language is very ancient, which suggests it is very old indeed. There is little within the content to place it at a particular moment in history.

It is also an astonishing piece of literature, and the poetry even in English is sublime. In Hebrew it's amazing, I'm told. According to Wikipedia, it has been 'extravagantly' praised and Tennyson called it 'the greatest poem of ancient and modern times'.

The poem is prefaced by a prose introduction in which Satan challenges God. He suggests that Job may be a faithful believer, but he's only doing it for what he gets from God. This is a picture of how many of us approach our faith. It's describing a transactional approach that says to God: 'I will believe in you and worship you if you look after me.' It has similarities with Jacob's prayer after his dream of the stairway to heaven. Satan challenges God: let me make him suffer and then we'll see if he really trusts you.

Despite the terrible things that Satan brings upon him, Job declares:

> Naked I came from my mother's womb,
> and naked I shall depart.
> The Lord gave and the Lord has taken away;
> may the name of the Lord be praised.
>
> (Job 1:21)

So then Satan says to God: 'But now stretch out your hand and strike his flesh and bones, and he will surely curse you to your face' (Job 2:5). God permits Satan to do this and Job suffers terrible illness. In response Job's wife tells him to curse God and die. But he tells her: 'Shall we accept good from God, and not trouble?' (2:10). Satan is being proved wrong; Job *will* trust God whatever happens, but he nevertheless demands that God give him an explanation.

Why?

Job's suffering is terrible. He has lost his wealth, his children have been killed, and now he suffers painful illness. Some friends come to comfort him, but they take the traditional view: you must have sinned terribly. In this they reflect that phrase uttered by so many people throughout history: 'What have I done to deserve this?' But Job refuses to agree.

His friends' blunt reasoning is that he must have been a naughty boy. Job protests his innocence. This dialogue proceeds for many chapters, until God himself intervenes, but not with an explanation. In the most profound and beautiful poetry of the book, God speaks for several chapters and asks Job who he thinks he is – can he do the stuff God can? Eventually Job apologizes for ever doubting, but God blesses him. He had questions, but he took them to God instead of abandoning faith. God tells him to pray for his friends whose comforting words were wide of the mark.

The reasons behind Job's suffering are never explained to him. Essentially, Job is told that God is amazing, and what makes him think he could understand? There are interesting echoes of Genesis 3 here; I wonder if the desire for an explanation of suffering has parallels with Eve and Adam's desire to be wise? Faith does not have all the answers.

The problem of theodicy – why do people suffer? – has been there throughout history. Ironically, at a time when we in the wealthy West are more comfortable than ever and live longer, it has been one reason why people reject God.

Why me?

I was ordained in Christchurch Cathedral, Oxford, in 1991 and served my curacy in Bletchley. About two years into my time there, my wife Carolyn was told that she had a meningioma – a benign brain tumour. We were reassured that the fact it was benign meant it was operable and would not be fatal. However, after an MRI scan we found out that it was massive – as big as an orange – and in the very centre of her head, making surgery challenging to say the least.

Within days, Carolyn had the first of two nine-hour operations. It was a success and the second op came a few weeks later. Although the tumour was completely removed, the surgery necessitated cutting facial nerves which were caught up in the tumour. She lost all feeling in the right side of her face, and all hearing in her right ear. Her right eye could see but not move, creating double vision. It had lost all sensation and any capacity to blink, so in a later operation it was sewn shut for protection.

Carolyn was only 34 when she was diagnosed. We had three children under 12 and I took six months off work to care for them. She was unable to drive for five years. Life was irrevocably changed. Every now and then, when I reflect on what she went through, I have a little cry to myself. But it could have been worse.

In the months just before my wife's diagnosis, I took the funeral of a six-month-old baby who was found cold and not breathing one morning by his parents. The father summed up the problem of theodicy perfectly: 'As far as I am concerned, if there is a God then he is not all-powerful or he doesn't care.'

I did not give him an answer. I just wept with the parents.

Jesus' surprising answer

In Luke 13, when Jesus is asked about suffering, he gives an answer that seems surprisingly stark and unsympathetic, though we should remember that he also wept at the grave of his friend Lazarus. He cares deeply. But here he is dealing with theoretical questions put forward by those not directly affected by suffering.

He is told about some Galileans who were killed by Pilate while offering a sacrifice at the temple. The question behind the question is this: these were good people doing their religious duties, so why did they die so horribly? Jesus responds: 'Do you think that these Galileans were worse sinners than all the other Galileans because they suffered this way? I tell you, no! But unless you repent, you too will all perish' (Luke 13:2–3).

Then Jesus reminds them of another incident in which a tower fell on eighteen people in Siloam. His question behind the question is: you asked me about evil actions carried out by an evil man, but why does totally random suffering happen? He responds to their silence by telling them again to repent.

The word 'repent' has become synonymous with street-preacher sandwich boards in a context where hellfire and condemnation is shouted at passers-by. But the word is not a religious term and simply means to turn and walk in the right direction.

Like God speaking to Job, Jesus does not give an answer to the question of suffering. He simply calls his hearers to turn and face God.

Is suffering sometimes a vocation? Might we even have a vocation to suffer?

Greg's story

When I was at theological college the first friend I made was Greg. He was such a lovely guy. After college we planned to keep in touch and formed a prayer triplet with Peter, another friend, hoping to meet regularly. Unfortunately we served our curacies a long way apart from one another and it didn't work out. Eventually our only communication was by Christmas newsletter, and neither Greg nor Peter used any type of social media.

The years passed. In January 2016 my wife sat me down one evening and I sensed something was wrong. She always opens our mail and she admitted she had hidden one Christmas card from me until things settled down after the festive period. Greg's wife Jackie had written to let us know that Greg had died of cancer after several months fighting the illness. I was devastated.

But I'm telling this tale because there's a postscript. Some weeks later I met someone from Greg's diocese who told me more. Apparently Greg was as extraordinary in death as in his previous years in ministry. He had been remarkably open with his congregation about his illness. He had shared the pain and challenges of his experience to help others. A popular parish priest, he had been truly priestly in his dying, talking about his struggles and faith.

I was reminded of David Watson, a major influence on my life, who shared his journey through cancer to his death in the book *Fear No Evil*, a little paperback which has helped many people. It seemed that Greg, like David, had seen his dying and death as a vocation – an opportunity to serve God and others. When my time comes, I hope I can aspire to that too.

A vocation?

Could dying be a *vocation*? Whoever wrote Ecclesiastes perhaps thought so:

> There is a time for everything,
> and a season for every activity under the heavens:
> a time to be born and *a time to die* . . .
>
> (Eccl. 3:1–2, my emphasis)

Whoever wrote Hebrews says: 'people are destined to die once, and after that to face judgment' (Heb. 9:27). Some translations use the words 'purpose' and an '*appointment*'. Death is a divine appointment. It is part of God's purpose in our lives. There is a sense in which God calls each person to die. He is sovereign over all of life, including the final experience of life. He calls us to face it with confidence in him and, where possible, love for others.

I once led a day conference at which we looked at the problem of pain from many angles and studied some helpful answers from Job. But eventually I took the focus to the cross, the place where the greatest inexplicable injustice proved to be the most wonderful thing that ever happened. Jesus is the true and better Job, who not only suffered but also, in his death, interceded for his friends and even his enemies.

'What did he do to deserve this?' Nothing; we deserved it and yet he takes our iniquity upon himself.

What did we do to deserve grace? Nothing.

FOR REFLECTION

- What would you hope people would say at your funeral?
- Does dying scare you? How could your death glorify God?

FURTHER READING

Blocher, Henri. *Evil and the Cross* (Kregel, 2005).
Greig, Pete. *God on Mute* (Kingsway, 2007).
Watson, David. *Fear No Evil* (Hodder & Stoughton, 2014).

43

Israel's Story: God's Chosen Stiff-Necked People

It's strange – for some people who don't know the whole story – that the nation that has suffered most from racism throughout history happens to be the one that God chose randomly to love:

> The Lord did not set his affection on you and choose you because you were more numerous than other peoples, for you were the fewest of all peoples. But it was because the Lord loved you and kept the oath he swore to your ancestors that he brought you out with a mighty hand and redeemed you from the land of slavery, from the power of Pharaoh King of Egypt.
>
> (Deut. 7:7–8)

In the ancient world, all nations had their gods. Israel was no exception in this, yet the whole mindset is different with Yahweh. There is no jingoistic nationalism, because Israel's Scriptures talk about the nation's unworthiness and insignificance. Compare this with such things as the second verse of the British national anthem, and phrases from across the pond such as 'Make America great again'. Ancient Israel knew its place; its people were small and insignificant, but their God Yahweh – creator of heaven and earth – chose and loved them despite their minor status.

The prophets have lots to say about the failure of justice and mercy in other nations, but they often reserve their greatest criticism for Israel. This seems to be because Israel has the law and the knowledge of God so should be behaving better than others.

'You know better'

I grew up as the older of two brothers, and when we sometimes fought I would be in bigger trouble because my mother used to say: 'You are old enough to know better.' Of course I waited until my brother was a few years older, and then when my mother came out with that same line, I pointed out that he was now as old as I was when she first started saying that, so surely now he too was old enough to know better. I was rewarded for my wonderful wisdom and wit with a clip around the ear.

Unlike the other nations mentioned above, Israel truly was a chosen race. But with that came accountability. Israel's failure to live up to its responsibilities is brought into sharp focus when its Messiah arrives. Jesus' acted parable of the Cursed Fig-Tree illustrates this.

Another acted parable is the overturning of the tables in the temple. This has often been thought to be about Jesus getting angry about money being exchanged in God's holy place. But a closer look will discover that Jesus quotes Jeremiah: 'And as he taught them, he said, "Is it not written: 'My house will be called a house of prayer for all nations'? But you have made it a 'den of robbers'"' (Mark 11:17). Jesus quotes a phrase from Isaiah 56 and joins it with a phrase from Jeremiah 7, and both the Old Testament texts are important. Matthew's gospel unfortunately omits the phrase 'for all nations', probably because he is writing to a very Jewish audience and they know the rest. But that's the point. The Jews ought to recognize that they exist for the sake of the whole world, going right back to the promise to Abraham that God would bless the nations through him.

In Jeremiah the passage comes from a longer section in which the prophet criticizes the people of Israel for thinking they can do what they like and carry out terrible injustice upon foreigners, orphans and widows just because they have a great God and a temple: 'Will you steal and murder, commit adultery and perjury, burn incense to Baal and follow other gods you have not known, and then come and stand before me in this house, which bears my Name, and say, "We are safe" – safe to do all these detestable things? Has this house, which bears my Name, become a den of robbers to you?' (Jer. 7:9–11).

Other spoken parables like the one about the tenants in the vineyard show how serious their rebellion has become and that it will lead to the murder of the owner's own son. This challenging judgement over Israel, however, shows the work of God's providential grace in action. The death of his Son will be the means of his grace.

A church for everyone

On pilgrimage in Israel we followed the traditional Palm Sunday route down from the Mount of Olives across the Kidron valley and up into Jerusalem. In the valley sits the garden of Gethsemane and there is a church built at the site where Jesus is said to have prayed before he was arrested. It's called the Church of All Nations.

As God's people called from every tribe and nation, Christians are collectively called to be radically inclusive of everyone from those tribes and nations. There is no place for a gospel that is not inclusive of all races. No nation can claim to be God's chosen race to the exclusion of others. At an individual level, there is no room either for a mindset that assumes being called means being special because we are chosen. Israel was chosen *because they were nothing special*. Paul reminds the Corinthians, who suffered with a spiritual superiority complex, that God chose the foolish things of the world to confound the wise.

Luke devotes all of Acts 10 and much of chapter 11 to the story of Peter and Cornelius. This story is vital because it tells how Peter's inbred understanding that the Jews were God's special people was turned around by God's clear intervention. When Paul hears about Cornelius's vision of an angel, he reflects: 'I now realise how true it is that God does not show favouritism but accepts from every nation the one who fears him and does what is right' (Acts 10:34–35). This is even *before* the Holy Spirit has fallen upon Cornelius and his friends, a moment sometimes called the 'Gentile Pentecost'.

Unconscious bias

We who think we are tolerant are probably not. It was while attending a training day on 'Unconscious Bias' that I realized the significance of the title: it was challenging us to admit that sometimes our bias is unconscious but still real. We daren't admit that we are not as loving and accepting as we think we are. Our call to follow Christ includes a challenge to love the unworthy, even our enemies.

And by the way, we are all called to love the biased and intolerant racist too, just as Jesus did. We don't have to agree with them but we have to love them too.

FOR REFLECTION

- Are you racist? Sexist? Homophobic? Ageist? It's hard to give a truly honest reply, so ask God to reveal your true heart.
- Bias is often unconscious. How might you become more self-aware?
- Consider: why are the three novels below all written by women? Is there something in the male ego that is blind? Is it because women are more aware of prejudice?

FURTHER READING

Cannon, Joanna. *The Trouble with Goats and Sheep* (The Borough Press, 2016) (novel).

Keller, Tim. *The Prodigal Prophet* (Hodder & Stoughton, 2018).

Lee, Harper. *To Kill a Mockingbird* (Arrow, 50th anniversary edn, 2010) (novel).

Picoult, Jodi. *Small Great Things* (Hodder Paperbacks, 2017) (novel).

44

Elijah's Story: Meeting God on the Mountain(s)

As I mentioned previously, in 2007 my wife and I went on a pilgrimage to Israel. As you can imagine, it was a trip of a lifetime, but it had the added bonus of an opportunity to see our son Matt, who was working in Haifa at the time. We ducked out of the pilgrimage group for 24 hours and he picked us up from our hotel. He drove us on the roads across the desert between Galilee and his home, with U2's 'Where the Streets Have No Name' turned up on the car stereo. Actually I think we were on Highway 77 but that would spoil the story. Special memories.

In Haifa, we took a lift to the top of a university tower block on the top of a hill and from the roof we could see for many miles around, even into Lebanon, which was slightly disconcerting because some rebels there had recently fired missiles in our direction.

Haifa is on a coastal range of hills which in biblical times included Mount Carmel. It's not on the usual Holy Land tour schedules because not much happened there except the story of Elijah's encounter with the prophets of Baal. The incident is the high point (excuse the pun) of a series of miracles that punctuate the story of an amazing prophet. He challenges the prophets of Baal to call on their god to send fire onto their sacrifice. They can't, but Yahweh does and it is a moment of great triumph for Elijah.

What's a little strange about Elijah is that, although he is called a prophet, he doesn't have a book named after him and he doesn't really prophesy in the same way as the other great prophets. In fact no prophet's ministry is exactly the same as another's. Prophecy in the Old Testament is not always about prophetic words but sometimes involves prophetic actions. Elijah's victory over the heathen prophets is a prophetic demonstration of God's awesome power. It also looks quite impressive on his CV.

And then he runs away.

The king in Elijah's time is Ahab and the prophet gives him a hard time about his behaviour. Actually, Ahab doesn't do much about it but his wife Jezebel does. She threatens Elijah with death. Within 24 hours, that is. This comes after his great triumph, and he runs for his life – hundreds of miles – in the days when the streets had no name and there was no Highway 77 or any other proper roads. This is a scared man. On the way, the Lord ensures that he has food and rest, but eventually God meets him on another mountain and gently asks him 'What are you doing here?'

Jeff Lucas wrote a book about Elijah called *Elijah: Anointed and Stressed*. That's pretty much how Elijah describes himself to God at this point. He complains that he has been zealous for the Lord but he is the only one left. In reply, the Lord says there are actually thousands like him, and then Elijah is recommissioned to return to Israel and anoint his successor and some new kings.

And he fails to do this.

God's care and restoration of Elijah is a great passage which preachers enjoy expounding, especially speculating on the mysteries of the 'still, small voice'. But the fact is, although God is gracious to him, Elijah does not fully carry out the instructions he is given.

At Spring Harvest 1998 I spoke to hundreds of people about Elijah at the Family Celebration each evening, and on the final day I asked everyone to consider the unpalatable truth that this great prophet had failed in his mission. I asked if, when they got home from this spiritual mountaintop experience, they would put into practice the things they had been promising to do for God during the week? I hope I didn't spoil their holidays.

There are those who are called by God and never actually follow through on the call. It's especially sad when someone has a great ministry and yet lets God down in later life. Yet God's grace is bigger than our failures and somehow God continues to use us despite our lack of obedience.

Another day of our Israel pilgrimage involved a slightly scary cable-car ride up into the mountains above Jericho. From there, we could look beyond the city, across to Jordan and Mount Nebo, where Moses died and was buried. I remember thinking: I'm standing where Moses wasn't permitted to go. He was not allowed to enter the promised land because of his disobedience.

Or was he?

Jesus often does things on mountains in the gospels, and in one significant incident he takes Peter, James and John up to a high place and before their eyes he is transfigured. They see a brief glimpse of his heavenly glory and he is joined by two others. In the Old Testament Moses and Elijah had meetings with God on mountains but it was too dangerous for them to see his true glory. Now here they are – seeing the full glory of Jesus, the man who is God. They had both 'failed' God during their ministries but now they are in the promised land, literally and metaphorically.

It is inevitable that we will sometimes fail God in our vocations, sometimes spectacularly. But the grace of God is bigger than our mess-ups. I for one am truly grateful for that.

One other thought. Sometimes people say: 'Why doesn't God just show himself to us?' It's the Christian claim that he has done that in Christ. But then people might respond: 'I would believe in him if I saw him.' However, if God revealed himself in power to everyone as he did at the transfiguration, we would worship him out of awe and fear – and maybe not even that would persuade us. In the parable of the Rich Man and Lazarus, Jesus says: 'If they do not listen to Moses and the Prophets, they will not be convinced even if someone rises from the dead' (Luke 16:31).

But God reveals himself in love, not on the mountain of transfiguration but supremely on the hill of Calvary, and we worship out of love. If there is any hint that our vocation as a response to God is based purely on fear, then we should question it.

FOR REFLECTION

- Have you let God down? Do you feel that any future ministry you might have is tarnished? Do you feel that he could never ask you to do anything again?
- Pray now that God would recommission you in his service. Be open for new opportunities to serve him. And follow them through.

FURTHER READING

Lucas, Jeff. *Elijah: Anointed and Stressed* (David C. Cook, 1998).

45

Elisha's Story: Handing Over the Mantle

After the England rugby team's amazing last-minute victory in the 2003 World Cup final, with Jonny Wilkinson's drop goal, I arranged to begin the Sunday morning service the next day by playing a recording of Ladysmith Black Mambazo's version of 'Swing Low, Sweet Chariot'. It had become the England team's theme song, and the fans have been s(w)inging it at matches ever since.

It would seem that the 'source material' for the old song comes from the moment when the great Old Testament prophet Elijah is taken up into heaven and hands over his prophetic power and authority to Elisha. I have this mental picture of a golden chariot, arriving like a celestial taxi to pick up Elijah. There's just one problem: that's not what happened. It was something rather wilder and windier.

The text does say that there was indeed a chariot, but that wasn't the only thing: 'As they were walking along and talking together, suddenly a chariot of fire and horses of fire appeared and separated the two of them, and Elijah went up to heaven in a whirlwind' (2 Kgs 2:11). It was the whirlwind that carried away Elijah, not the chariot. In fact, we were already told that this was the plan in verse 1 of the same chapter. It also explains why a group of fifty fellow prophets insist on going to look for Elijah ('Perhaps the Spirit of the LORD has picked him up and set him down on some mountain or in some valley'), even though Elisha tells them they are wasting their time.

Afterwards, Elisha sees Elijah's cloak (or mantle) and soon uses it to work a miracle similar to one that Elijah performed earlier. The phrase 'take on the mantle' is in common usage and means to take over the role of your predecessor. It's frequently used in sports commentary when a superstar steps down and a new person needs to take on their role. Who would take over from Jonny Wilkinson?

We touched on apprenticeship in the earlier chapter about Joshua. The parallels between Moses/Joshua and Elijah/Elisha are fascinating. Moses and Elijah are the ones who meet Jesus on the mountain of transfiguration, but they also hand over their ministry to their apprentice at the River Jordan, on the edge of the promised land.

When it comes to Jesus, he too takes up the mantle from his predecessor – John the Baptist – also at the Jordan river, but in Jesus' case, the 'apprentice' will go on to do much greater things.

Handing over

During my second curacy my vicar became unwell and was off work for many months until he retired for health reasons. Eventually I took his place officially and became the new vicar, but I will always be grateful for the way he handed over the mantle when he first was taken ill. He stood me at the front of the church in a service, laid his hands on me and blessed me, and told the congregation that I was the leader now.

He was a hard act to follow. He had actually taken over the church many years earlier, with instructions from the bishop to work towards its closure, but just before he was installed as vicar he had a deep experience of the Holy Spirit and his ministry was transformed. Dozens came to Christ through him, and the church grew to be a significant centre of worship and renewal.

With our vocation, there are seasons when we are in just the right place, but a day often comes when it's time for someone else to take up the mantle. I don't remember his exact words, but I recall Tony Blair saying that he did not want to stay in office beyond his time and become unpopular. Ironic.

The church has often been quite good at starting new initiatives, but has not been great at stopping when the time has come. We start a project – a group for young mums, a fellowship for men – but it stagnates, it has 'had its day', yet we keep going and much energy is wasted that could be used in a new and better thing.

Vocation can seem to be all about being the right person in the right place, but sometimes it's not the right time, or no longer the right time. Elijah had struggled in his later years, as we read in the previous chapter. God intervened to hand on his role to his apprentice, and it turns out that Elisha is a brilliant replacement for Elijah, and he does more amazing things.

FOR REFLECTION

- Is it time for you to move aside from your current role?
- Is there someone who should be taking on your mantle? How might you encourage them?

FURTHER READING

Ling, Tim, ed. *Moving On in Ministry* (Church House, 2013).

46

A Little Girl's Story

At the time of writing, the civil war in Syria is in the news, especially the terrible events in Aleppo. In Bible times, this region was known as Aram, which is linguistically connected to the word for bandits. During the Elisha story, in 2 Kings 5, we meet a man called Naaman who is commander of the army under the king of Aram. Soldiers acting like bandits under his command have raided Israel and captured a little girl, who has become a slave to Naaman's wife. We are never told her name.

Naaman has leprosy, and this little girl bravely suggests that if he goes to Samaria he can find a great prophet who will cure him. Naaman is desperate for healing, so with his king's permission, he sets off for Samaria with a sack full of gifts and a letter from the king. Cutting a longer story short, Elisha tells Naaman to bathe in the River Jordan seven times. He takes some persuading, but when he does so, he is healed. The heart of one of the enemies of God's people was transformed by the compassionate actions of the little Israelite girl who loved her enemy.

It's interesting that the gospels tell us very little about Jesus' life from birth to the age of 30, when his ministry began, but we do hear from Luke about his trip to Jerusalem when he is only 12 years old. After his parents lose him, they find him in the temple courts, sitting with the teachers and asking questions. Luke tells us: 'Everyone who heard him was amazed at his understanding and his answers' (Luke 2:47).

Later, when his disciples tried to 'protect' him from parents bringing their children to be blessed, Jesus was 'indignant' (Mark 10). Previously, in Matthew 18, the disciples had been arguing about who was the greatest in the kingdom of heaven. They were of course assuming that this kingdom would be political, but Jesus shocks them by saying that they must change and become like little children – or they will never enter the kingdom.

'Just a kid?'

Just before I wrote this, I watched the BBC *Songs of Praise* programme, which featured an initiative to help the homeless in Preston. The project, run by a local church, provides 'Hope Bags' which people purchase and can then offer to those sleeping on the streets, instead of giving money or buying them a coffee. The bags contain a toothbrush, toothpaste, thermal hat, foil blanket, moisturizer, socks, tissues, shampoo and body-wash sachets, wipes and mints.

The project was the brainchild (appropriate word alert) of Megan Holmes, aged 13, who was only 11 when she first had the idea. A confident young lady, she also explained that her Christian faith was the motivation for her desire to help. We don't know the name of Naaman's wife's servant girl, but at least we know Megan's name and her work is acknowledged nationally.

In my role as Director of Ordinands and Vocations, I often see candidates for the priesthood who tell me that they first began to sense God's call when they were a child. My son Paul led a church service when he was 7 years old. This is not to say that we should have lots of teenage vicars and pastors; but we should not be too quick to dismiss the thoughts of children and young people. The discernment criteria used by the Church of England when assessing candidates for ordination talks about 'potential' in younger candidates rather than evidence.

Jeremiah was not discouraged by others because of his age. He himself thought he was too young, but the Lord said: 'Do not say, "I am too young"' (Jer. 1:7); we will have more to say about that in his chapter later. We need to watch for the children and young people in our churches whom God is raising up, and encourage them. This must not be done in a patronizing way. As someone has said, the Holy Spirit in children is not a baby version.

FOR REFLECTION

- Do you need to become 'like a little child' in some way? What do you think this means?
- Do you consider yourself too young to do something that God might be asking you to do?
- Is there someone you know who is young now but shows great potential? Do you need to encourage them? Pray for them.

OTHER

The Hope Bags project website is at:

- https://www.crossgate.church/hopebags/

47

The Minor Prophets' Stories

A few years ago, the London School of Theology and *Christianity* magazine ran a competition to find the 'Rising Theologian of the Year'. To enter you had to write a talk on the future of Christianity in the UK. Over a hundred people entered and three were chosen to deliver their talk at a special event at the college. Our son Matt entered the competition and won it. His parents are obviously very proud and would like to claim all the credit, though we can't because we didn't help at all. Matt's prize was to study for a degree with the college for free. As he already had a degree in theology, he chose to take a master's and his chosen area of study was . . . (fanfare please) . . . 'The Contemporary Relevance of Obadiah'.

Can you remember anything Obadiah wrote? Be honest. No, me neither. But he's there in the Old Testament, along with several other prophets whose words are rarely remembered unless they are quoted elsewhere in the Bible. Obadiah's message is a warning of judgement on the neighbouring country of Edom – the descendants of Jacob's brother Esau. But the judgement upon them is a picture of God's judgement on all nations.

Essentially, although all of the Minor Prophets have some things in common, each is unique and worth reading, although we're not going to look in great detail at all of the so-called 'minor' prophets in this little book.

Remember that prophets generally do not foretell; they forth tell – they tell forth God's message. They look back as much as forward – calling Israel back to faithfulness to God's covenant. Remember too that the vision they speak about is like someone looking at distant hills and describing what they see. They cannot know for certain what is near and what is far. They talk of things that may have already happened, or are about to happen, or would happen when the Messiah comes, or when he comes again.

Jesus warned that a prophet is not welcomed in his home town. He himself was rejected by his own village and briefly even by his own family. There are different views about Obadiah's home town; one view actually says he's a converted Edomite, which would make his oracle against Edom even more unpopular. Amos, meanwhile, was a southerner called to go to the northern kingdoms and pronounce judgement. Jonah was called from Israel to go to Nineveh, which someone has described as like a Jew standing up in Berlin in the mid-1930s and denouncing the Nazis.

Theology of place

In the Anglican Church there is a particular theology of place. The Church of England has a parish system, which means that each local church has a patch of land in which to minister. There is less of a 'members only' approach to church life. We are there for everyone who lives in our parish. We routinely baptize, marry and bury those who live there.

There are questions to be faced post-Christendom as to whether this model is still appropriate or workable in the twenty-first century when geographical space is much less relevant to people's lives. Many people live in one place, work in another and shop somewhere else, and they don't live there for life. When I researched my family tree, I found ancestors going back several centuries who all lived and worked in the same area of Lancashire, and whose names are in the registers of their local churches. They would be surprised to discover that my children had lived at times in Israel, South Korea and – most shockingly of all – Yorkshire.

The prophets teach us about a willingness to speak out for God wherever he calls us to be. To go to a far-off land if necessary, or sometimes to stay where we are, which can have its challenges too. Sometimes it's harder to minister among those we have grown up with.

Lights to the world

John writes in his great prologue to the gospel: 'The true light that gives light to everyone was coming into the world. He was in the world, and though the world was made through him, the world did not recognise him. He came to that which was his own, but his own did not receive him' (John 1:9–11).

Even Jesus faced rejection. He expected it. And he expects it of the church too. But he also said: 'You are the light of the world. A town built on a hill cannot be hidden' (Matt. 5:14).

We can be prophets wherever we are, sent or not. We 'cannot be hidden' unless we choose to hide. If our faith and calling are real, we won't be able to help ourselves. The light will leak out.

FOR REFLECTION

- Is it hard in your context to serve God? Do you need to move?
- Or is God calling you to stay and be his presence in that place?

48

Isaiah's Story: Making a Great Prophet

Isaiah's vision and call in chapter 6 of his book are significant for any study of vocation, although once again we must be wary of making the text too prescriptive. Here is a glorious revelation of God and Isaiah's sense of unworthiness.

I was invited to preach about vocation in the grandeur of Ripon Cathedral, a good place to reflect on Isaiah's spectacular vision. I was expected to follow the set Church of England lectionary readings for the day, which was great because Isaiah 6 was the Old Testament passage. What follows is adapted from my sermon.

We know this incident probably really happened because Isaiah roots his experience in a real time and place. Like the Gospel of Luke, which tells us who were the kings and governors when Jesus was born, Isaiah says he had this vision in the year King Uzziah died. And in the vision Isaiah sees the Lord himself, with his robes filling the temple – even bigger than Diana or Meghan's wedding dress. Here is someone with infinitely greater splendour than even royalty.

Isaiah's vision is also his call to be a prophet – perhaps the greatest prophet ever – certainly the one who gets the most pages of the Bible. What can we learn from Isaiah about hearing God's call?

First, he has a vision of God – and how awesome he is. This doesn't begin with Isaiah but with God revealing his glory to him. Calling begins with God, not us.

Second, Isaiah has a recognition of God's holiness. As part of the revelation, Isaiah glimpses the worship of heaven where the living creatures are proclaiming God's holiness – his otherness – another book in itself.

Third, Isaiah uncovers an awareness of his own unworthiness. Seeing God's holiness, Isaiah realizes that he is totally inadequate. He is a man of unclean lips. He is a sinner.

Fourth, Isaiah becomes aware of the state of the world. Yes, I am a man of unclean lips – but so is everyone else. The world is a mess. All have sinned, as Paul says in Romans 3.

After a friend preached recently, a woman paid him a visit a few days later. In his words: 'Her bottom had not quite reached the sofa' when she commented: 'I didn't like your sermon on Sunday.'

He politely asked why.

'Well, you said we were all hypocrites,' she said, 'that we are sinners.'

'Yes,' replied my friend. 'Isn't that what the text says? Aren't we all?'

'Well, I'm not!' she replied gruffly.

But fifth, Isaiah is in receipt of forgiveness. Isaiah is helpless to help himself, so God does something about it. As Paul later would say: 'while we were still sinners, Christ died for us.'

Finally, Isaiah has a willingness to respond. Having received forgiveness, when God calls for someone to go and tell people about him, Isaiah says: 'Here am I, send me!'

Do I need to say more?

Here endeth the sermon. But in case I *do* need to say more, Isaiah's response is, as we mentioned earlier, '*Hineni* – here I am.'

But I also said we must beware of making any text prescriptive. Is it valid to preach the point above purely from this one text? Well, there is New Testament support for these points too.

In Luke 5, when Jesus works the miracle of the large catch of fish, Peter reacts in a very similar way to Isaiah. Jesus reveals his glory, Peter realizes his own sinfulness, Jesus tells him not to be afraid and commissions him, Peter gives up everything and follows him.

Any sense of God's call on our lives needs to begin with a revelation of who he is and his glorious holiness and majesty. Is your God too small?

FOR REFLECTION

- Have you got a sense yet of just how awesome God truly is? Are you aware of his piercing holiness?
- Have you truly understood what Christ did for you and how he dealt with your need for forgiveness?
- Has God begun to do something within you – recently or even today – or is there something that has been building maybe for years? Are you willing to say 'Here am I, send me'?

49

Cyrus's Story: God Uses Unbelievers

The book of Isaiah is a staggering work of ancient literature. In an odd quirk – and we shouldn't read too much into this – Isaiah displays a strange relationship to the whole Bible. Just as there are 66 books in the whole of the Christian Scripture, there are 66 chapters in Isaiah. But just as the Scripture divides into two – 39 books in the Old Testament and 27 in the New – Isaiah divides in the same way numerically and chapter 40 marks a complete change of tone and atmosphere, beginning with a prophecy about John the Baptist.

The final 27 chapters contain some of the most remarkable and most loved passages in the whole Bible. In particular, they contain four 'songs' about servanthood that are helpful for those reflecting on vocation. The songs are centred on chapters 42, 49, 50 and 52, and these four servant songs are regarded by most Christians as prophecies about the Messiah, the Christ.

But commentators also note that there seem to be four different servants in these chapters. Apart from Jesus Christ, another one is Israel, often called 'Jacob' here, another is the church, and then the fourth is Cyrus. There were several kings called Cyrus; this is Cyrus the Great, who was king of Persia.

Cyrus is described in Isaiah 44 and 45. Several times he is called 'my chosen one' or 'my shepherd'. Then Isaiah says:

> This is what the LORD says to his anointed,
> to Cyrus, whose right hand I take hold of
> to subdue nations before him and to strip kings of their armour,
> to open doors before him so that gates will not be shut . . .
>
> (Isa. 45:1)

Cyrus is actually called God's servant and his anointed, even though he is a pagan king. We hear more about him at the end of the book of 2 Chronicles and the beginning of Ezra. The context for his actions is introduced starkly by the author of 2 Chronicles in chapter 36.

Even when God sends Israel his messengers, the prophets, he is ignored. But that isn't going to stop him rescuing the nation. The writer continues: 'This is what Cyrus king of Persia says: "The LORD, the God of heaven, has given me all the kingdoms of the earth and he has appointed me to build a temple for him at Jerusalem in Judah. Any of his people among you may go up, and may the LORD their God be with them"' (2 Chr. 36:23). Although Cyrus calls God 'the LORD, the God of heaven', he hasn't become a monotheistic believer. As with most ancient people, especially kings, he believes in many gods. He rules over a vast empire but is happy for each local nation to have its own gods. He seems to be impressed with Israel's god and orders that the temple in Jerusalem should be rebuilt. The rebuilding is told in the book of Ezra, which follows 2 Chronicles.

Our simple but vitally important point here is that God uses unbelievers, including rulers, to bring about his purposes for his world. They have a vocation, even if they don't know it.

Paul talks about this in Romans 13, where he tells us that the governing authorities in each nation are placed there by God and bring law and order to society: 'They are *God's servants*, agents of wrath to bring punishment on the wrongdoer. Therefore, it is necessary to submit to the authorities, not only because of possible punishment but also as a matter of conscience' (Rom. 13:4–5, my emphasis). Some may say that Paul overstates his case; Hitler and many like him don't seem instinctively to be rulers raised by God, do they? And in the case of Cyrus, he was in other ways one of many 'bad' kings, including those reigning in Israel and Judah at the time.

But for all their faults, kings and rulers do bring a kind of order to societies. We only need to look at the chaos that has followed modern conflicts when there is a power vacuum in post-war countries, such as Libya and Yugoslavia. These are perhaps surprising examples of our sovereign God at work in an apparently godless world.

But remember that governments are accountable to God, and Paul is not suggesting that we cannot criticize and call to account those in authority over us, press for reform and justice, or seek democratic change. As a friend pointed out to me, some American evangelicals have unfortunately used Cyrus's story as justification for supporting Donald Trump.

God at work, at work

The great Protestant Reformer Martin Luther challenged the separation of vocation into a purely spiritual realm in which ministers, monks and missionaries (Steve Walton!) are 'spiritual' and the rest of the people are 'secular' or second class. He talked of the 'masks of God'. It's an odd phrase but he meant that God is at work, often unseen or 'masked', in his world. He cites the milkmaid and tells us that God provides for our need for milk through her. He might have underlined his point by showing how the prayer 'Give us this day our daily bread' is answered by the farmer and the baker. These days we might add the supermarket, the delivery driver, and so on. This is God at work in his world, even through unbelievers. How big is God?

God does not *need* anyone to do anything. He is omniscient, all-powerful. But in his gracious love he involves the creatures of his creation and gives them vocations, often without them being aware. Most paid jobs will not be 'religious' and many will be mundane. In fact, the curse of the fall means that work requires hard labour and toil. But behind his 'mask', God is at work in each of us, even the unbeliever.

I recently saw a photo of one of the vehicles owned by a street-cleaning company based in Manchester. Painted discreetly on the side are the words: 'I will sweep away everything in your land' – a quote from Zephaniah 1:3, obviously taken out of context but amusing nonetheless.

Any division of the world into sacred and secular risks creating 'no-go zones' for God, which would be illogical, since God by definition is all-knowing, all-seeing and omnipresent. He is at work in his world in unlikely places.

If you are tempted to call your current workplace 'God-forsaken', then you do have my sincere sympathies, but look for him at work there anyway. You might be surprised.

FOR REFLECTION

- Can you see God at work wherever you go?
- In your place of work?

FURTHER READING

Cosden, Darrell. *The Heavenly Good of Earthly Work* (Baker, 2006).

Costa, Ken. *God at Work* (Bloomsbury, 2007).

Higginson, Richard. *Called to Account* (Eagle, 1993).

Oliver, David. *Work: Prison or Place of Destiny?* (Authentic, 2000).

——. *Love Work, Live Life* (Authentic, 2006).

Schumacher, Christian. *To Live and Work* (Christian Research, 1987).

Veith Jr, Gene Edward. *God at Work: Your Christian Vocation in All of Life* (Crossway, rev. edn, 2002).

Witherington III, Ben. *Work: A Kingdom Perspective on Labor* (Eerdmans, 2011).

50

Josiah's Story: One Good King

King Josiah is hardly the most famous or well-known person in the Bible, despite the fact that it has some very positive things to say about him: 'Neither before nor after Josiah was there a king like him who turned to the LORD as he did – with all his heart and with all his soul and with all his strength, in accordance with all the Law of Moses' (2 Kgs 23:25).

Please could I have something like that for my obituary or gravestone? As if that wasn't praise enough, Lamentations 4 is a whole-chapter dirge of grief at the death of Josiah, who seems to have been greatly mourned when he departed. Lamentations was probably written by Jeremiah, whose prophetic ministry was contemporary to Josiah's reign.

Of course, this is the part of the Bible that few people read, and if you are reading this book in bed, you may be ready to switch out the light and rest your weary head on the pillow. But wait – please hang on a little longer. Josiah is significant because he is different. He's a good apple in a basket of bad ones.

They say that history is written by the winning sides. But this is where the Bible is unique, and it's another reason to believe it. As we have repeatedly said, the only hero in the Bible is the guy who died on the cross. The writers of the books of Kings and Chronicles don't pull their punches when telling us the truth about those who reigned in their nation, supposedly the people of God. There's no fake news here.

To save you reading through this sorry tale, check the links at the end of this chapter to biblestudy.org and gotquestions.org. These web pages give lists of the various kings of Israel and Judah from the time when the nation was divided in two in 930 BC after Solomon's reign, to 586 BC when the Babylonian captivity ended the separate nation of Judah.

There are no good kings in the northern kingdom of Israel. The southern kingdom, Judah, is rarely better with a few exceptions. But please look again at the commendation from 2 Kings mentioned above. Why is Josiah a good king? He is not commended for winning wars, like Churchill. He does not turn round the economy after a period of austerity. He didn't preserve a fragile peace after civil war. He simply turned to the Lord with all his heart and with all his soul and with all his strength. Isaiah wrote about God's view of his servants: 'These are the ones I look on with favour: those who are humble and contrite in spirit, and who tremble at my word' (Isa. 66:2).

King of Kings

But Jesus is the greater Josiah, the greatest king of all. There is irony in the fact that Pilate arranged for a sign above his crucified head: 'The King of the Jews' – in Hebrew, Latin and Greek, so that everyone knew it. Jesus Christ was never a political king. He never held any public office, led a political party, or sought to change the world by any other means than his own death.

If we want to know what greatness looks like, if we want to know about our mission in life, it is this. If we want to be truly great, then it must be to be great in the sight of God. This begins as we turn to the Lord and love him with all our heart, soul and strength, as Josiah did. It's what Jesus himself said was the greatest commandment – the call to everyone – so whatever else I have written in this book, I know I am right about this.

FOR REFLECTION

- In your quest for a vocation, do you desire greatness or to humbly serve God?
- What would you do if you were 'king for a day'?

OTHER

The lists and assessments of the kings of Israel and Judah are at:

- http://www.biblestudy.org/prophecy/israel-kings.html
- https://www.gotquestions.org/kings-Israel-Judah.html

51

Jeremiah's Story: Too Much Too Young?

When I was at theological college, we had a mantra that went 'exegesis, exegesis, exegesis'. It has served me well as a constant reminder to ensure I read the Bible very carefully so that I don't assume I think I know what it says. Exegesis means the interpretation of a text, from the Greek words meaning 'lead out'. The text must *lead* our thinking as we tease the meaning *out*, and we must not come to the text with our own ideas and import them.

Jeremiah's book begins with his call. He is to be a 'prophet to the nations'. His response is to say: 'Alas, Sovereign LORD . . . I do not know how to speak; I am too young.' This is ironic because God has already said to him: 'Before I formed you in the womb I knew you, before you were born I set you apart'. However young Jeremiah might be, God had started work on him before birth. So God simply responds by saying 'Don't say that'.

One of the ways this passage has been used, perhaps unhelpfully sometimes, is to say God can use anyone of any age, which is of course true. Nothing is impossible with God. But I have sometimes heard church leaders taking this thought and making it a slogan to stir up young people, as though they all are ready now to do some significant thing – like being a prophet to the nations – even though they are teenagers. But Jeremiah may be the exception to a more general rule that such things require a degree of maturity.

Some people are definitely not ready. As someone very unkindly said, God can speak through an ass but that doesn't mean you should ordain donkeys. It's true that God calls everyone – the title of this book, after all. It's true that he uses us in small ways every day. It's also true that God can work through a child – see the chapter about the little servant girl who helped Naaman to get healed. But we need to learn the art of waiting for God's timing. Sometimes there may be something significant that God wants us to do for him, but not yet.

God's bigger plans

The need for careful exegesis is perfectly illustrated later on in Jeremiah. If you've been a Christian for more than 10 minutes, it's quite possible that you have received an encouraging card at a difficult time with a quote from Jeremiah 29:11, which says: '"For I know the plans I have for you," declares the Lord, "plans to prosper you and not to harm you, plans to give you hope and a future."'

While working on this chapter, my wife has just shown me a Christian charity gift catalogue which includes a mug and coaster inscribed with these words that were addressed to Jeremiah 2,600 years ago. The accompanying text says this gift set 'makes an encouraging gift, ideal for youngsters facing exams'. What . . .?

Text in context

Jeremiah 29:11 is indeed encouraging and I don't want to be too cynical. Nevertheless we need to look at the context for this great verse. The people of Judah and Jerusalem in particular had been taken into captivity in Babylon. Imagine, then, what they would think if Jeremiah arrived and said: 'I know the plans I have for you, plans to prosper you and not to harm you, plans to give you hope and a future.' Would they not think that rescue from slavery was immediate or soon?

But no. In the preceding verse, the Lord says through Jeremiah: 'When seventy years are completed for Babylon, I will come to you and fulfil my good promise to bring you back to this place.' In other words, yes, there will be a better future – *in seventy years' time*. This is beyond the lifetime of nearly everyone who might have heard Jeremiah's message.

But the context set by earlier verses makes this even clearer:

> Build houses and settle down; plant gardens and eat what they produce. Marry and have sons and daughters; find wives for your sons and give your daughters in marriage, so that they too may have sons and daughters. Increase in number there; do not decrease. Also, seek the peace and prosperity of the city to which I have carried you into exile. Pray to the LORD for it, because if it prospers, you too will prosper.
>
> (Jer. 29:5–7)

Here is a basis for a vocation in politics or many other spheres of life. Politicians and other leaders are called to seek the peace (*shalom*) and prosperity of our town, our country and our world, because then we all benefit. In recent years Christian writers have begun to talk of doing what makes for 'human flourishing'.

Vocation outside church

We need to get serious about valuing Christian vocation outside the church. We need Christians in politics, the media, sport, social activism, local councils, town planning, counselling, medicine, education and, well, everything else. As Jeremiah says: 'Build houses . . . plant gardens.'

Anyone who thinks that the work of the ordained is more vital than jobs outside the church is missing the meaning of vocation. There are so many things that need doing in our modern society to make it function, from assembling cars to making roads, to keeping them safe, to keeping them clean.

We visited Petra in Jordan recently, one of the wonders of the world. To get to the site, we walked through the *sik*: a narrow passageway over half a mile long with high rock-faces on either side. Many tourists travel through it every day and in recent years it has been paved with concrete. This has enabled horse-drawn carts to take the less able visitors to the wonders of the city. But it also means that horses and camels pass through very frequently, with inevitable results. Our guide told us that nine men are employed to scoop up the droppings. Yes, that's their job, which they do all day, whatever the weather. Without them, we tourists would have a horrible experience.

In the past, most labour was agricultural, or people had associated jobs such as being the blacksmith. Others might have been fishermen or clothes makers. But industrialization brought factory work and capitalism. Our ancestors would never have dreamt of the kind of jobs we have now, from hedge-fund manager to cinematographer to petrol-pump attendant. On TV recently I saw a woman whose first job was answering the fan mail for Kermit the Frog. How do we find any sense of worth in these professions?

This time tomorrow

The challenge to church leaders is to find ways to affirm so-called 'secular' work in our Sunday worship. Some churches have been running 'This Time Tomorrow' slots in their services, where people share what they will be doing on Monday morning and the congregation prays for them. The title is useful because it does not assume paid employment and can include homemakers, the retired and those unable to work. It's a start . . .

FOR REFLECTION

- How might you seek the peace and prospering of your neighbourhood/town/nation?
- If you are exploring a call to a specific ministry or role, is the time right or should you be waiting?

FURTHER READING

Greene, Mark. *Imagine* (Authentic, 2004) (on DVD also).
——. *Thank God It's Monday* (Muddy Pearl, new edn, 2019).

52

Daniel's Story: A Daringly Different Diet

In *Star Trek: The Next Generation*, the most frightening enemy are the Borg, who travel across the universe conquering worlds and assimilate each vanquished race into their collective consciousness, thus making them even more powerful and removing any renewed threat from those they defeat.

Long before Jean-Luc Picard and his crew were a twinkling star in Gene Roddenberry's eye, the Babylonians were already doing this. Having defeated God's people Judah, they did not obliterate them completely but took the elite among the young men back to Babylon to be assimilated into Babylonian ways and lobotomize their defeated foes' culture and religion.

I recently visited the British Museum to see a great exhibition called 'I Object', curated by Ian Hislop, the editor of *Private Eye* magazine. The display included various ancient and modern 'relics' that typify resistance against repressive governments. One amazing item was from Iraq in about 600 BC and was described as 'part of Nebuchadnezzar II's building programme'. The brick is officially stamped with the king's name, but an Aramaic name has been scratched into a corner, possibly as an act of rebellious graffiti by a captured worker from Jerusalem.

Veggie tales

Daniel is one of those taken from Judah to serve in the court of Nebuchadnezzar, along with three of his friends whom we will hear about in the next chapter. The Judeans are given new names and are expected to eat the food provided for them at the king's table. But it's not kosher, and although they never had the email asking if they had any special dietary requirements, they manage to persuade the chef that they're vegetarians. He agrees to give them a trial and, by God's grace, they grow more healthily than their Babylonian colleagues.

Daniel lives through the reign of several kings, acquiring a fine reputation as an advisor and interpreter of dreams, though he is always careful to ascribe his wisdom to the Lord. Under King Darius, however, the indigenous Babylonian officials have grown jealous of Daniel's success and they persuade the king to sign a law that will catch Daniel. He is found guilty and, despite the king's reservations and regrets, he is thrown into a pit with hungry lions.

After Daniel survives, his enemies are thrown into the pit and are eagerly devoured by the lions who, like teenagers arriving home from school, have turned out to be really hungry after all. God's people, even in captivity, have defeated their enemies, and their culture and religion survives.

Another Daniel

Centuries later there would come a man whose enemies plotted to assassinate him. He would be accused of wrong, but the ruler would find no fault in him. Nevertheless he would be thrown into the pit of death and actually die, yet come out alive, because he was found to be innocent.

Our collective vocation is to live uncompromisingly for God in the circumstances we each find ourselves in, while remembering what God did in Christ, as he willingly was taken as a slave in a foreign land but refused to compromise. His vindication came after his suffering, and we may find ourselves in similar situations in this life as we seek to live for him and perhaps stand out as different in our culture.

Blending in?

In Romans 12, Paul writes: 'Do not conform to the pattern of this world, but be transformed by the renewing of your mind. Then you will be able to test and approve what God's will is – his good, pleasing and perfect will' (Rom. 12:2). Paul says 'Do not conform to the pattern of this world'. We are supposed to be different. We are not residents of this world any more. We should not let ourselves be assimilated. He tells us that this is the prerequisite for discerning God's will.

We should not expect to blend in. In fact Jesus warned: 'If the world hates you, keep in mind that it hated me first. If you belonged to the world, it would love you as its own. As it is, you do not belong to the world, but I have chosen you out of the world. That is why the world hates you' (John 15:18–19). A couple of chapters later, he prays for his disciples and for us: 'My prayer is not that you take them out of the world but that you protect them from the evil one. They are not of the world, even as I am not of it' (John 17:15–16).

If you are seeking a vocation for your life, if you want to know what God's will is, then this is where it begins. Whatever others do, focus your thoughts on what God wants. Train yourself to think like him. Let the Holy Spirit renew your mind. Don't conform to anything else but Christ and his word. It may not make you popular, and who knows, it might endanger your life. But it is the right thing to do.

FOR REFLECTION

- Are you just like those around you when it comes to: justice, gossip, sexual behaviour, swearing, priorities, money, drinking?
- How is your life different from those around you? Should the difference be more noticeable? Is anything you do too much of a compromise to the ways of this world?
- Would doing what God wants mean swimming against the tide?

FURTHER READING

Wright, Tom. *Virtue Reborn* (SPCK, 2010).

53

Daniel's Friends' Story: 'Even If God Doesn't Rescue Us . . .'

Daniel's three friends who were taken into captivity with him by the Babylonians are called Hananiah, Mishael and Azariah. As with Daniel, they are being assimilated into Babylonian ways, and these were their Hebrew names before the Babylonians imposed new names on them. My kids think it's probably my worst ever 'dad joke' in a sermon, when I said that if they had been captured by the Welsh they would have been renamed Shadwell, Meshach and Abednegogogoch. In Babylon they were called Shadrach, Meshach and Abednego. For the purposes of this chapter, I think I will just call them the 'three friends'.

The three friends of Daniel have their own story about refusing to become assimilated. I'm not sure where Daniel was when this was going on, but they are required to bow down and worship a statue of Nebuchadnezzar whenever music plays. Being Jews, they will only bow before the Lord so they reject Nebuchadnezzar's command.

As punishment, the king has them bound and thrown into a 'fiery furnace', but instead of burning to death they are unharmed. Nebuchadnezzar orders them to come out. They are happy to oblige the king and obey his command this time.

The king notes that there is not even a smell of burning on their clothes and is so suitably impressed that he orders that no one should ever say anything bad about the God of the three friends. He also promotes them within his household.

The bit I've conveniently missed out (for dramatic effect of course) is that in the fire the three friends are seen 'walking around' with a fourth figure, who looks like 'a son of the gods' according to Nebuchadnezzar. Commentators assume this is an Old Testament appearance of Christ himself.

But I want to draw our attention to something else I omitted from even earlier in the story. When the three friends stand defiantly before the king, he asks: 'what god will be able to rescue you from my hand?'

They reply:

> King Nebuchadnezzar, we do not need to defend ourselves before you in this matter. If we are thrown into the blazing furnace, the God we serve is able to deliver us from it, and he will deliver us from Your Majesty's hand. But even if he does not, we want you to know, Your Majesty, that we will not serve your gods or worship the image of gold you have set up.
>
> (Dan. 3:16–18)

No guarantees

Here we learn that we must never presume upon God. Although all ends well, this story makes no guarantee that we will be spared suffering if we trust the Lord. As we saw in the last chapter, Jesus warned: 'If they persecute me then they will persecute you.' There is much in the New Testament that talks about suffering, and much of it is about persecution for our faith.

Paul writes:

> To this very hour we go hungry and thirsty, we are in rags, we are brutally treated, we are homeless. We work hard with our own hands. When we are cursed, we bless; when we are persecuted, we endure it; when we are slandered, we answer kindly. We have become the scum of the earth, the garbage of the world – right up to this moment.
>
> (1 Cor. 4:11–13)

Many Christians today and throughout history have not had the luxury of choosing a vocation. Instead their vocation has been to suffer and it has been thrust upon them through no choice of their own. Some have died for their faith. In fact, it's said that more Christians have been martyred for their faith in the last century than in the previous nineteen.

Precious in the sight of the Lord

At the Spring Harvest event in Harrogate in 2018, after I spoke at a seminar about vocation, I was privileged to hear a talk – translated into English – by Hae Woo, a North Korean Christian who had spent years in a labour camp because of her faith. Hae Woo is not her real name because of the risks to her family. There are many thousands like her in North Korea. It felt a privilege to say '*Anyoung haseyo*' ('Hello') to her later. Although that was the total extent of my Korean language skills, she smiled graciously as we bowed to each other. I felt I was in the presence of something (or rather someone) precious. She has survived persecution, but many Christians throughout history and even today have not.

'Precious in the sight of the Lord is the death of his faithful servants,' says Psalm 116:15. It's clear from the Bible, especially in Revelation, that those who are martyred for their faith in Christ are treasured by him. We should never discount the possibility that we might also face such a fate and that it could be our vocation, individually or collectively.

FOR REFLECTION

- If you could choose a new name for yourself to sum up the real you, what would it be? Why?
- What might God call you?

FURTHER READING

Endo, Shusaku. *Silence* (Picador, 2015) (a novel that has also been made into a film by Martin Scorsese).

54

Ezekiel's Story: A Vision of Dry Bones

> I will put my breath into you, and you shall live again, and I will set you upon your own soil.

These words come from Ezekiel 37:14. They also appear on a giant memorial gateway to a museum just outside Jerusalem. I took a photograph of the inscription when we visited. The museum is called Yad Vashem, and it is Israel's memorial to the victims of the Holocaust. Few people visit there without tears.

It is understandable that the new state of Israel that arose from the embers of World War II would find the words of Ezekiel 37 appropriate for the memorial, although the name 'Yad Vashem' actually comes from Isaiah 56:5. It means 'a monument and a name'.

The verse quoted above comes from the best-known passage in Ezekiel and is often called the 'valley of dry bones' reading. In a vision, the prophet is taken to a valley full of bones and he walks among them. God tells him to prophesy to the bones and they come together into skeletons which are then covered in flesh, but they have no breath. Ezekiel is told to prophesy again – this time to the breath, not the bodies – and the breath (the word is the same word as for spirit) enters the bodies, who stand up – 'a vast army'. The Lord then reminds Ezekiel that the people of Israel have been saying that their bones are dried up and hope is all gone and they are 'cut off'.

Has God forgotten?

Ezekiel was prophesying at a dreadful time in Israel's history – maybe worse than the Holocaust, if that is possible. The divided nations of Israel and Judah have now both been taken into captivity and there seems no hope. All that is left is dead bones. But God has not forgotten his people.

In the rest of the chapter there are more visions. Ezekiel is told to take two sticks and write the names of Israel and Judah upon them, then hold them together in his fist as though there was one stick. He is told to hold this up before the people as a sign that one day both nations will return as one, with one great Davidic king on the throne – one king and one shepherd. That king will make an everlasting covenant with them, and God himself will come and live with them.

Restoring Israel

Once again Jesus is the interpretative key. It is he who will 'restore Israel' (see Acts 1:6) and unite God's people, but there will be one tribe from all the nations of the earth, not just Jews but Gentiles too. This began at Pentecost and will come to full fruition when Christ returns.

In the New Testament Paul frequently refers to a 'mystery', but he is not talking about a secret or 'mystery religion' purely for those secretly initiated. This is a mystery that has now been revealed, and it is not just the gospel but the gospel of peace between the Jews and the rest of the nations – two sticks joined as one, if you like – brought about by Christ's death and resurrection.

For example, in Ephesians 2:11–22 Paul sees his vocation as a calling to not only preach the gospel to the Gentiles but consequently to reconcile them to God along with the Jews, thus reconciling them to each other. This would surely be the ultimate memorial for Israel, and the fulfilment of God's promise to Abraham to bless all the nations through him.

Whatever our vocation, we need to remember Paul's words: 'Let us therefore make every effort to do what leads to peace and to mutual edification' (Rom. 14:19).

Everyone's vocation

In Ephesians 4, Paul talks about our (collective) calling, but he does not talk about a task or role. Instead he says:

> I urge you to live a life worthy of the calling you have received. Be completely humble and gentle; be patient, bearing with one another in love. Make every effort to keep the unity of the Spirit through the bond of peace. There is one body and one Spirit, just as you were called to one hope when you were called; one Lord, one faith, one baptism; one God and Father of all, who is over all and through all and in all.
>
> (Eph. 4:1–6)

If we are searching in the Bible for references to 'call' and 'calling', we will find the greatest concentration of those words here in Ephesians 4. We are called to live out our collective calling – by working hard to keep (not attain) the unity of the Spirit.

Down the centuries the church has often been infected by the spirit of the age and by the cultures in which it has found itself. Paul's letters are often combating Gnosticism. The church was influenced by the dualistic thinking of Greek philosophy, by the legal systems of the Roman Empire, by Norse tales of bravery at the time of the Crusades, by the rise of academic liberalism, and in many other ways. The modern world places huge emphasis on the individual, including the way human rights legislation is worded.

The message of the New Testament carries a healthy balance between the value of the individual and that of the community. See, for example, Paul's reflections in 1 Corinthians 12, where he stresses both oneness and diversity, and locates both in God. We are all members of a body, but it is Christ's body. We are all different, but that difference is the work of the Holy Spirit. The bottom line is that whatever our vocation, we also value the vocation of all our brothers and sisters.

FOR REFLECTION

- Read Ephesians 2:11–22 a few times and reflect on its meaning.
- Do the same with Ephesians 4:1–6 and 1 Corinthians 12.

55

Esther's Story: For Such a Time as This

There are sixty-six books in the Bible. Only two of them are named after women, one of which is Ruth. The other is hardly a feminist tract, with a first chapter describing drunken men leering at a woman, and later a king who apparently sleeps with candidates to be his bride until he finds the one he likes. But look a little more closely and the two women are a long way ahead of their time. The Bible is invariably more pro-women than we first realize.

King Xerxes, also known as Ahasuerus, is the king of the Persians about five hundred years before Christ, a period in which the Jewish people are in captivity to the Persian Empire. Xerxes has a liking for wine and women, something confirmed by sources outside Scripture, and the story begins with him throwing a lavish party. When he and his all male guests have partaken liberally of the wine, he calls for his wife Vashti to come and parade before them. She is not impressed – and refuses.

The king is advised to rid himself of this rebellious wife and hold a sort of beauty contest to choose her replacement. There are several movies telling the story that follows, one of which is called *One Night with the King*, starring Luke Goss as Xerxes. I kid you not.

Although it's not explicit, it seems likely that Esther had to sleep with Xerxes, but she had no choice in this.

I could continue with the rest of Esther's story but it's a bit too long for this book. Can I suggest you read the book for yourself? It's only ten chapters and I'll be here when you come back.

Just a quick note about something you may have missed. The book begins with a misogynistic king throwing a banquet and encouraging other men to leer at his queen, who refuses to do what he wants. Later in the story the new queen holds a dinner (two in fact) and gets the king to do what *she* wants. But that's an amusing side story. Our main point here is to think about choice and chance.

Providence

The key theme of the book of Esther is Providence. So many things happen at the opportune moment. God is never mentioned in the book of Esther, but he is in control, even of the 'bad' stuff. He is working out his purposes for his world. There are clear echoes of the story of Joseph in Genesis. Like him Esther finds herself in the courts of power and is able to save her people.

This story of perfect timings begs the question: is the whole course of history already determined from the moment creation begins? Many scholars have argued about this down the centuries. The Bible seems to teach both free will and God's absolute sovereignty, as though both coexist.

Sin demonstrates human freedom because God does not sin or cause it; yet in the Bible God somehow always uses it for his greater purpose, although that greater purpose may not be seen immediately or even in our lifetime.

It just so happened . . .

In November 2015, I was a few weeks into my new role as the Director of Ordinands and Vocations, reading lots of stuff about guidance but also looking forward to a special treat. My son had managed to obtain tickets for U2's concert in Dublin, their home town. We lived in different cities, so we flew there separately.

Arriving at the airport, I realized I had brought nothing to read on the flight, but in the airport shop I spotted a New Scientist publication called *Chance* which happened to be on special offer. Then I prayed that I would not be stuck on the plane next to someone who wanted to chat. When I boarded the plane I discovered that not only was there no one next to me but the whole row was empty, as were the rows in front and behind. Providential.

I settled down to read my book about chance. One of the core questions was: is the universe completely random or is everything that happens inevitably determined from the Big Bang onward? Let me briefly summarize the answer the scientists gave:

'We don't know.'

How does this help us to consider vocation? I don't believe in coincidences, or rather I do believe in them in the sense that *for God* such events are not random. He is in control – even when I don't understand what he is up to.

As we explore our callings, it's vital that we understand that God has a much bigger purpose than our minds can fully comprehend. We can't always say why we believe.

Paul writes:

> No, we declare God's wisdom, a mystery that has been hidden and that God destined for our glory before time began. None of the rulers of this age understood it, for if they had, they would not

> have crucified the Lord of glory. However, as it is written: 'What no eye has seen, what no ear has heard, and what no human mind has conceived' – the things God has prepared for those who love him – these are the things God has revealed to us by his Spirit.
>
> (1 Cor. 2:7–10)

This calls for humility. The Spirit may or may not show us glimpses of what God is up to. We may sometimes see those 'God-incidences' when we realize that his timing is perfect. But it is always perfect, even when we don't see it and even when his timing seems wrong.

In my role as Director of Ordinands and Vocations, I ask the question: 'Is this person called?', but I also have to ask: 'Is this person called now – at this moment?' A better way to word this might be: 'What is God doing and where does this person fit into that?' They may be the ideal candidate, but it may be that God has some more preparation work to do before they are actually ready. It may be that the banquet tomorrow night is a more suitable time.

FOR REFLECTION

- Can you think of instances when God's timing seemed wrong? Or times when you realized his timing was just right but you didn't know it until later?
- Is there something you have been putting off doing that you need to do now? Are you in a place or position for such a time as this?

FURTHER READING

Gutting, Gary. 'What Makes Free Will Free?' *New York Times* (2011): https://opinionator.blogs.nytimes.com/2011/10/19/what-makes-free-will-free/

56

Ezra and Nehemiah's Story: Rebuilding

In recent years leadership has become a major topic for Christians. There are seminars and books and courses. This is probably no bad thing; the church in the West needs to move from maintenance mode to mission-mindedness as soon as possible and there is much catching up to do. We need leaders at a time like this who will be strong, visionary and entrepreneurial.

I've been to a few seminars on leadership over the years and noticed a few times that Ezra and Nehemiah are used as models, but these days I'm not as sure about that as I once was. There is a risk of taking Scripture and using it to sanctify business methods – with some success, but at what cost?

The Bible books of Ezra and Nehemiah were originally a sort of box set (called 1 Ezra and 2 Ezra) on one scroll but were separated in medieval times. Both men are remembered as rebuilders, as Ezra supervised the rebuilding of the temple in Jerusalem and Nehemiah the city walls. But their background is different as Ezra was a priest and Nehemiah was the king's cupbearer. They lived at the time of the Babylonian exile when most of God's people had been killed or enslaved, and their work was vital in beginning the restoration. By the way, there is a third person whose name has been missed from the book titles – Zerubbabel, who began the work before the other chaps got involved. Unfair.

Previously, earlier prophets had promised that despite the mess Judah was in, God would restore things: he would send his Messiah, the temple would be restored, his kingdom would grow to encompass the nations, and all the promises made to Abraham would be fulfilled. Unfortunately, although the ministries of Zerubbabel, Ezra and Nehemiah show some promise, this doesn't happen (yet). It's almost as though Yahweh gives his people one last chance to renew themselves before he steps in to do it properly.

Here's one of those many places in the Bible where names seem to have significance. Zerubbabel means 'sown in Babylon' and there may be a hint that the project is not going to succeed. Ezra means 'helper' and Nehemiah means 'comforter' or 'Yahweh comforts'. In the New Testament, we learn that although there is no longer a temple where God's people can worship him, now the people themselves are the temple, and it's another 'helper' who does the building.

Another helper

The night before Jesus' death, after the Last Supper, he prepares his disciples for his later departure at the ascension. His physical presence will only be with them for a few weeks after the resurrection. He tells them: 'I will ask the Father, and he will give you another advocate to help you and be with you for ever – the Spirit of truth' (John 14:16–17). The words 'another advocate' are important here. We are reading an English translation of John's Greek words which themselves are translating Jesus' teaching in Aramaic, so we need to get back to what he was saying. Who is this 'advocate' and why is he described as 'another'?

Without getting into the technicalities of the Greek text, Jesus is saying that after he goes, another person like him will come. And the word 'advocate' is a Greek word which is translated differently in the various translations: advocate, comforter, or helper. The word literally means 'someone who gets alongside you to help you'. So Jesus is essentially saying: 'I will pray and the Father will send another person just like me who will get alongside you to help you, and he'll always be with you.' And so it proves: in fact in Acts 16 when the Holy Spirit is guiding the apostles he is called 'the Spirit of Jesus'.

The book of Acts is often called 'The Acts of the Apostles' but could be called 'The Acts of the Holy Spirit'. Acts 1 begins with Luke saying: 'In my first book I told you what Jesus began to do . . .' This is now the sequel, starting after Jesus' resurrection and before his ascension, and it begins as he leaves instructions for his disciples: 'Do not leave Jerusalem, but wait for the gift my Father promised, which you have heard me speak about. For John baptised with water, but in a few days you will be baptised with the Holy Spirit' (Acts 1:4–5).

In Acts 2 the day of Pentecost arrives, fifty days after Passover, when Jesus was crucified, and now this festival celebrates the 'first fruits' of the harvest, in May in the modern western calendar. Waiting for something to happen, the disciples experience fire and wind, symbols of the Spirit and presence of God from the Old Testament. They are filled with the Spirit and cannot help but spill onto the streets, praising God. Suddenly the church is being born as dozens of men and women are infected with joy and worship, and many in the crowd that gathers are converted.

The renewal that stalled in the days of Zerubbabel, Ezra and Nehemiah will succeed this time because God himself has come down (see the chapter on Babel) and changed people's hearts. Now the temple will be built – not with stone bricks but in the hearts of the church. Peter writes: 'you also, like living stones, are being built into a spiritual house [or temple]' (1 Pet. 2:5).

Experiencing the Spirit

After my wife and I married in 1980, we hosted a house group every Friday night. A group of young people in their teens and twenties met together. We would read the Bible, pray together and sing worship songs. Late in the evening we often sent out for a takeaway and then after midnight parents would ring to ask where their children had got to.

It was fun and a lot was good, but somehow the group drifted and was starting to falter by the mid-1980s. Then my wife suggested I should go to a week-long conference in Sheffield City Hall, called 'Signs and Wonders and Church Growth', led by an American called John Wimber. (Fun fact: Wimber was the keyboard player with 1960s superstars The Righteous Brothers.)

The conference has passed into legend because of its extraordinary influence on the Anglican Church in the UK. Events such as New Wine and Soul Survivor grew from the aftermath, as did the Alpha Course. Wimber's approach was simple: 40 minutes of contemporary sung worship, 40 minutes of teaching and 40 minutes of Holy Spirit ministry. It was not exactly the Book of Common Prayer.

At the first session, this pattern was established. When it came to the 'ministry' time, Wimber prayed 'Come, Holy Spirit', put down his microphone and sat down. Around us, manifestations of God's work began. People wept, shook, spoke in tongues, fell to the floor, laughed and did other strange things. Lives were being changed.

On the third day I too experienced the Spirit's touch. I felt extraordinary warmth gently surge through me from head to toe. My hands trembled. I felt deeply loved. Nearby people lightly put their hands upon me and prayed. My good friend Paul prayed a prayer about God's call on me to be a leader, which at the time was news to me. When the sensations ended, I felt drunk with joy. We made our way to lunch and it took me several hours to recover a sense of normality. Some people call this sort of thing 'the baptism of the Spirit', though the phrase is much debated. Whatever it was, whatever you want to call it, it was precious to me.

Returning home, I began to share these experiences with our house group and we listened to some tapes of John Wimber's teaching. We began to experiment with the gifts of the Spirit. We learned how to pray for one another. The group grew.

Some months later, I was leading an after-church gathering. At the time, all the services in our parish were strictly Book of Common Prayer with a robed choir, but once a month we were permitted to have a Sunday night meeting with little liturgy and a music group. As I led that evening, I felt prompted to pray 'Come, Holy Spirit'. Then I sat down and left it to him. In the meeting of about fifty or sixty people, we saw the same manifestations occur as I had seen during the week in Sheffield. Some were healed. One person became a Christian. As I looked around, everyone was being prayed for and ministered to by the young members of our house group.

Our house group ended when I left for ordination training in 1989, but it's interesting to see that the fruits continued to grow. Two of the group have since sadly died, but most of the others are heavily involved in church life today, in a whole variety of ways. One is a church organist; one is a Reader; others do youth work. Another currently leads a large free church in the south of England. That house group was a living temple in which God dwelt by his Spirit.

True vocation requires the Spirit to be at work in us. Before I was touched by the Spirit, my witness and teaching were faithful and sometimes fruitful but there was a dimension missing. Afterwards, I was not perfect and I know there remains lots of my 'flesh' in what I do, but something more was happening.

There have been further movements of the Spirit in the UK and around the world since the 1980s of course, though I have had some concerns about the sensationalist approach sometimes. What ultimately matters is the fruit of the Spirit, not the outward and unusual manifestations, exciting though they may be.

Not in our own strength

The Church of England ordination service ('The Ordinal') asks those about to be ordained a number of demanding questions to which the candidates respond in the affirmative, but then there is a further paragraph read by the bishop, which recognises that this calling is so weighty that it is actually impossible for anyone to manage it in their own strength, so they will need God's grace and help. The bishop tells the candidate to pray for an enlarged heart (every day!), a deeper understanding of Scripture and for the gift of the Holy Spirit. Then the bishop lays his or her hands on the candidate and calls down the Holy Spirit upon them.

I love these words and, despite having been at several ordination services, the hairs on the back of my neck always stand up at this point. We can make promises, but it still all comes back to God. It's a shame these declarations are reserved for priests and deacons because they could be used by any Christian.

The Spirit of God is not just for 'holy' people. No one merits the Spirit and he is not exclusive to those who have a special role. He is a gift to every Christian. In the confirmation service, the bishop lays hands on each candidate and asks that the Lord will 'confirm' them with the Holy Spirit.'

If Jesus told his followers to wait for the Spirit to come, then we cannot manage without him. Whatever our collective or individual calling, we will need the Spirit more than we ever dare admit, but if we allow him to fill us, we will find that he can do more than we ask or even imagine.

'If you ask . . .'

One hot summer's day, I conducted a funeral in the modern surroundings of the Milton Keynes crematorium. After the service ended and the mourners filed quietly out of the building, I turned to chat to Max, the attendant on duty. At that exact moment, he froze and pointed to the floor. 'Look at that!' Walking towards us across the floor was a small scorpion. It had probably come from a bunch of flowers brought by mourners. If we'd had mobile phones in those days, I think we would have taken a picture to share with friends, but instead Max stepped on it firmly with his heavy-duty boots.

Jesus said: 'Which of you fathers, if your son asks for a fish, will give him a snake instead? Or if he asks for an egg, will give him a scorpion? If you then, though you are evil, know how to give good gifts to your children, how much more will your Father in heaven give the Holy Spirit to those who ask him!' (Luke 11:11–13). This is one of those times when Jesus uses the phrase 'how much more'. If you sinful parents can manage to be kind to your children, how much more will Father God be kind to you. The Holy Spirit won't hurt you.

The Holy Spirit is called 'the gift', and if we ask, God is more willing to give than we dare believe. You cannot serve him without his help.

FOR REFLECTION

- Kneel down and close your eyes. Pray that God would fill you with his Holy Spirit to overflowing. Give him time.
- If you are with others, or using this book for group study, pray for one another to be filled with the Spirit. If you've never prayed out loud before, there is always a first time. Go for it!

FURTHER READING

Packer, J.I. *Keep in Step with the Spirit* (Baker, rev. edn, 2005).

Pytches, David. *Come, Holy Spirit* (Hodder & Stoughton, rev. edn, 1987).

Volf, Miroslav. *Work in the Spirit* (Wipf & Stock, repr. 2001).

Williams, Jane, ed. *The Holy Spirit in the World Today* (Alpha International, 2011).

Wimber, John. *Power Healing* (HarperOne, repr. 2009) (contains an appendix with a report from an independent observer at the Signs and Wonders conference in Sheffield mentioned above).

Wimber, John, with Kevin Springer. *Power Evangelism* (Hodder & Stoughton, 2013).

57

Jonah's Story: A Reluctant Vocation

The story of Jonah appears in many books of Bible stories for children, though it is an odd little book, included among the Old Testament prophets even though it's not really like any of the other books in that series, and Jonah is not really a prophet in the conventional sense.

Jonah is called by God to go and preach repentance to the people of Nineveh, a heathen nation. Jonah runs away, catching a boat in the opposite direction. The text does not say he is scared, as you may have heard some people say or preach. He has a quite different and shocking reason for not wanting to go to Nineveh, which we will discover soon.

God is very determined to make Jonah obey his calling. When a terrible storm hits the boat, the sailors believe that someone has upset their god. They're right – it's Jonah. Lots are drawn to see who is to blame and Jonah is identified. Despite their protests, Jonah insists that the others should push him overboard. Eventually they do this and the storm subsides.

Jonah is saved from drowning by God. A big fish swallows him and three days later spews him up on the land. After singing a psalm of thanksgiving (chapter 2), Jonah reluctantly heads for Nineveh. He brings the people God's message and to our delight and surprise they respond. They repent of their behaviour and God forgives them. But instead of being delighted, Jonah sulks. He's not pleased.

Now we discover Jonah's *real* objection to his call and the actual reason he ran away. He's a racist. He tells God he didn't want to go preach because the people *would* repent: 'I know you are a gracious and merciful God.' In his view, the Ninevites should have been wiped out.

At the end of the book, God gently points out to the sulking Jonah that he was right: the Lord cares for everyone – even for the cattle in the city of Nineveh. Jesus would later declare that God cares even when a sparrow falls from a tree.

The sign of Jonah

Jesus has some interesting things to say about Jonah. Religious leaders are demanding a 'sign' from him – a miracle to prove he is truly from God. It's rather ironic, since he's often doing miracles and when he does they ask him what authority he has to do them. Jesus refuses to perform for them and instead tells them that the only sign they will be given is the 'sign of Jonah'. What does he mean?

Jesus continues:

> For as Jonah was three days and three nights in the belly of a huge fish, so the Son of Man will be three days and three nights in the heart of the earth. The men of Nineveh will stand up at the judgment with this generation and condemn it; for they repented at the preaching of Jonah, and now something greater than Jonah is here.
>
> (Matt. 12:40–41)

Jesus may simply be reminding these people who are very sure of their own holiness that God cares for even their enemies. But there is something more profound here. As Jesus says: 'something greater than Jonah is here.'

Remarkably, the book of Jonah shows what we are like and, by contrast, what Christ does. We are like Jonah, and Jesus is like Jonah but in a different way. We are riddled with prejudice and often want God's fierce justice to fall on others.

Jesus, however, is the true and greater Jonah. Justice was done on someone else instead of us – the one who came knowing that people would *reject* his call for repentance. Jesus could calm the storm with a word. But when Christ was 'thrown overboard' by Pilate, he really did suffer death, thus saving everyone 'in the boat' with him. Nevertheless, after three days in the 'belly' of the earth, he rose again.

'Shall we call down fire?'

In the Sermon on the Mount, Jesus said: 'If you love those who love you, what reward will you get? Are not even the tax collectors doing that? And if you greet only your own people, what are you doing more than others? Do not even pagans do that?' (Matt. 5:46–47).

When Jesus set out resolutely towards Jerusalem, he was not made welcome en route at a Samaritan village. His disciples knew what to do: 'When the disciples James and John saw this, they asked, "Lord, do you want us to call fire down from heaven to destroy them?" But Jesus turned and rebuked them' (Luke 9:54–55).

Earlier in the same chapter of Luke, James and John were on the mountain when Jesus was transfigured and Moses and

Elijah appeared. Being versed in Israel's history, they would remember Elijah calling down fire from heaven on the sacrifice he had prepared. But Jesus rebukes them. This is not the way of the kingdom of God.

Elsewhere in this book I write about the justifiable anger and judgement of God upon evil. But it is not for us to be the judge, as Romans 12:19 (quoting Deut. 32:35) points out – that only appears on God's job description, not ours. We don't have the wisdom or knowledge for it. He does.

Jonah divides easily into two and it's as though the story of chapters 1 and 2 is repeated in 3 and 4. For example, chapter 1 begins with God calling to Jonah to go to Nineveh, as does chapter 3. In chapter 1 Jonah preaches to pagans – in the boat (see how God even uses us in rebellious moments?) – and he does the same in chapter 3.

It's interesting to spot these kinds of literary connections, but it's even more exciting to see them picked up in the New Testament. When Jesus is confronting some self-righteous judgemental people, he tells three stories about things that were lost and the party that follows them being found. They are a lost sheep, coin, and son. But in the third story there are two sons, and what we call the parable of the Prodigal Son has two halves that show remarkable similarity to the book of Jonah. It's as though Jonah is the young son, running away but somehow surviving in chapters 1 and 2, and the older son, resenting the Father's grace to his undeserving brother in chapters 3 and 4.

What happened next?

Strangely, both stories are unfinished. What did Jonah do next? Did he accept that the repentance of the people of Nineveh was something to celebrate? What did the older brother do next? Did he join the party celebrating his brother's return to the family?

And our lives are unfinished too. What kind of Christians are we?

I am saddened that my fellow evangelicals can be so much like those Pharisees who found it hard to see Jesus 'compromising' by eating with sinners. Some of my brothers and sisters seem to have a Jonah-like faith that knows the truth about grace but do not show it with their lives. There is an obsession with being right that can be quite ugly, especially on social media. Social media is also where I found the quote from Francis Schaeffer that I mentioned in an earlier chapter: 'Biblical orthodoxy without compassion is surely the ugliest thing in the world.'

John says: 'For the law was given through Moses; grace and truth came through Jesus Christ' (John 1:17). We are all called to be a community of both grace and truth, reflecting our master.

And one more amazing, sobering thought: God used Jonah despite his hard heart and God can do the same with us. Having a 'successful' ministry does not mean we are super-saints with better prayers and better gifts. We might be terrible racists or secretly adulterous, but the fruit of our ministry is produced by God, not us. While God looks for clean hearts and pure lives, he nevertheless can use anyone. We cannot claim the credit.

FOR REFLECTION

- How would you like people to think of you – now or when you are being remembered at your funeral? Would you like to be someone known for their achievements or for their grace?
- Assuming it is the latter, pray for God to mould you into a truly gracious person.

FURTHER READING

Keller, Tim. *The Prodigal Prophet* (Hodder & Stoughton, 2018).
Kendall, R.T. *Jonah: An Exposition* (Send the Light, new edn, 1995).

58

Malachi's Story: The Distant Future

When I worked in information technology in the late 1970s, computers were fed with punched cards. I used to write lines of computer code on paper (yes, really) and send it to the 'punch room' where a small army of women – I'm afraid there were no men – would input the code to a mechanical device which produced the punched cards. Hi-tech or what? Then came an exciting development: they typed the code on a special keyboard with a green-screen computer monitor. And productivity went down.

Why? Because there was no pile of cards on each desk to prove how hard the girl had been working. No evidence of the great speed at which she was producing results. What was the solution? The bosses simply arranged for the keyboard to 'beep' every time the typist pressed 'return'. There were noticeable results again. Productivity went back to normal.

It's hard to work on a job without a feeling that something is being achieved, especially in the modern 'instant' world. We should remember that many great cathedrals took several generations to build, although the builders could at least see progress as the walls rose up. At a conference for church leaders, I heard a speaker talk about 'horizon mission-planning' – looking for what God is doing on the far 'horizon' of the distant future. What might our church look like in a hundred years' time, and what should we do now to prepare for it?

We have already seen plenty of evidence to show that God works on a different timescale. In Jeremiah we noted that God's plans for a more prosperous future would take seventy years to come to pass. Moses spent forty years in the palace and forty years in the desert before spending another forty years in the desert with thousands of moaners.

Malachi's prophecy

Malachi is the final prophet of the Old Testament in the order that we have in the Bible, but it seems probable that he was active around the same time as Ezra and Nehemiah were working in the construction industry.

Some Bibles have the Apocrypha (the word means 'hidden') in between the Old and New Testaments, especially the editions used by Roman Catholics and some High-Church Anglicans, but not Protestants. It's not the remit of this book to debate the status of these apocryphal books, but if we assume they should be omitted, then there are several hundred years between the Old and New Testaments.

Before the long silence begins, Malachi challenges Israel and Judah, especially the priests. There is food for thought here about those who are specially called as leaders in the church and their greater responsibility. In Luke 12, in a passage discussing stewardship (see Chapter 2), Jesus says: 'From everyone who has been given much, much will be demanded; and from the one who has been entrusted with much, much more will be asked' (Luke 12:48).

Malachi has good news that the Lord will send his messenger, but who will be able to stand against him? That messenger will bring a word of judgement and refining fire. At the end of the book, we discover that the messenger will be a second Elijah. We will meet him in the next chapter of this book.

Working for change in a future generation

After the terrible wars in the Balkans in the early 1990s, a charity was set up to build long-term relationships among Christian and Muslim young people in Bosnia and Herzegovina. It was called Novi Most, which means 'new bridge'. Their website currently says: 'Talk to people in Bosnia and Herzegovina about the future, and fear and fatalism are never far away. There may be reasons to justify this pessimism, even defeatism, but we believe a better future is possible. We must show it is possible to believe and act differently.'

Our church supported Novi Most's work, and one of the people who set up and led the charity came to preach. He recalled driving down a motorway and finding himself overwhelmed by the size of the challenge. There are those who say that conflict has been a fact of life in that region for a hundred generations. As he drove he found himself weeping and had to pull to the roadside for safety. As he continued to pray he felt God say: 'Are you prepared to work for something knowing that you will not see the fruits in your lifetime?'

God's call is not some guarantee of immediate results. Far from it. As someone has said, we are not called to be successful, but to be faithful, although this should not excuse us from working and praying to see church growth and God's kingdom coming.

After progressing from punched cards, things moved on in the world of IT and eventually I was working with consultants from around the world and even using the first Apple Macs in the UK. But then I was called by God to leave and train for ordination. Several work colleagues asked me why I would do this. I always responded with a smile: 'Because God has a bigger project'.

Once again, the message here is that it is God who has a mission and a plan for his world, and vocation for everyone is about discovering how we can be involved in what he is already doing. Sometimes our calling will be to work for something that will not see fruit for decades or centuries to come. He has a bigger project.

FOR REFLECTION

- If God calls, are you prepared to work for something knowing that you will not see the fruits in your lifetime?
- Give thanks for all those who went before who had the vision and obedience to bring about many of the benefits we enjoy today because of their work.

The New Testament

Author's note: The New Testament is only one third of the whole Christian Scripture, but this section of this book will be even shorter than that, partly because we've actually covered quite a lot of the New Testament as we've looked at the Old Testament.

As I have explored the story of the Old Testament, I have referred frequently to the New, because so much is fulfilled and interpreted by Jesus. So we do not need to repeat that now, but there are still some reflections that I need to add as we look at the gospels, the letters and the final revelation. I'll do that by telling the stories of those involved.

59

John the Baptist's Story: Who Is the Greatest?

When my wife and I were recently in Jordan, we visited Machaerus, where John the Baptist was imprisoned and beheaded. But the significance of John's story was brought home to me on another holiday, in Malta. Malta has a magnificent cathedral in Valetta, which is the southernmost capital in all of Europe. It's called St John's Co-Cathedral, which means it is one of two cathedrals where the same bishop has his 'seat' – the other one is St Paul's in Mdina, the old capital of Malta. If this has started to sound like a BBC2 documentary, I'll explain why I'm telling you this stuff shortly.

Our holiday was in fiercely hot weather and we went into the cathedral partly to escape the heat and very bright sunlight, but I really wanted to see a very significant painting by Caravaggio, my favourite Renaissance painter. As far as we know, it's the only painting he ever signed and the biggest he ever produced. When we got outside, I commented to my wife: 'That picture was very dark.' She looked at me with that look that wives reserve for their husbands and said: 'Well, you did have your sunglasses on the whole time.'

Even without sunglasses, the picture *is* very dark. There is a lot of darkness, typical of Caravaggio, who was noted for his 'tenebrism' style – exaggerating the dark areas, which dominate the picture, and highlighting the subject with a ray of light. But it's also a very dark subject: the beheading of John the Baptist. The beheading obviously fascinated Caravaggio, because he also painted two pictures of Salome carrying John's head on a plate. One of them is in the National Gallery in London, hung next to Caravaggio's amazing painting of Jesus breaking the bread at Emmaus.

It might beg the question: of all the subjects in the Bible, why choose to paint something so gruesome and unpleasant – and surely discouraging? In the cathedral the painting is not in the main part of the building but in an oratory or side chapel, where it dominates the room. A quick search on Wikipedia will reveal that many other artists have painted this scene too. In fact only this week I've seen a painting by early Renaissance artist Bellini which depicts John's severed head; the canvas is round and painted to look like a plate. Maybe it's as a reminder that we might have to suffer for the sake of the gospel. That's certainly true, but I believe there's more.

The significance of John the Baptist

John's beheading takes up a whole section of fifteen verses in Mark's gospel, which is surprising since Mark only has sixteen chapters, and he likes to be brief and keep the action flowing. He clearly thinks it's important. Matthew has twelve verses on the subject; Luke has only three but he does begin his gospel with the story of John the Baptist's birth. John the apostle and gospel writer doesn't mention John the Baptist's death at all, but he does give John pride of place in his glorious first-chapter prologue – John is introduced as early as verse 6, and Jesus is only named when he is finally revealed to be 'the Word' in verse 17.

This all gives us a hint as to the significance of John's beheading and the reason Mark devotes a section to it: John is preparing for and prefiguring Jesus' death. Note that immediately after he hears the news of the execution, Jesus withdraws for a time from public ministry, or attempts to. This is a man grieving for his own relative and friend, but perhaps also anticipating his own death.

John is a man with a clear vocation: his role is to prepare the way for the Messiah. At one point John says: 'He must become greater; I must become less' (John 3:30). In a sense, John is the final Old Testament prophet, prefiguring and preparing for the Messiah. Despite this, he is a man with occasional doubts, especially when he is imprisoned and sends his disciples to ask Jesus if he is really The One. Nevertheless, Jesus declares: 'Truly I tell you, among those born of women there has not risen anyone greater than John the Baptist; yet whoever is least in the kingdom of heaven is greater than he' (Matt. 11:11).

Hands up anyone who finds this puzzling. How can the man Jesus declares to be the greatest person who ever lived be less than the least in the kingdom of heaven? What Jesus seems to be saying is that even John's greatness is not enough. He has only been preparing the way. Until Jesus' life, death and resurrection, and the pouring out of the Holy Spirit, no one could truly enter the kingdom of God that was to come.

We have frequently said in this book that the people we hear about in the Bible have unique vocations and we must be wary of considering them as examples. We can only learn principles, not practices. It is obvious that we are not called to dress like John, who himself was copying Elijah. Nor are we called to baptize people 'for repentance'. John's baptism was a symbolic washing as a sign of repentant preparation for the Messiah's arrival, whereas Christian baptism is a sacramental joining ceremony as we are symbolically incorporated into Christ and his death and resurrection.

No, John's example to us is more basic. It's about being willing to point to Christ. Any vocation that gives the glory to us instead of the Messiah is questionable at best. This may be obvious, but the lesson of many fallen Christian leaders is that once people start telling you how great you are, you start to believe them. John and Paul now have cathedrals named after them in places like Malta (I told you I would explain why I went on about the cathedrals at the beginning of the chapter), but in their lifetime they knew what was required of those who follow Christ. Paul humbly declared: 'I am the chief of sinners.' And he was willing to die for the sake of the gospel.

Repenting of our good works

Paul talked a lot about reluctantly boasting when defending himself against his critics. Much of this is in 2 Corinthians, but in Philippians he also writes: 'But whatever were gains to me I now consider loss for the sake of Christ. What is more, I consider everything a loss because of the surpassing worth of knowing Christ Jesus my Lord, for whose sake I have lost all things. I consider them garbage, that I may gain Christ and be found in him' (Phil. 3:7–9). Paul's point is staggering and vital: he uses the picture of a financial ledger and says that everything he used to list in the spiritual credit column he now has moved to the debit side. These are his good deeds, but he says that when it comes to salvation, they are actually worthless. The

Greek word is more like 'crap'. Any credit comes from Christ and knowing him by faith. As Tim Keller often says: 'We need to repent of our good works.'

I have already mentioned several 'starting points' for vocation. This one is vital and one of the hardest – acknowledging that our best works are 'filthy rags', as some translations say in Isaiah 64:6. The Hebrew word used is a religious term for ceremonial/ritual uncleanness, indicating that we cannot approach God. Isaiah and Paul are saying that what we might have thought creditable is pathetic in God's sight. We can only stand in the merits of Jesus Christ.

So let's make all we have said so far clear once and for all: it's not about us; it's all about Jesus. I must decrease and he must increase.

FOR REFLECTION

- John says: 'He must become greater; I must become less.' What would this look like in your life? Does something need to change?
- John also says: 'I am not worthy to untie his sandals.' Do we have that level of reverence for Christ?

60

Mary's Story: There's Something about Her

Mary is a key player in the nativity story, of course. In fact her role is central and much has been written about her willingness to play her part in God's extraordinary plan of salvation. So here let's just focus on one aspect of Mary's extraordinary story. Her vocation was to give birth to the Son of God.

What an awesome responsibility! Some have seen in her story an affirmation of the vocation to motherhood. Motherhood often takes over a woman's life – as the one who carries the child, frequently with physical side-effects, as the one who breastfeeds (until the modern era and powdered milk), and in many societies the one who raises and nurtures their offspring.

I could get into trouble for sounding politically incorrect here, but I am describing, not advocating. We need to value the vocation to motherhood – and fatherhood – much more than our modern society allows, with its emphasis on work rewarded by payment and status. At the same time, we need to have a special place in our hearts for those who are unable to have children, recognizing their yearning to respond to a call they feel but cannot fulfil, and pray for them.

The household code

In an earlier chapter about stewardship, I quoted the passage in Ephesians 5 and 6 which is Paul's version of the 'household code' penned by several other writers of that era. The great difference is that Paul's code is not some misogynistic rant at women to submit to their husbands. Unfortunately some translations, such as the New International Version, insert a paragraph heading in the text after Ephesians 5:21 which exaggerates this misunderstanding. In fact, the Greek text says: 'Submit yourselves to one another, out of reverence for Christ; wives to husbands as to the Lord.' There is no repeat of the word 'submit' in the second half of this quote. The key thought is *mutual* submission.

In fact, other household codes of the time were only addressed to men, as the husband, father and master, and were very patriarchal. Aristotle, for example, declared (in *Politics*): 'the courage of a man is shown in commanding, of a woman in obeying.' He also added: 'Silence is a woman's glory, but this is not equally the glory of man.'

On the other hand, Paul's version is staggering in that it begins by addressing women, then children, then slaves. Modern readers miss this and can think of Paul as old-fashioned. In fact he was way ahead of his time. In Paul's view, the wife is as important as the husband, though their roles may be different simply by virtue of biology. Men will never have the awesome privilege (and pain) of giving birth.

So back to Mary. She is an example to all of us in her humility and willingness to submit to God's plan. But she is also an example to mothers and fathers in her care for the Christ child and her devotion to him, not only as her son but as the Son of God.

FOR REFLECTION

- Mums and dads: do you recognize your parental calling as a gift from God and a responsibility he has given you?
- Everyone: do you recognize that a calling to motherhood is as valuable as any paid role, if not more? Pray for those you know who are fulfilling this demanding task.
- Pray for those you know who struggle because they are childless, that God will affirm their value in other ways.

OTHER

For more on household codes, see Ian Paul's blog Psephizo at:

- https://www.psephizo.com/life-ministry/aristotle-and-the-household-codes/

61

Jesus' Story (Part 1): Nativity – God Incarnate

Although there are four gospel biographies of Jesus' life, death and resurrection, only two of them tell the Christmas story – Matthew and Luke. Mark is very keen to get to the action so he jumps straight to Jesus' ministry. However, John goes much further back to 'In the beginning . . .', with echoes of Genesis 1.

In his prologue (1:1–18), John takes until verse 17 to reveal the name of the person he is telling us about. Having introduced us to 'The Word' in verse 1, in 14 he says: 'The Word became flesh and made his dwelling among us' (John 1:14). As you may know, this is a translation of Greek words that actually say: 'And the word flesh became and *tabernacled* among us.' These are exciting words for a first-century Jewish reader. A tabernacle was a tent, and Jews still look back during the Feast of Tabernacles to their time wandering in the desert living in tents. But *the* tabernacle was the precursor to the temple and it was the portable place where the high priest met with God's overwhelming presence. This meeting will now happen in the form of a person. What if God was one of us?

In case we miss it, however, the first half of John 1:14 is rather good too: 'The Word became flesh'.

What if God was one of us?

Remember that Jesus was born into a world dominated by Roman and Greek thought. The Romans were content to have lots of gods and didn't mind who you worshipped, as long as you understood that Caesar was a god in human form. Everyone in the empire was supposed to declare 'Caesar is Lord'. And meanwhile, the Greeks were into dualism, a belief that physical matter – especially the body – was bad, and spirit was good.

Jesus arrived into this world, born of the Spirit and Mary's flesh. As Christians would later formulate into a key doctrine: Jesus Christ was wholly man and wholly God. The ancient Nicene Creed says he was 'of one substance with the Father'. Jesus breaks down a lot of walls, but this one is key: his incarnation shows us (as we heard in the creation story at the beginning of the Old Testament) that creation and physical matter is good, even if spoilt by sin.

As a child, I received mixed messages from my parents. They loved gardening and wanted me to discover their passion for myself. But gardening involved digging and weeding and getting my hands dirty, and they also stressed the need for cleanliness, which I was often reminded was 'next to godliness'. Clean hands won in my case (OK, I was lazy, I admit it). But theologians have noted that Christianity rejected the Greek dualism by declaring that in the incarnation 'God gets his hands dirty'.

For our thoughts about vocation, this is vital. There must not be any separation into sacred and secular. There must not be holy work and ordinary jobs. Holiness is not about living apart from the 'dirty' world but getting stuck into it. Yes, some individuals might be 'set apart' by the Spirit (see Acts 13) to serve a particular role, but *all* work, done in the service of God and others, is sacred. Our collective vocation as the church is to tabernacle in the world, continuing the presence of Jesus. This is often called 'incarnational ministry'. Jesus prayed for his 'holy' apostles that they would be *in* the world, though not *of* it.

Jesus' emptying

Back to Jesus. In Philippians 2, Paul shares a great hymn of praise to our Saviour and his humility. Jesus 'appeared in human likeness', says Paul. This translation should not be taken to mean that Jesus pretended to be human. As we have seen, mainline Christian doctrine teaches that he was and is fully God and fully man. Baptized and then filled with the Holy Spirit, we are told that before his ministry began he was 'thrust out' into the wilderness where he was tempted by the devil.

Temptation by manipulation

Whenever I'm in London during the summer months, I try to get to a play at Shakespeare's Globe Theatre. It's fantastic to be a 'groundling' – one of those who stand in the courtyard around the stage, for just a fiver. Recently it was a special pleasure to see *Othello*, with the part of Iago played by Mark Rylance, who the Internet Movie Database says is 'widely regarded as the greatest stage actor of his generation'.

In the play, Iago wants to cause the downfall of his master Othello and subtly does so by cleverly persuading him that his wife is unfaithful. There is a real sense in which he is 'devilish' in his manipulation. At a key moment, as Iago's plan begins to work, he pauses to reflect on the situation.

At this point, Rylance moved to the edge of the stage, just where I was standing, and took hold of my hand. Then he looked me deep in the eyes, and said 'Divinity of hell!' As you can imagine, the hairs on the back of my neck stood up. In this key moment in the play, Iago is admitting that his scheme is something the god of hell would be proud of.

Whenever I have talked or preached about the devil, people seem to be especially interested. In fiction and movies, the 'evil' characters are often more interesting than the good guy/girl. But we must not give demons too much credit, as C.S. Lewis warned. They have a tiny role in Scripture, and this is true of even Satan himself. The demon stories seem to cluster around Jesus as his light exposes their darkness.

When Satan comes to Jesus in the wilderness, he tempts him. Like Iago in *Othello*, he is trying to use subtle manipulation, just as he did in the garden of Eden. The temptation scene has been preached about numerous times, and sometimes I've heard it used to teach us how to resist temptation. Of course this makes some sense. Jesus responds to each suggestion with words from Scripture, and it has been suggested that this is how we combat the temptation. Not much wrong with that – although note that Satan quotes Scripture too.

There's something different here. Although we are told elsewhere that Jesus was tempted just as we are, the temptation of Christ here is unique. Adam and Eve were tempted by Satan to be 'like God', but here the Son of God is being tempted not to be human – to use his divine power instead of 'making himself nothing, taking the form of a servant'.

Eve was told 'You can be like God', but Jesus was challenged 'You can't just be human. You might as well use your awesome power. Show it, and everyone will bow down to you.' The crowd would later mock Jesus on the cross, shouting: 'Come down and then we'll believe in you!'

Paul's challenge to the Philippians and to us is to have the same attitude as Jesus – to give up the power that we have, in absolute humility. In the Gospel of John, after the Last Supper, Jesus washes his disciples' feet. Then he tells them that since he, their master, did this, they should do the same. Elsewhere, in a different context, Jesus says: 'Whoever can be trusted with very little can also be trusted with much, and whoever is dishonest with very little will also be dishonest with much' (Luke 16:10).

While writing this book, I contacted a bishop in another diocese from mine, asking if I could meet him to discuss vocation, as he had some important national responsibilities on the subject. Not only did he agree to see me, but he also invited me to lunch. He picked me up at the railway station, drove me to his house, made a lovely soup for lunch and gave me over two hours of his valuable time before dropping me back at the station. He didn't wash my feet but he served me sacrificially. A few weeks later I met him again at a meeting where he was the main speaker, and he greeted me by asking what I would like to drink. He was serving the tea and coffee to people as they arrived.

We are all called to this vocation. Mother Teresa said: 'Be faithful in small things because it is in them that your strength lies.' Be willing to take the servant role, whatever your vocation proves to be.

FOR REFLECTION

- What acts of service have you done today/will you do tomorrow?

FURTHER READING

Green, Michael. *I Believe in Satan's Downfall* (Hodder & Stoughton, 2nd edn, 1995).

62

Jesus' Story (Part 2): Mystery – Parables and the Kingdom

In this book we've been seeing how the Old Testament points to and is fulfilled by Jesus, so now you may be thinking: 'Finally we've reached the New Testament and Jesus himself so it will all be straightforward.' But when we read the gospels and Jesus' teaching in particular, it turns out that he often speaks in parables and they are hard to understand. The good news is that we can still use the same interpretative key as we have been using all along.

There are nearly fifty parables in the gospels, depending on how you define a parable. Some are just brief comments; others are extraordinary tales that could be turned into movies. The traditional explanation of 'parable' is that it is a story with a meaning. But this does not mean they are teaching a simple moral point.

You may have noticed this if ever you have tried to do a school assembly about a parable. They are rarely little moral tales with a simple lesson about how to behave. Jesus' parables are stories about a person (guess who?), and this points to the way we should understand them. Even the gospels must be interpreted by the gospel.

What I mean is, we should come to every Bible passage in the light of Jesus and all that he did and will do. This can be less obvious than it first appears when it comes to the gospels. We need to interpret them in the light of Jesus and his death and resurrection. So, for an easy example, the parable of the Vineyard Tenants is obviously about Israel rejecting the prophets, and the owner's son who is killed must be Jesus. Similarly, the bridegroom in the parable of the Ten Virgins is also Jesus. Jesus explains the point of the Wise and Foolish Builders: wisdom is to hear *his* teaching and put it into practice. More subtly, while the story of the Good Samaritan does teach us to love our neighbour who may be different from us, it's also a picture of a saviour who helps the unloved stranger at cost to himself, and having done so, promises to return to complete what he has done. Sound familiar?

After surprising us by saying that he uses parables so that some will not believe, Jesus explains: 'If anyone has ears to hear, let them hear' (Mark 4:23). Parables will only be understood through him. Only if you 'get' the gospel will you truly 'get' the parables. Very occasionally he explains the meanings, but it is usually just to his disciples. He is not being deliberately obtuse; the parables draw in the listener and encourage faith, but often can be puzzling for those who don't believe.

The kingdom of God

A lot of parables are about the kingdom of God. We heard a bit about kings in the Old Testament, and learned that the true king is the Lord himself. When Jesus arrives, the true kingdom begins, but God's rule will come fully when Jesus returns. The parable of the Wheat and Weeds shows God's kingdom growing alongside the 'weeds' of this world's kingdoms. The various parables about kings and masters returning home and demanding an account from their servants are about the second coming of the king and our accountability.

Another book would be required to really unpack all this, but what does this mean for vocation? Every Christian is called to 'seek first his kingdom and his righteousness' (Matt. 6:33). So we can ask ourselves the question: are my actions working towards this?

When God's true reign begins, there will be an end to poverty, injustice, pain, inequality and many other evils of this present age. Our collective vocation includes working to see God's kingdom come, even though it will not fully come until the return of Christ. So organizations like Tearfund or Christians Against Poverty are working for the kingdom of God. These are specifically evangelical Christian charities, but at their best the work done by secular charities such as Oxfam or Macmillan Cancer Care also contributes towards the bringing of the kingdom.

In passing, we might note that many major charities were founded by Christians, from Samaritans to the RSPCA. The Jubilee 2000 'Drop the Debt' campaign was the idea of Christians. The abolition of slavery (which was unfortunately initially defended by some church people) was the work of Wilberforce and the Clapham Sect, a group of evangelical Christians.

Why are so many schools and hospitals named after Christian saints? Because Christians founded them. Further, community work, teaching, nursing and many other professions are doing kingdom work without being overtly Christian or even carried out by believers. This is common grace at work. I am certainly not claiming above that Christians have a monopoly on good works, but for Christians their faith is their motivation and their engine as they seek the kingdom of God, consciously or not.

If we can see our individual role in the light of the call to seek the kingdom, we may not then fall into the trap of thinking our work is 'second class' or unspiritual. Working for God does not mean being called into a specifically 'Christian' job in the church. Like God, vocation is bigger than you think.

FOR REFLECTION

- Is God calling you to get involved in some kind of charitable work in your spare time?
- Full time?

FURTHER READING

Kirkby, John. *Nevertheless* (Christians Against Poverty, 6th edn, 2010).

Tomkins, Stephen. *The Clapham Sect: How Wilberforce's Circle Transformed Britain* (Lion, new edn, 2010).

63

Jesus' Story (Part 3): Identity – 'Who Do You Say I Am?'

We will shortly be thinking about Jesus' death and resurrection, the centre of our study and what it all means for our calling. But first we must establish who Jesus was and is. The Romans crucified thousands of individuals until the practice was ended by Constantine in AD 337, so the significance does not come from the manner of his death but from the identity of the one who was crucified.

Reading the gospels with the simple quest to find out who Jesus is, or who he thinks he is, we find things just a little confusing sometimes. First of all, John the Baptist makes it plain from the start that this is the Messiah. But when John is imprisoned, he sends messengers to ask if he really is 'the one who was to come', and Jesus' reply is to point to his miracles and actions. Sometimes when Jesus works miracles, he tells people to keep this quiet, and yet at other times he tells them to go and tell everyone what God has done for them. Why?

This is known as the 'Messianic Secret'. Generally speaking, before his death and resurrection, Jesus wants people to keep quiet about him if they are Jewish but not if they are Gentiles. It seems he is worried that Jews will realize he is the

Messiah but then have wrong expectations about him. When Peter declared that Jesus was 'the Christ [Messiah], the Son of the Living God', he had in mind someone who would come and revolutionize Israel, but as usual God had a much bigger project in mind, and it was necessary for the Messiah to suffer and die. This didn't fit with Peter's concept at all. Meanwhile, Gentiles were not waiting for any Messiah.

'Who do you say I am?'

Peter's declaration came in response to Jesus' question: 'Who do you say I am?', and this is the question that we all must answer in order to give the crucifixion its proper significance. It was the famous question C.S. Lewis asked his readers to consider, summed up by the even simpler question: was Jesus mad, bad or God?

Bono has drawn attention to the same question when probed by interviewers about his Christian faith. He recalls Lewis's point that everyone loves Jesus as a popular rebel figure who cares for the outcast and loves the unlovely, and whose teaching is widely regarded as some of the best moral teaching ever produced. Even outright atheists are drawn to Jesus; Richard Dawkins has a whole chapter on him in *The God Delusion*, and he finds it difficult to say anything bad about him. He joked that he wants to have T-shirts printed that say 'Atheists for Jesus'. Search the web and you will find pictures of him wearing one that someone made for him.

But, as Bono says, the 'problem' is that Jesus demands more – he claims to be the Son of God, and wants us to believe in him and give absolutely everything for him. So Lewis says that this leaves us with only three options: Jesus is totally mad, he's totally evil, or he is who he claimed to be. The religious authorities decided that he was bad. His own family believed for a time that he was mad. What will we decide?

My story

I grew up going to my local Methodist church. My brother and I were sent there before we had even started school, with our parents staying at home. Most children left in their early teens but I kept going for reasons I have never worked out (oh, OK, there were some attractive girls there). At 16 I was the oldest teenage boy and the leaders asked me to help with Sunday school. I wonder now what I used to teach. I think it was basic 'be nice to each other' deism, but whatever it was, it was not the gospel.

When I was 19, a friend started challenging my rather vague beliefs and she lent me a book. The book was called *In Search of God* by David Watson and I read it in a few hours. I was gripped from the first page and particularly taken with his thoughts about Jesus. He highlighted Jesus' words at the Last Supper: 'I am the way and the truth and the life' (John 14:6). The Holy Spirit brought these words alive; I truly grasped that Jesus was who he claimed to be and I literally knelt by my bed and told God that I believed this stuff and wanted to give my life to him. I would like to tell you that a bright light shone in my room and that I could hear angels singing, but nothing like that happened. Yet everything had changed.

Back to C.S. Lewis, who expanded on his thoughts about Jesus by recounting how the thing that really won him over was Jesus' claim to forgive sins. It was this that persuaded him that there was something more about this man. Everything about him was so good, but this additional claim to be God must be true, however unlikely it first appeared.

So this is our common calling and perhaps most important vocation: to answer Jesus' own question: 'Who do you say I am?' It makes all the difference. If you haven't answered that, then there is no point considering any more specific purpose for your life. Put this book down right now and pray that the Holy Spirit will make this clear to you.

FOR REFLECTION

- Who do you say Jesus is?

FURTHER READING

Lewis, C.S. *God in the Dock* (Eerdmans, 2014).
Watson, David. *In Search of God* (Falcon, 1st edn, 1974).

64

Jesus' Story (Part 4): Passion – The Suffering Servant

Jesus' 'passion' is the term usually used to describe what happened to him in the last 24 hours of his life – from after the Last Supper to his burial. While the cross is at the centre of our faith, it would be unfortunate if we neglected the important events that led up to it. Certainly the cross, and the salvation it achieves, is the absolute 'high and low' point of Good Friday. We will come to it in the next chapter, but before that there are some significant things to think about.

Three key things happen between the Passover meal and midnight. There is Judas's betrayal, Peter's denial and Jesus' trial. I'll be looking at Peter's denial and restoration in a later chapter, and the trial is when Jesus has been 'handed over to sinful men', so here I want to look at Judas.

Interesting people?

One of the bestselling books of recent years was *Girl on the Train*, later made into a film. Before the book became very high profile, I went to a talk and book signing by the author, Paula Hawkins. I asked her about her characters, none of whom are especially nice people. 'Do you have a fascination with bad people?' I asked.

Her response was to say: 'Not exactly. I have a fascination with interesting people.'

Whatever our perspective, evil people often seem to fascinate us more than good ones; isn't it odd that the TV schedules seem every day to have at least one programme about Hitler? In *The Lord of The Rings*, while Frodo seems to lack personality, readers are fascinated by Gollum. Similarly, Judas has intrigued writers through history. The problem of evil, predestination and freedom and other mysteries find a focus in him. Was his rebellion in some senses a vocation? Is it blasphemous to even consider it? Bob Dylan posed the question in one of his songs, 'With God on Our Side'.

It certainly seems that Judas's betrayal of his Lord was his destiny. Centuries beforehand, the psalmist predicted it: 'Even my close friend, someone I trusted, one who shared my bread, has turned against me' (Ps. 41:9). Jesus quotes this at the Last Supper in John 13 and tells his disciples that this is about to happen, and that he's pointing it out beforehand so it will actually encourage their faith – because it shows that this was all part of God's greater plan. Peter alludes to all this in his sermon at Pentecost: 'This man was handed over to you by God's deliberate plan and foreknowledge; and you, with the help of wicked men, put him to death by nailing him to the cross' (Acts 2:23).

So was Judas guilty if this was always God's intention? But Judas does have a choice. When John discreetly asks Jesus who the betrayer will be, Jesus replies: '"It is the one to whom I will give this piece of bread when I have dipped it in the dish." Then, dipping the piece of bread, he gave it to Judas, the son of Simon Iscariot. As soon as Judas took the bread, Satan entered into him. So Jesus told him, "What you are about to do, do quickly"' (John 13:26–27). Jesus has offered him the choice; when Judas takes the bread, his mind is made up. It's only then that Satan enters him. His role is God-given, but Judas takes it.

There has been much speculation as to Judas's motives. We won't rehearse them all here but go back to the Scriptures. What we do know is that Judas was a thief who took money from the 'common purse' that the disciples shared as they travelled. It also seems that Judas somehow believed that Jesus would not be condemned, because when he is found guilty and sent to Pilate by the chief priests and elders, Judas seems to be shocked and regrets his actions: 'When Judas, who had betrayed him, saw that Jesus was condemned, he was seized with remorse and returned the thirty pieces of silver to the chief priests and the elders. "I have sinned," he said, "for I have betrayed innocent blood"' (Matt. 27:3–4).

Bono wonders about this in the lyrics of U2's powerful song 'Until the End of the World', in which the three verses are written from the standpoint of a bewildered (and dead) Judas. But between the second and third verse, there is a different voice – either Jesus responding with a repeated cry of 'love', or maybe it's Judas crying out for it.

When it comes to the question of who is 'saved', we are drawn to Paul's words: 'if you declare with your mouth, "Jesus is Lord," and believe in your heart that God raised him from the dead, you will be saved' (Rom. 10:9).

Who is saved, then?

With Paul's well-known statement in mind, I am not a universalist, but I do hold out the hope that many more will be saved than at first appears – I cling to phrases like 'even though only as one escaping through the flames' from 1 Corinthians 3:15.

I believe in the apparent paradox of God's absolute sovereignty and purpose for his world and our responsibility for our free-will choices, which mysteriously he uses to bring about his will. This is not to say that the world is perfect but to say that in some mysterious way even our bad decisions are going to work out for good in a manner that we cannot now understand.

Judas's mysterious vocation to betray his Lord and so bring about the salvation plan of God is important for our understanding of calling. It is liberating because it means we can make wrong choices but God will still be at work. It is challenging because we still have responsibility to seek to make the right choices.

Gethsemane

Before he is kissed by Judas in the moment of betrayal, Jesus goes to the garden of Gethsemane to pray. The darkness of night makes this a good time and place for his arrest, instead of broad daylight in the temple where there was a risk of crowd trouble. He takes his disciples with him and leaves them in two groups. Peter, James and John come a little further with him. He becomes anxious and troubled, and he asks them to keep watch.

Perhaps this is where we see Jesus at his most human. At times before this he seems to know everything – including his betrayer – but at this dreadful hour it's as though he knows what is coming yet wrestles with the tiny possibility that there may be another way. He sweats blood in prayer as he asks his Father if the cup he's about to drink might be taken away. When he checks on the disciples he discovers them asleep.

I find it interesting that sleep overcomes Abraham in Genesis 15 when God 'cuts' the covenant and promises that if it is broken he will face the penalty himself, as we heard in Chapter 9. And the same three disciples here also fell asleep on the mountain when Jesus was transfigured.

I have heard sermons on this passage that warn us against laziness and highlight Jesus' words: 'Couldn't you keep watch for one hour?' But this feels like another moralizing message that uses the text as an excuse to beat up the congregation spiritually. We do not know if the tone of Jesus' words was accusing or compassionate. I suspect the latter.

In Matthew's version of events, Jesus says: 'Watch and pray so that you will not fall into temptation. The spirit is willing, but the flesh is weak' (Matt. 26:41). Here is someone who is concerned for the welfare of his friends. There may be some disappointment, but there is also understanding and protectiveness.

We are like the disciples, with all our human shortcomings, and we must not allow ourselves to feel unnecessarily condemned when we read such passages. A key point of the passion narrative is the failure of the disciples as evil does its work, but the grace of God overcomes. Look at Peter starting to throw his sword around and cutting off someone's ear – the typical human response to enemies; then when Jesus intervenes to stop him, he and all the other disciples run away. Wouldn't we do the same?

Even if we forsake him, he promises that 'he will never leave you nor forsake you' (Deut. 31:8, quoted in Heb. 13:5).

Forsaken

A careful study will show that every single time Jesus prayed, he called God 'Father', except in one particular place. Having endured his passion, Jesus cried out on the cross: 'My God, my God, why have you forsaken me?' (Matt. 27:46). Here is the terrible but joyous truth about grace. In that moment, Jesus was abandoned even by his Father, so that we are never abandoned.

Being a disciple is not about success or failure. It is about faithfulness, to some extent of course. But if we mess up, it will never be the end: 'if we are faithless, he remains faithful, for he cannot disown himself' (2 Tim. 2:13).

When I discuss vocation with individuals or speak to groups, I will often quote something I heard someone else say many years ago: 'God's will is not a tightrope.' In other words, we must not get the idea that if we get things wrong, either in terms of guidance or in moral failure, it means that life is over. He will still be with us.

To be blunt, you and I are not so important that our failures somehow spoil God's plan. Grace always overcomes. How big is God?

FOR REFLECTION

- Do you feel that God could never forgive you for something you once did?
- Pray now, asking him to assure you that forgiveness is not based on the depth of your repentance but the height of Christ's love on the cross.

LISTEN

- U2, 'Until the End of the World', from the album *Achtung Baby* (1991). Lyrics version here: https://www.youtube.com/watch?v=t7ElEHJpvNs

65

Jesus' Story (Part 5): Death – What It Achieves

I recently heard a Christian speaker recount a rather interesting exercise she undertook in which she showed a variety of pictures of Jesus to a group of Christian young people, asking which one most appealed to them. She noted that the different reactions depended on the race and cultural background of the viewer. The white westerners all chose an image of Jesus hugging someone. Non-white non-western people all chose pictures of Jesus on the cross.

Jesus' crucifixion is not a pleasant image compared to a hug, but it is where we see God's love demonstrated most profoundly and powerfully – in weakness and suffering. It has been noted many times that the symbol of the Christian faith is a picture of pain, torture, undeserved death and punishment. I have had good cause to write about it extensively and frequently earlier in this book because, along with the incarnation and resurrection, it is the lens through which we interpret everything else in Scripture.

What the cross means

In the earliest days of the Internet I explored some of the new possibilities that were being opened up by this new media.

I was an AOL user and dipped into some of the text-based chat rooms where more or less anything was discussed and acceptable. If you didn't like it, go somewhere else.

One such room was a New Age and Spirituality forum and I chatted to various people for a while before coming across a woman (it could have been a man of course – who knows?). She claimed to have psychic powers and could predict the future. We talked about faith and meaning and then I asked her what she thought about Jesus' cross.

She told me it was a powerful symbol. I asked her what it symbolized and her answers became vague. She seemed to believe that a great man called Jesus Christ had died a horrible death but I asked: if it was only symbolic, what was the point? When Jesus cried out 'It is finished!' what had he achieved? Was it no more than a symbolic hug?

For me, one helpful way of thinking about the cross is to distinguish between God's love and his justice – and then to discover how they come together at Calvary. We touched on this in previous chapters, but let me explain further. God's love for his world and for each person is very real, but so is his justice and holiness. God's love never changes or diminishes, but he cannot really ignore sin and rebellion. Although the parable of the Prodigal Son (in which the son is welcomed home with a hug) seems to suggest otherwise, that parable is not so much about the mechanics of salvation but about the certainty of the Father's love for his two sons, both of whom think their dad's love for them is dependent on their performance. It isn't.

What the cross achieves

What the cross achieves is the forgiveness of sins in what theologians call a 'forensic' sense. Jesus' death is 'for us' in that it deals with the 'righteous requirement of the law' (Rom. 8:4). To see this from an imaginative literary perspective, read about Aslan's death in *The Lion, the Witch and the Wardrobe*, or for a robust intellectual explanation, read Fleming Rutledge's *The Crucifixion: Understanding the Death of Jesus Christ*.

Rutledge helpfully quotes John Calvin, who is in turn quoting Augustine. The quote is lengthy so I won't reproduce it here, but let me summarize it: the cross doesn't turn a God who hates us into a God who loves us. He always loved us, but it was necessary for the sake of God's justice for a price to be paid.

What does this mean for our vocation? As we have seen, it is the very basis for our understanding of Scripture and it is also the basis for our response to God's word. If God loved us that much, what can we add, what can we owe him, except our very lives? The gospel of grace is totally free and demands everything. In the words of the hymn: 'Love so amazing, so divine, demands my soul, my life, my all.' This understanding must be wrapped around anything we might offer him as our service.

FOR REFLECTION

- Get the words of 'When I Survey the Wondrous Cross', find a quiet place where no one can hear you, and sing the hymn – prayerfully if you wish or loudly if you prefer.

FURTHER READING

Lewis, C.S. *The Lion, the Witch and the Wardrobe* (HarperCollins, 2009).
Rutledge, Fleming. *The Crucifixion: Understanding the Death of Jesus Christ* (Eerdmans, repr. 2017).

66

Jesus' Story (Part 6): Resurrection – Surprise!

The great biblical scholar Tom Wright has pointed out that the resurrection of Jesus was totally unexpected. Even though Jesus talked of it beforehand, his return from death stunned the disciples. This is one of several reasons we should believe it really happened.

The Jews did not have a developed theology of the afterlife. Indeed the very religious Sadducees actually sound remarkably like modern atheists, declaring: 'When you're dead, you're dead.' Their rivals, the Pharisees, did believe in life after death, although not in the way Christians usually think of it. The evidence is unclear, but the ancient Jewish historian Josephus, who was himself a Pharisee, writes about believing in the death of the body but continuation of the soul, even hinting at a sort of belief in reincarnation.

I have come across a common misunderstanding in the contemporary world when taking funerals. Many people believe that the body dies and the soul ascends to heaven – or descends to hell. There's some support for this idea in 2 Corinthians 5, but it's not the full Christian understanding of death, as we will see.

There is a vague belief among people I've met that our soul is immortal and only the body dies. However, let's remember the most famous verse in the Bible: 'For God so loved the world that he gave his one and only Son, that whoever believes in him shall not perish but have eternal life' (John 3:16). This verse is so full of good news that it's easy to miss the reason why it's good news. Only God is eternal *in himself*, but Jesus' death enables his people to have eternal life too. We are born mortal and life after death is not automatic. As we will see, the Christian hope is for physical bodily resurrection, not just a ghostly soul hanging around in the clouds.

Paul's explanation

In 1 Corinthians 15, Paul responds to consternation among some of the people in the Corinthian church because some of them had died. There was an expectation that Jesus' return was imminent, so what was the status of someone whose death occurred before he arrived? It's a long chapter, but we can sum up what Paul has to say fairly briefly.

First of all, he assures his readers that Jesus *has* been raised and there is good, reliable, eyewitness evidence for it (vv. 3–7). Second, he stresses that this matters a lot, because if Jesus isn't raised then our faith is in vain (vv. 12–19). Third, Paul says that Jesus' death is the 'first fruits' of what he achieved on the cross, and that just as Adam's sin brought death to everyone, Jesus' death and resurrection makes the resurrection possible for everyone (vv. 20–34).

In verse 34 onward, Paul then talks about what will actually happen when we die. It will be as though we have gone to sleep in heaven, hence the expression 'Rest in Peace'. John Donne's famous poem written in about 1610, 'Death Be Not Proud', ends with the comforting words:

> One short sleep past, we wake eternally,
> And death shall be no more; death, thou shalt die.

The image of death as a long snooze is a metaphor, but it is a really helpful one, because our experience of sleep is that we lose consciousness and then regain consciousness later but have no sense of time passing in between.

Paul's other metaphor is from the garden. He points out that seeds are buried in the ground – apparently dead. But then in spring they burst forth as a flower or other plant. The resurrection is like this; our new bodies will be physical like our old ones but they will be as different as a seed and a flower. The old body was ugly, weak and perishable, but the new body (actually the same body transformed) will be beautiful, strong and imperishable, and suitable for the new world in which we will live (this world transformed) – and it will be a physical world, though different in ways which we cannot yet conceive.

The resurrected Jesus had a transformed physical body: he still had his scars, and he ate fish in the presence of his disciples – but he could somehow pass through locked doors. John tells us in his letters that we don't quite know yet what we will 'become' after the resurrection, but we do know that we will be like Jesus.

Just a brief thought: isn't all this wonderful?

Paul adds that when Christ returns, those who are dead and 'are his' will rise first and those who are still alive will join them to meet and greet him. This will happen very suddenly – in the twinkling of an eye – which is why Jesus' parables about this are all concerned with being ready. I'll say more in the chapter about the book of Revelation.

But finally, what does all this have to do with vocation, I hear you ask? Yes, it's comforting and reassuring, but what should we do now? Well, as we have just said, we are to be ready. Paul sums it up neatly with a very surprising end to his thoughts about death, the resurrection of Jesus and our own resurrection. He says: 'Therefore, my dear brothers and sisters, stand firm. Let nothing move you. Always give yourselves fully to the work of the Lord, because you know that your labour in the Lord is not in vain' (1 Cor. 15:58).

Riches in heaven

By now, most people have heard the apocryphal tale of the pope's reply when he was asked how to prepare for Jesus coming back suddenly tomorrow: 'Look busy!' He probably never said it, but it's almost good advice. We should be busy, but not pretending to be busy, because the work we do has value for eternity. In Chapter 9 we heard how Abram was told that his true reward for faithfulness was God himself. Nevertheless, there are 'additional benefits' (sometimes called *rewards*) in the Age to Come.

Jesus said: 'store up for yourselves treasures in heaven' (Matt. 6:20), and Paul said:

> For no one can lay any foundation other than the one already laid, which is Jesus Christ. If anyone builds on this foundation using gold, silver, costly stones, wood, hay or straw, their work will be shown for what it is, because the Day will bring it to light. It will be revealed with fire, and the fire will test the quality of each person's work. If what has been built survives, the builder will receive

> a reward. If it is burned up, the builder will suffer loss but yet will be saved – even though only as one escaping through the flames.
>
> (1 Cor. 3:11–15)

Paul says something similar in 1 Timothy 6:17–19.

What we do now builds the kingdom, and when the king returns and the kingdom is complete, it will include the kingdom work we have done in this life. This adds another dimension to our sense of vocation. We should be looking to do work that will last for all eternity.

FOR REFLECTION

- What are you building for the Age to Come?

FURTHER READING

Tolkien, J.R.R. 'Leaf by Niggle' (1945) (short story). You can buy this, but it can also be found as a free download in various places on the web. It's said that Tolkien wrote it when he was struggling to complete *The Lord of the Rings*, and it inspired him to go on.

Wenham, John. *Easter Enigma* (Wipf & Stock, repr. 2005).

Wright, Tom. *Surprised by Hope* (HarperOne, repr. 2018).

67

Jesus' Story (Part 7): Ascension – 'Please Be Seated . . .'

A couple of years ago, a friend joked that the church was suffering with ADHD – ascension deficit hyperactivity disorder. We are so busy celebrating Easter and Pentecost that we forget all about Jesus' dramatic ascension into heaven – forty days after Easter and ten days before Pentecost. I tend to think that the main problem is that it falls on a Thursday, and we don't get a bank holiday.

And yet this important event has some significant things to consider when it comes to vocation. Here's the Bible text of Jesus' last words: 'you will receive power when the Holy Spirit comes on you; and you will be my witnesses in Jerusalem, and in all Judea and Samaria, and to the ends of the earth' (Acts 1:8).

The gospels end with similar words. Matthew ends with the 'Great Commission', which is an instruction to go out into the whole world and make disciples. Here, and at the end of Luke, Jesus is not instructing but foretelling. This is how it will be. The church will go to the ends of the earth with the message of salvation.

Certain hope

But there's something else about the ascension that I want to draw your attention to. Paul writes: 'And God raised us up with Christ and seated us with him in the heavenly realms in Christ Jesus, in order that in the coming ages he might show the incomparable riches of his grace, expressed in his kindness to us in Christ Jesus' (Eph. 2:6–7). This is incredible. Paul tells us that we have already been seated (past tense) with Christ in heaven. This is the way he often writes; we can regard something in the future as though it was in the past because it is so certain.

Recently Manchester City, the richest football club in the world, played lowly Burton Albion in a two-legged cup match. City won the first leg 9–0. The aggregate win after the second leg was a foregone conclusion. The outcome was absolutely certain (FYI City won the second leg, but only 1–0).

Now, in football anything can happen, such as Leicester City winning the Premier League, but with God some things are totally certain. We *will* be seated with Christ in heaven and this is absolutely 100 per cent, no-doubt-about-it, cast-iron, nailed-on certain to happen, even more than tomorrow's sunrise. This is because everything depends on Christ's finished work on the cross, his resurrection and ascension, and nothing depends upon us.

In Christ

Paul has another way of describing this, summed up in the little (and often therefore overlooked) phrase 'in Christ'.

I won't quote the whole text here, but get your Bible, read the first chapter of Ephesians with a fluorescent marker pen, and highlight the times Paul says 'in Christ' or 'in him'. Don't miss the one in the first verse.

When speaking about this I sometimes use an illustration that I think originates with Watchman Nee. I take a piece of paper and put it in various places – on the floor, on my head, on a table, and so on – asking each time: 'Where is the paper now?' Then I put the same piece of paper inside a book, and put it in those places again. The point is, wherever I put the book, that's where the piece of paper is. And for Christians, wherever Jesus is, that's where we are. When he died, rose, ascended and began to reign, that's where we are if we are 'in Christ'. Baptism is symbolic of our incorporation *into* him.

This is incredibly liberating when we consider vocation. Our salvation is certain and we can offer our lives in the confidence that we are secure because of Christ's finished work. If we fall, we will never fall out of his arms.

FOR REFLECTION

- Pray that God will give you complete assurance regarding your salvation.
- Pray for those who seem to lack this.

68

Peter's Story: Even after Failure

We all have different tastes, especially when it comes to art. I live in Wakefield where the Hepworth Gallery contains many of Barbara Hepworth's iconic sculptures. I wonder what she would have made of the statue of Jesus and Peter that stands at the site of Peter's restoration on the shore of Lake Galilee? Personally I'm not a fan. In fact I think it's almost, well, unforgivable. Peter seems to be cowering on his knees.

Peter is often portrayed by preachers as someone with a big heart and a big mouth, into which he often puts his big foot. This may be unfair as Scripture does not set out to give us a comprehensive personality portrait. Nevertheless, he does have some memorable up-and-down moments.

Having been praised for his significant declaration 'You are the Christ, the Son of the Living God', Peter is reminded that this wasn't due to his genius but came by a revelation from heaven. And soon afterwards when he tries to talk Jesus out of the idea that he will suffer and die, Jesus' response is somewhat brutal: 'Get behind me, Satan!'

At the Last Supper Peter and the others boldly declare that they will never let Jesus down, but Jesus warns him that before the cock crows in the morning, he will have already managed to deny his friendship three times. Jesus is never wrong, of course.

As Jesus is violently interrogated overnight, in the high priest's house, Peter is casually interrogated outside by bystanders and eventually swears an oath that he doesn't even know who Jesus is.

Peter's restoration is well known. Three times Jesus asks Peter if he loves him. Three times Peter responds 'Yes, Lord'. And three times Jesus commissions him as someone who will feed his 'sheep', the church. The text says that when Jesus asked the third time, Peter was sad, but he acknowledged 'You know everything'. Peter was being restored, but that didn't mean he was confident that he wouldn't mess up again. And Jesus takes that on board. Peter has learned humility. He's learned that his love is inadequate. Jesus accepts us as we are. He knows that we are fallible.

Of course Jesus also loves us so much that he wants us to change and will work with us to make that happen, but the beginning of true calling is an acknowledgement of our failings and frailties. Vocation is not ultimately 'I can do it!' but 'He can do it through me, and despite me.'

When Jesus had told Peter about his own impending suffering and death, Peter had chided him. But now, after the resurrection, Peter is told that he will one day suffer for his faith and he quietly accepts that this is sometimes God's way. Later, in one of his letters, he warns that we too might be called to suffer, even if we are doing the right thing: 'But if you suffer for doing good and you endure it, this is commendable before God. To this you were called, because Christ suffered for you, leaving you an example, that you should follow in his steps' (1 Pet. 2:20b–21).

So, be assured that when we (inevitably) slip up, we can be restored, but be warned that serving God and doing good might mean martyrdom. This may not seem like good news at the end of this chapter, but consider this verse too: 'The apostles left the Sanhedrin, rejoicing because they had been counted worthy of suffering disgrace for the Name' (Acts 5:41).

FOR REFLECTION

- On a scale of 1–100, how morally good are you? Be brutally honest with yourself.
- Now consider what God's 'pass mark' is for you to be used by him. Are you above or below it? If you think you are above the pass mark, read this chapter again. If you think you are below, read this chapter again.

69

The Apostles' Story: What Jesus Did Next

This chapter will be a long one and it will be noticeably different from other chapters. As we continue our overview of the whole Bible story, we need to look at Acts. Acts tells the story of the early church in the years immediately after Jesus' death, resurrection and ascension. It is not a story of a perfect church by any means, and some writers have made it more prescriptive than perhaps they should. As the story unfolds, I'll mention some of the Old Testament people we have already considered, to show some of the connections between Acts and the Hebrew Scriptures.

I was surprised to realize that, as the author of the gospel and Acts, Luke actually wrote more of the New Testament than Paul. His gospel takes us from Jesus' birth to his resurrection, and Acts begins with his ascension. We heard in the earlier chapter about *Gideon* that the disciples decided to draw lots when seeking guidance, something that the coming of the Holy Spirit changed, but they have to wait for his arrival until Acts chapter 2.

Pentecost means 'fiftieth' and comes fifty days after the Feast of Passover. As we heard in a previous chapter about *Moses*, the Passover supper celebrates the escape from slavery in Egypt and finds its great fulfilment in the Last Supper. Pentecost was a spring festival that celebrated the first harvest. It came early because there are multiple harvests each year in the Middle East.

The festival also celebrated the giving of the law to *Moses* at Mount Sinai, even though three thousand people died at the foot of the mountain. But at the first Christian Pentecost three thousand people were born again. The disciples celebrated the spring (first) harvest of souls. And as a bonus they also demonstrated the reversal of confused languages that began at *Babel*, as we saw earlier in Chapter 6.

Luke began Acts by talking about his first book which described 'all that Jesus began to do and to teach'. Now the work continues in the same vein through the apostles and other believers. In Acts 3 we see the continuation of Jesus' healing ministry through Peter, and in Acts 4, as Jesus predicted, we see the continuation of his persecution. One other thing of note in Acts 4, when it comes to vocation, is the religious leaders' assessment of the apostles: 'When they saw the courage of Peter and John and realised that they were unschooled, ordinary men, they were astonished and they took note that these men had been with Jesus' (Acts 4:13). I don't think I need to labour the point here, but I do think we overplay the need for academic learning rather than the Spirit's empowering.

In the story of *Joshua* we heard about Achan's sin and how it is paralleled in the story of Ananias and Sapphira in Acts 5. We looked forward to the appointment of the seven administrators in the story of *Moses* and Jethro, and how one of them became the first Christian martyr, in Acts 6 and 7.

Acts 8 is the story of Philip and the Ethiopian official, which we unpacked in the story of *Isaac*, and in our chapter about *Samuel* we talked about Saul/Paul's conversion in Acts 9.

The significant story of Peter and Cornelius follows in Acts 10 and 11, as we heard in the chapter about *Israel*, and Acts 12 tells about Peter's miraculous escape from prison.

Acts 13 begins with the setting aside of Saul and Barnabas that we examined in an earlier chapter about *David*, and continues into Acts 14 with some of their adventures that follow, including Paul cursing Elymas with blindness, which we spoke about in the chapter about *Moses* and the ten plagues.

We talked about the Jerusalem council of Acts 15 in the chapter about *Moses* and the law.

In Acts 16, Paul takes on Timothy as his apprentice. We mentioned his circumcision in the chapter about *Moses* and the law, and the apprenticeship model in our chapters about *Joshua* and *Elisha*.

Acts 16 also contains Paul's vision in which a Macedonian man begs Paul to come and help. A few verses earlier we are told that the Holy Spirit ('the Spirit of Jesus') would not let them go where they thought they should be going (Bithynia). Here is guidance at work, although it is not clear how the Holy Spirit prevents them, or if Paul had any guidance other than his vision. In the absence of other factors, a candidate for ordination would have to show that they had other reasons than a dream for us to take them seriously.

Acts 17 tells of Paul's difficulties in Thessalonica and Berea. He has a tougher time in the first of these, but the Bereans are commended for listening to Paul's message and examining what he says in the light of the Scriptures. There are a lot of conversions – 'many of them believed' – and interestingly Luke notes that this included many 'prominent' women and also some men. Luke frequently writes positively about women, against the misogyny of his age, as do many Bible writers. Scripture isn't as male-centric as is often supposed, as we realized in the chapters about *Ruth* and *Esther*.

But troublemakers have followed Paul from Thessalonica so he flees to Athens. In Athens he becomes 'distressed' to see the widespread idol worship. As is his habit, he goes first to the Jewish synagogue and debates with the locals, but also heads to the market square for further opportunities to debate. He meets some Epicurean and Stoic philosophers, who take him to the Areopagus and ask him to speak to a meeting.

The context here is a bit like debates at the university student union; the discussion is mostly intellectual. The people there love having debates. Luke tells us: 'All the Athenians and the foreigners who lived there spent their time doing nothing but talking about and listening to the latest ideas' (Acts 17:21).

The debate at the Areopagus is often seen as a useful model for evangelism in the modern world. Up to this point, much of Acts has been taken up with mission among the Jews and then debate about what is required of Gentile converts. But Paul's ministry in Athens has a more contemporary feel to us. He latches on to his surroundings. He notes the statues and poetry of his context and uses them as illustrations in his speech. I'm not suggesting that Christians should be avid viewers of Saturday night television, but I am saying that Christians who never pick up a newspaper or watch the news channels run the risk of being seen as irrelevant. Missionaries to other cultures know this of course, but we might need to wake up to our own missional context in our own country. By the end of the chapter Paul has won 'a number' of converts.

What else might this have to say about vocation? Speaking at the Leeds Diocese clergy conference in 2016, Paul Bayes, the Bishop of Liverpool, commented: 'The church's vocation is to be distressed by idols – but not moan about them in a curmudgeonly way from the sidelines. How can we speak prophetically with grace to a society that is having vain hope in things that will not satisfy, and offer them the one true hope?'

There is much we could say about Acts 18, but we might particularly note that, as Paul arrives in Corinth, Luke tells us that he is a tentmaker and he meets with Aquila and Priscilla, who are in the same line of work. They've just fled persecution in Rome and so the three of them set up business together.

In the Church of England we have Self-Supporting Ministers ('SSMs'). These are marvellous people who do not take payment from the church for their ministry, and of course there are many in the 'new' churches who have similar financial arrangements.

Luke tells us: 'When Silas and Timothy came from Macedonia, Paul devoted himself exclusively to preaching, testifying to the Jews that Jesus was the Messiah' (Acts 18:5), which suggests that Silas and Timothy's arrival somehow enabled him to 'go full-time'. But this also coincided with his rejection by the synagogue.

Paul turns to the local Gentiles and his ministry is successful. He stays for a while, then travels to Syria with Aquila and Priscilla. The narrative suddenly accelerates and Paul and his companions move rapidly through Ephesus, Caesarea, Jerusalem and Antioch, before a summary verse about him travelling all around 'Galatia and Phrygia, strengthening all the disciples' (Acts 18:23).

In Ephesus Paul and his companions meet a man called Apollos, who oddly 'knew only the baptism of John' but seems to know all about Jesus and is proving to be a great evangelist. This is interesting, since there are those who believe conversion happens at our baptism into the Trinity, and I have even heard it suggested that those in the Salvation Army are not Christians because they don't practise water baptism – an outrageous thought! If this bizarre idea is true, then how come:

1. Apollos is already a great evangelist before he's a baptized Christian?

2. Cornelius and his friends receive the Holy Spirit before their baptism?
3. the dying thief next to Jesus on the cross is told that he's headed for paradise, with little opportunity to pop down to the river to be dunked?

Nevertheless, Priscilla and Aquila take Apollos under their wing and straighten out some of his beliefs and teaching. We have the beginnings here of apprentice ministry, where more experienced Christians take younger Christians and school them in the faith. Growing mature disciples and growing leaders are much neglected aspects within the church. We are not exactly brilliant at evangelism in the UK, but we are even less proficient these days at producing mature disciples. It should surely be the vocation of more of us to build the vocation of others.

In Acts 19 Paul and his friends arrive at Ephesus, where they meet more believers who had 'received John's baptism' but have 'not even heard that there is a Holy Spirit'! These people – about twelve in all – are baptized 'in the name of Jesus', and we are told that 'When Paul placed his hands on them, the Holy Spirit came on them, and they spoke in tongues and prophesied' (Acts 19:6).

Some have suggested that this shows, together with other similar texts in Acts, that tongues and prophecy are normal for every believer, but it is more likely that Luke wants us to see that the Spirit is authenticating his ministry as the gospel spreads from Jerusalem to Judea, Samaria and the ends of the earth, as Jesus foretold.

After this we have the usual scenario in which Paul goes to the synagogue, and when the Jews begin to reject him he moves on to witness to the Gentiles in the area. It's very easy to get the impression that things move very quickly in Acts and that Paul is always on the go, but often we miss the long periods when Paul stays for a while in the same place. Here we learn that he gave daily talks in the lecture hall of Tyrannus for two years.

Just as we settle down to thinking that mission is all about preaching, we hear that Paul was also doing extraordinary miracles – stuff that would make us uncomfortable if TV evangelists did it – such as healing people through contact with his aprons and handkerchiefs. Perhaps we should not be too quick to condemn the vocation of some people who seem wacky to us?

As though to underline this, we go on to read about the seven sons of a Jewish priest called Sceva, who are casting out demons in the power of Jesus' name, even though they are apparently not believers. But one day a possessed man attacks them and they run off naked and bleeding – a sort of reversal of the gospel story about the Gadarene demoniac healed by Jesus. Nevertheless, God is at work in all this, and many fearful people who have demonic scrolls bring them in vast quantities to be burned.

Paul begins to plan to go to Jerusalem and then Rome but stays a little longer in Ephesus, where a riot occurs when the local gift-shop owners realize that their trinkets of the goddess Artemis will not sell well if people become Christians.

Acts 20 continues with Paul leaving Ephesus for a while but eventually arranging for the church elders from there to come to him in Miletus. Before a tearful farewell, he gives a final speech reviewing his last three years with them and kneels to pray.

We hear of several prophecies in Acts 21, each suggesting Paul's life is at risk if he goes to Jerusalem, but he persists. Prophetic messages that warn us of danger ahead do not have to be a reason to give up. Jesus was aware of the suffering that lay ahead of him when he set out for Jerusalem. And as we have heard, Jesus also prophesied to Peter regarding the way he would die a martyr, but Peter went ahead.

Sadly, much of what passes for prophecy in charismatic circles can be weak and innocuous. Sometimes it's true and powerful, but it can be rare to hear someone share much beyond 'God loves you and he's very nice', though it would be a brave woman or man who predicts a gruesome end for someone, like Jesus' words to Peter.

Inevitably, soon after arriving in Jerusalem, Paul's arrival provokes a riot and he is arrested, though he is allowed to speak to the crowd. He shares his conversion testimony, which is all very fine until he mentions that Jesus commissioned him to preach to the Gentiles. This reignites the riot, and the confused Roman centurion sends him to the barracks to be flogged. Paul mischievously waits until the last moment to mention that he is a Roman citizen. The centurion is horrified because it's illegal to chain up a Roman citizen until he or she is proved guilty in a trial.

What follows in Acts 23 is almost comical, as Paul defends himself before the Sanhedrin, provoking yet another riot, and eventually he is escorted by 200 soldiers, 70 horsemen and 200 spearmen to protect him on his journey to stand before Felix, the governor of Caesarea. Paul could have made his own way to Rome – his eventual intended destination – but now he has a vast armed guard!

But it's not all plain sailing (sometimes literally – see below). After Paul speaks to Felix in Acts 24, he is left to wait in jail for two whole years until Felix is replaced by Festus. Note, however, that Paul is not wasting his time while in prison. It's evident from some of his letters that he is using the opportunity to witness to the other prisoners and guards. If you feel as if you are currently 'marking time' while waiting for God to use you in a special way, are you missing opportunities to share your faith or do other work for him?

Jesus had told his apostles that they would testify before kings, and now in Acts 25, Paul – the 'twelfth apostle' – testifies not only before Festus but also in the presence of King Agrippa, the grandson of Herod, whom we last saw in Acts 12.

We hear Paul's important testimony for the third time in Acts 26. Agrippa decides that he must be sent to Rome because he has appealed to Caesar, and the first half of Acts 27 concerns the voyage across the eastern Mediterranean. This time it is Paul who prophesies disaster, for it's not really safe to set sail at this time of year. It seems likely that was not so much a Spirit-inspired message as plain common sense and wisdom. But they sail anyway and the ship is wrecked in a storm. Paul has reassured the crew and passengers – this time probably inspired by the Holy Spirit – that no one will perish, and he is proved right as they all wash up in Malta, on the shore of St Paul's Bay. What a coincidence.

In Acts 28 the islanders welcome the castaways and we read the amusing tale in which Paul is bitten by a snake, though not amusing for Paul at the time. At first the superstitious islanders think this is a certain sign that he has murdered someone and he's getting his just deserts. But when he casually shakes the snake into the fire, they swing to the opposite extreme and decide he is a god. Sometimes our ministries will be misunderstood because of prior expectations.

Arriving in Rome, Paul meets with the Jewish leaders and once again he moves on after they reject him. The book ends with him continuing to share the gospel: 'For two whole years Paul stayed there in his own rented house and welcomed all who came to see him. He proclaimed the kingdom of God and taught about the Lord Jesus Christ – with all boldness and without hindrance!' (Acts 28:30–31).

More chapters?

These are the last two verses of the book, and also in a sense the end of Bible history. Is this the end of God's big story? Well, we might add a few things. First, Paul tells us where this is all going in a previous verse: 'Therefore I want you to know that God's salvation has been sent to the Gentiles, and they will listen!' (Acts 28:28).

Second, the story – God's big story – will be truly completed when we read Revelation. Although that book is mostly about the events of the time it was written, it will finally tell us how God's big story ends in chapters 20–22. We'll get there shortly in this book.

Third, as this book is about God's story and discerning where we fit in, perhaps one day Luke will write an ending to Acts, and we will be in it. By Acts 28, the gospel had only reached Rome, so Jesus' prophetic words about the gospel being preached 'to the ends of the earth' were still to be fulfilled. Over to you.

FOR REFLECTION

- If you can get the time, sit down and read the whole of Acts in one go. Alternatively read it over several days and note as you go along how Jesus' words about the spread of the gospel in Acts 1:8 are being fulfilled.
- Watch out for Luke's six summary verses: 6:7; 9:31; 12:24; 16:5; 19:20; 28:31 (seven if you include 1:8).
- If Luke writes more chapters one day, in the Age to Come, what might he say about you?

70

Paul's Story: Power in Weakness

Although Luke was the one who wrote the most words, the two great giants of the New Testament are Peter and Paul. Having covered Paul's adventures in Acts, we turn to his letters. We have quoted him extensively elsewhere, but although there is so much more we could say about Paul and his teaching, we are going to limit ourselves to a couple of important things that have special relevance for vocation: one of his key themes, and one particular thing about Paul himself.

Peter describes Paul's letters in this way: 'His letters contain some things that are hard to understand, which ignorant and unstable people distort, as they do the other Scriptures, to their own destruction' (2 Pet. 3:16). Notice that Peter is already calling Paul's letters 'Scripture', even in his lifetime. As he says, Paul's letters can be challenging to read, probably because many of them were written in response to problems in churches that he had founded. We only see part of the correspondence, so, with the exception of Romans and Ephesians, Paul is not writing about theology in a systematic way. He's dealing with very specific issues.

Nevertheless, there are some things that Paul talks about that are his key themes. Two of them are apparent opposites, but in fact both are vital. There are two sides to Christ's work expressed in two simple statements.

First, you and I are *in Christ*. We covered this in the earlier chapter about Jesus' ascension.

Second, *Christ is in you and in me*.

Every fruit of our union with Christ is governed by these two statements of what God has done. Jesus himself puts this in a concise sentence which says: 'Abide in me, and I in you' (John 15:4).

The thorn in the flesh

One great mystery about Paul concerns what he calls his 'thorn in the flesh', which he discusses in 2 Corinthians 12. There are various views about what Paul's thorn actually was. The Good News Bible boldly translates it as 'a painful physical ailment' but we can't be sure. One strong theory is that he suffered partial blindness as an ongoing consequence of his Damascus road experience. Galatians hints at this:

> As you know, it was because of an illness that I first preached the gospel to you, and even though my illness was a trial to you, you did not treat me with contempt or scorn. Instead, you welcomed me as if I were an angel of God, as if I were Christ Jesus himself. Where, then, is your blessing of me now? I can testify that, if you could have done so, you would have torn out your eyes and given them to me.
>
> (Gal. 4:13–15)

The dreadful 'health and wealth' teaching that has permeated many areas of the western church is not only unbiblical but also extremely damaging. A Christianity in which we expect God to make us healthy and wealthy because we are his followers forgets what happened to the founder, a man of sorrows with nowhere to lay his head. As we heard in the chapter about *Job*, a transactional relationship with God is not the gospel.

It's also deeply distressing for anyone with ill-health or disability, because guilt is loaded upon their other troubles as they feel they have inadequate faith. The chapter on Job reflects on this, but also note that such unscriptural teaching neglects the power that God can demonstrate through people who are suffering.

God's power in our weakness

Mabel was a member of the preaching team when I was a vicar. She had been a Methodist lay preacher and she preached for us occasionally with the bishop's permission and encouragement. Mabel had been totally blind for many years and all her sermons were carefully memorized. Somehow her weakness gave her preaching an extra dimension. The congregation seemed to listen especially carefully when she spoke.

When I was a curate, I worked a lot in local schools, especially our local church school. One week we had a visitor called Alyn Haskey in the parish and I took him into the school to speak in assemblies. His talks had a lot more power than mine. I used props, jokes, stories, songs and a whole array of gimmicks to get attention, but this guy just spoke quietly. He was difficult to hear. His words were slurred and sentences were hard to follow at first. But the children and staff listened with rapt attention.

Alyn was born with severe cerebral palsy. He could not walk, had to be fed by a helper, drink with a straw, and needed to be carried to the toilet. He was written off as a child and education was seen as a waste of time. In his early teens, through a radio programme he heard, he became a Christian. Because

God believed in him, he began to believe in himself. He began to write and study, not only managing O levels but eventually gaining a BA in theology. He won a bronze medal at the 1984 Paralympics in the seven-a-side football squad.

In Alyn's *Church Times* obituary (29 February 2012) Rachel Farmer writes about one of the books he wrote: 'In the book, he refers to his disability as a means of encouragement, never clouded by self-pity, but in a conversational style that is gentle and humorous. It was this approach that made him effective in sharing his faith with young people. He worked across the country, visiting schools, running holiday clubs, and engaging in parish missions, and much else besides.'

Alyn was a diocesan evangelist and was ordained into the Church of England, later becoming an advisor in evangelism. God worked in him and through his disabilities, not despite them. I counted it a privilege to minister with him. We neglect those around us who are differently abled at our peril.

FOR REFLECTION

- What weaknesses/disabilities do you have that might actually be part of your vocation?
- At the end of his week in our local schools, Alyn preached at a Sunday service in my church. The text he chose was the second half of John 10:10. I'm not going to quote it; go and look it up and then sit quietly reflecting on what you think he might have said.

OTHER

There are various Christian charities working with disabled people. You could consider supporting their work through giving, prayer or direct involvement. Through the Roof is one example:

- https://www.throughtheroof.org/

71

John's Story: Does God Have Favourites?

In John's gospel there are references to 'the disciple whom Jesus loved'. It's not absolutely certain, but it is widely assumed that this is John the writer of the gospel, not John the Baptist but John the apostle, brother of James and, along with Peter, one of the 'inner three' whom Jesus occasionally takes with him at key moments, such as on the Mount of Transfiguration, the time when he raises Jairus's daughter, and in Gethsemane.

There are reasons why I think this probably is John, which I won't go into here, but the more interesting thing is the thought that Jesus had a favourite disciple. Why not? We all have friends and we all have friends we prefer. It's not a sin, just a matter of circumstances and taste. I have favourite friends – I'm just not going to say who they are.

But for me, the best bit about John is actually in the passage where Jesus restores Peter, which we looked at previously. After Peter has been forgiven and recommissioned, he notices that John has been lingering nearby, probably to find out how much trouble his friend was in! Now he's been restored, Peter gestures towards John and asks 'What about him?' Jesus' reply is blunt and amusing: 'What about him? What if I want him to live for ever? You follow me!'

The text adds that rumours about this arose later, suggesting that in fact John really was going to live for ever. This is unsurprising since the early church literature suggests that John was the only apostle to escape martyrdom and reach old age. But we digress. What we need to note is that when Peter starts to ask about someone else, Jesus draws the focus back upon Peter: *you* follow me!

Self-worth

One of the particular curses of modern life is the problem of self-image and self-worth. Those who run advice columns, those who are trained counsellors, will tell you that a high percentage of problems come from how we feel about ourselves. And that often springs from comparing ourselves with others. If we are not spending our time wishing we were like someone else, we spend it looking down on those we feel superior to.

In 1 Corinthians chapters 12–14 Paul examines the Corinthians' attitude to spiritual gifts. It's apparent that they have all decided that to be truly spiritual you must speak in tongues. The same problem plagued the early years of Pentecostalism and then charismatic renewal. Anyone who spoke in tongues often thought themselves to be 'better' than other Christians. Those who didn't do it felt themselves to be second-class Christians. Paul later points out that tongues is the least of the gifts and he would rather people prophesy.

Ephesians 4 declares that we are all one in Christ. 1 Corinthians 12 says that although we are all one, we are all different. The church is one body with many parts. And just like a body, all those parts are necessary. Every part belongs, no part is excluded, and they are all different.

When we were in Ghana a few years ago, we noticed that there were quite a few cars and vans with Bible verses written on them. But my favourite was not a direct quote from any part of Scripture. It simply said: 'I am who Jesus says I am.' A biblical version of this could be: 'I care very little if I am judged by you or by any human court; indeed, I do not even judge myself. My conscience is clear, but that does not make me innocent. It is the Lord who judges me' (1 Cor. 4:3–4).

Although he had been restored and recommissioned, Peter needed to learn that he was not John, and John was not Peter. There is a similar lesson here for all of us. We all need to know and understand this vital principle: if God calls you and you can get to that place where you know your specific personal vocation, be content with it. Don't compare yourself with someone else and wish that was your calling. Be yourself. No one else is qualified to be you. Don't try to be someone else. You are not qualified to be them. Seek first the kingdom of God, and everything else will be added.

FOR REFLECTION

- Who do you wish you were? One of your friends? A famous person? Prayerfully recognize that they are who they are and you are who you are. God calls you as you, not someone else.
- Thank God for who you are. Offer that person – you – to God afresh, to be used for his glory.

72

Jesus' Story (Part 8): 'I'll Be Back'

Imagine reading all the Harry Potter books but when you get to the final book (*The Deathly Hallows*), you completely forget everything you read before. You decide that the story is really all about Europe or the USA. Voldemort is either the American president, the pope, or a personification of the European Union. Hogwarts is the church, the UK, or the European Union. It would be fun to go on, but I have already made the point. It may seem silly but people do this kind of thing with the Bible and especially with Revelation.

I witnessed this first-hand with a group of intelligent Christian friends when we studied Revelation together. I had to keep reminding the group (and myself, I admit) that we must let Scripture interpret Scripture, and not try and read our modern context into Revelation. Revelation (and other parts of Scripture, especially Ezekiel and Daniel) uses a special genre of literature called 'apocalyptic', which involves the use of strange imagery.

The Bear

Towards the end of April in 1986, a major disaster occurred at the Chernobyl nuclear power plant in the Ukrainian area of the

Soviet Union. As the news about the leak . . . er . . . leaked out, everyone was worrying about the short- and long-term effects. Could we in Britain be in any danger?

At the time, I was working with a team of computer consultants whose on-site manager had previously been the captain of an American nuclear submarine. He called his team into his office for a briefing, saying: 'I just want to let you know what the Bear's up to.'

'The Bear' would be instantly recognizable to those who followed serious news media around that time but maybe not so much nowadays. It was a symbol of Russia going back several centuries, but in political cartoons, especially during the Cold War, the Bear was shorthand for the USSR.

This illustrates the problem we have when we interpret apocalyptic writing. The authors are using almost cartoon-like imagery which would have been much better understood by their contemporaries. The most famous stage direction in any play is from *The Winter's Tale* by Shakespeare, which says: *'Exit, pursued by a bear.'* Did Shakespeare have Russia in the twentieth century in mind? Of course not. If Revelation mentioned a bear (it doesn't) it would be very unlikely to symbolize the USSR in the twentieth century. It does mention a dragon, but that does not mean Wales.

The end times . . . now?

A few years ago, an experienced church pastor confidently told me that the seven churches of Revelation represent the seven eras of Christianity and that we are now in the final Laodicean era, as evidenced by the current lukewarmness of the church. He went quiet when I gently pointed out that outside western

Europe the church across the world is stronger and flourishing more than ever. His interpretation is rather parochial at best.

I have a book that was published early in the twentieth century, called *Light for the Last Days*. It has an impressive pull-out chart which outlines all of human history, and ends when Jesus returns in about 1958. Apparently that didn't happen. See your local Jehovah's Witnesses for further examples.

The Rapture

The return of Christ was a much hotter topic when I was growing up in the 1960s and 1970s than it is today. In the Christian subculture, heavily promoted in the USA, there were books such as Hal Lindsey's *The Late Great Planet Earth*, films such as *Thief in the Night* and songs like Larry Norman's 'I Wish We'd All Been Ready'. Even today there are ripples of this in books/films such as the Left Behind series. It's a significant part of the American evangelical mindset for some people.

Although Jesus warned that no one would know the time of his coming, the Cold War atmosphere created a climate of expectation that The End Is Near and we'd better be prepared. Poor exegesis also created an emphasis on the 'Rapture', with an expectation that millions of Christians would all suddenly float up to heaven, leaving behind the heathen to suffer a terrible Armageddon. I confess that I believed it myself for many years.

The sad thing about all this is that bad theology can create bad practice. If Christians are being taken out of the world, why should we care what will happen to it? We don't need to worry about the environment or using up all the natural resources. God's going to wipe it all out and start again, isn't he?

Death and afterwards

Let's sort a few things out, but keep in mind that there is much we don't know and maybe don't need to know. Jesus warned that no one, not even him, knew the day or hour of his return. Other parts of Scripture say that we don't know too much about what happens afterwards either. For example: 'Dear friends, now we are children of God, and what we will be has not yet been made known. But we know that when Christ appears, we shall be like him, for we shall see him as he is' (1 John 3:2).

As we have already seen, 1 Corinthians 15 is an extended meditation on death and what happens afterwards. Here there is no rising to sit on fluffy clouds and play harps for ever. As the great theologian Bart Simpson pointed out, that would be very boring. Instead Paul tells us that death is like sleep, and when the last day comes, those Christians who are dead/asleep will rise and join those who are still alive, together meeting Christ. Heaven is currently a place of rest until Jesus returns, as we have said previously.

The biblical mindset is not about escaping earth to go to heaven but about the 'Age to Come', a concept that existed before the time of Christ. In fact, in Acts 1 the disciples thought that Jesus was bringing in the New Age immediately after his resurrection. In one sense he was – but this was just the start and he was expecting the disciples to help. The work would not be completed until his return.

When Christ does return, he is coming to earth to stay and bringing heaven with him. The verses about going up to meet him use the language of the citizens of a city going out to meet their victorious king and his army returning from battle. The kingdom of God that we pray and work for has begun (theologians use the term 'inaugurated'), but when Jesus returns, his kingdom will come fully. It will literally be heaven on earth. 1 Corinthians 15 makes it clear that this will be different from the world now, but it will nevertheless be a physical existence.

A new heaven and earth – together

This is the image in Revelation:

> Then I saw 'a new heaven and a new earth,' for the first heaven and the first earth had passed away, and there was no longer any sea. I saw the Holy City, the new Jerusalem, coming down out of heaven from God, prepared as a bride beautifully dressed for her husband. And I heard a loud voice from the throne saying, 'Look! God's dwelling-place is now among the people, and he will dwell with them. They will be his people, and God himself will be with them and be their God. "He will wipe every tear from their eyes. There will be no more death" or mourning or crying or pain, for the old order of things has passed away.'
>
> (Rev. 21:1–4)

The point of much of the biblical teaching about the return of Christ is readiness for whenever he appears. Because we don't know when that will be, we are called to be ready: 'Now, brothers and sisters, about times and dates we do not need to write to you, for you know very well that the day of the Lord will come like a thief in the night. While people are saying, "Peace and safety," destruction will come on them suddenly, as labour pains on a pregnant woman, and they will not escape' (1 Thess. 5:1–3).

Here comes the bride

One of the joys of being a vicar is conducting weddings. I used to enjoy the rehearsal a few days beforehand, especially having some fun to help relax the couple's inevitable nerves. I would take the bride and her father to the entrance and ask them to practise walking slowly down the aisle. Then, returning to the front of the church, I would tell the groom to turn and enjoy the sight of his beautiful bride walking towards him. I would add: 'Remember, she's spent hours getting ready – she'll never look this good again.'

Many of the weddings I have conducted were between couples already living together, but in the past the wedding night was often the first time the groom saw his wife undressed. The white wedding dress symbolized virginity and purity. Remember back in an early chapter, when we talked about the fall and Adam and Eve's nakedness? God provided animal skins to cover their shame.

In Revelation, John writes:

> Hallelujah! For our Lord God Almighty reigns.
> Let us rejoice and be glad and give him glory!
> For the wedding of the Lamb has come, and his bride has made herself ready.
> Fine linen, bright and clean, was given her to wear.
>
> (Rev. 19:6–8)

Our collective vocation and the way we live our individual lives involves the responsibility to prepare for the Groom. We do have to be ready, not for departure as we are raptured away from this world, but instead ready as a bride for the grand arrival of our husband, wearing the clothes given to us. As John writes: 'All who have this hope in him purify themselves, just as he is pure' (1 John 3:3).

FOR REFLECTION

- 'Purity' is an unfashionable word these days. Reflect on your life and how this word makes you feel.
- What should we do to be ready for Jesus' return?

FURTHER READING

Holmes, Stephen, and Russell Rook, eds. *What Are We Waiting For?* (Paternoster, 2008).

Paul, Ian. *Revelation* (IVP, 2018).

Thiselton, Anthony C. *The Last Things* (SPCK, 2012).

Wright, Tom. *Surprised by Hope* (HarperOne, repr. 2018).

73

Your Story: God's Story

So what?

Earlier in this book I told some of my own story. A new curate came to my church, preached about vocation and suggested to me that God was calling me to consider ordination. About a dozen Christians whom I respected made the same suggestion. At Spring Harvest 1987 our friend Denise became the latest to push me to consider it. In the afternoon of the same day a complete stranger challenged me about getting out of my comfort zone.

The evening meeting was a big celebration in a big circus tent. The speaker was Caesar Molebatsi, a South African preacher from Soweto. I knew from hearing a talk by the late David Watson that Caesar had been through some tough times and was not a triumphalist. He had lost his leg in an accident caused by a white man, and when he sought compensation from the government, the official turned to him and said: 'Why should I care if a dog dies?' And yet here Caesar was, a gentle, grace-filled Christian.

He spoke (you guessed it) about God's calling on our lives and challenged us to consider that we might be being too individualistic about it. He described this as being like a soldier marching on a parade ground refusing to obey orders because the drill sergeant doesn't speak to us personally, by name. There is a need for people to serve God, so get on with it.

He also talked about a picture he had in his mind of the day of judgement, when God will burn up in fire all the useless things we have done, leaving only the treasures we have stored up by our good works carried out in response to God's grace in Jesus Christ and his cross and resurrection.

I'm sure he was thinking of Paul's words from 1 Corinthians 3 that we quoted earlier. He says that our works will be 'tested' by fire on the last day. What will be left of what we have done? A pile of ash?

So what should I do?

I hope this book has taken some pressure off you, and you've recognized that vocation is not all about being a superstar for God, an ultra-holy saint surrounded in light, and that the Bible is primarily about Jesus first, not us. The Bible is God's great story from creation to the new creation, and vocation is finding our part in that marvellous unfolding plan.

At the same time I also want to encourage you: God does not call super-spiritual superstar Christians, but he does call everyone. Yes, it's all about him, but his big plan includes you in some way, big or small.

An Internet meme currently circulating says: 'I've just bought my friend a card that says "I hope you get better." He's not ill; I just think he could make more effort.' Although I have been stressing that it is all about God, we have a part to play, some choices to make and some work to do. Sometimes we could make more effort.

Vocation: joining in

As I write these words, only a few hours ago I heard Rowan Williams, the former Archbishop of Canterbury, speaking about prayer. One of his key points was that prayer is not primarily about us asking God to do something. Prayer is already going on. The Son is interceding for us, and the Holy Spirit is our advocate – enabling us to cry '*Abba*, Father' (Rom. 8:15). Instead, when we pray we are slipping into this stream of communication that is already happening.

Similarly, when it comes to mission and evangelism, writers such as David Bosch and Lesslie Newbigin have said that mission is not primarily something we do but something God does and which he invites us to join in with.

And so vocation (if you want another really short definition) is really about seeing what God is up to and joining in. This is very different from the common image of vocation as 'God speaks directly to me and I do it', which is very individualistic. I spoke with Archbishop Rowan about this, suggesting that maybe we in the Church of England need to take this on board in the way we assess vocation. He agreed, but added with a wink: 'Good luck with that!'

It's all about God

I hope that one thing this book might have done is give you a bigger vision of God. Ultimately, he is in charge. If I've read

Scripture right, so many of the stories we've heard are about God moving sovereignly in his world and in individual lives almost before people have had time to think. When it comes to the 'heroes' of the Bible, things sometimes seem to happen to them, not through them, at times against their will. In our modern world where 'choice' is the god of . . . er . . . choice, we risk ignoring this.

Having made a big career change from the world of IT to train for ordination, my second most significant step was moving from running a parish church to being Diocesan Director of Ordinands and Vocations. On my last day in the parish, after my emotional farewell service ended, a friend drove me to Manchester, where I was blessed to see a concert by Canadian singer-songwriter Bruce Cockburn, whom I much admire. I spoke to him after the gig and commented: 'Thank you, Bruce, for sharing yourself in your songs.'

He smiled at me and replied: 'As if I had a choice . . .'

Serious discipleship

And yet . . .

Although it's God's big story, this does not let us off the hook concerning serious discipleship and God's command to love him with all our heart, soul, mind and strength, and our neighbours as ourselves. I heard someone preaching recently say: 'Jesus' vocation has implications for our vocation.' When he explained to his disciples that it was his vocation to go to Jerusalem, suffer, die and rise, he added that his disciples must deny themselves and take up their cross daily.

What now?

So what will you do now you've read this book? If you are seeking guidance about your future, here are some thoughts:

1. Pray.
2. Keep reading the Bible, remembering it is God's story, not yours, and you are looking for your place in what he's already done and is doing – in history, in your nation, town, neighbourhood, church, home and life.
3. Actively seek those things we are told to pursue in the Bible: holiness, wisdom, spiritual gifts, the kingdom of God, Jesus himself.
4. Don't rush into any life-changing decision.
5. Go back through the questions for reflection at the end of each chapter and use them in whatever way they help you to reflect.
6. Ask God to speak to you – and be open to ways he might do that. Give him time!
7. If God speaks to you, say '*Hineni*'.
8. Surround any decisions with good common sense (unless there are really clear indicators otherwise – which will be rare).
9. Discuss with others, especially people who love you and will give you an honest answer and say what you might not want to hear.
10. Remember that God's will is not a tightrope. If things don't work out, it's not the end. He can restore you and use you.
11. Reflect: if I can see myself as serving God in Christ in what I am doing now, then maybe that is enough. Blossom where you are planted, as someone once said.

12. Wherever you find yourself, love God with all your might and love your neighbour as much as yourself.
13. Put Jesus before your family, but put family before your church.
14. Remember that it's not about you.
15. Remember that it's all about Jesus.

And finally . . .

I will be praying for everyone who reads this book. If you've found it helpful, perhaps you could encourage others to read it. You could buy them a copy . . .

'We always thank God for all of you and continually mention you in our prayers. We remember before our God and Father your work produced by faith, your labour prompted by love, and your endurance inspired by hope in our Lord Jesus Christ' (1 Thess. 1:2–3).

Acknowledgements

Thanks to . . .

My wife Carolyn and my children Matt, Paul and Sarah and their families. I'm incredibly proud of you all.

Those who have influenced my life and the writing of this book in so many ways. There are really too many to mention but they include:

My brother Roy; Barry, Jean, Peter, Cliff and Betty Chivers, Joanne and Chris (RIP) Booth, Maxine Coupe, Sue Munslow, Paul and Nicky Parkinson, Anji and Greg Thomson, Graham and Rona Helliwell, Rose and Simon Hart, Diane Komorowski, Jenice Guild, Karl and Sue Jones, Sheila Robinson, Howard and Jane Carter, Steve and Revd Fran Grasham, Andrew and Val Steele, Michael and Audrey Parkinson, Vera Jackson, Revd Michael and Daphne Savage, Revd Keith and Mary Knight, Joanne Meehan, Steve and Julie Green, John and Sue Ritter, Joanna Cannon, Norman and Christine Hall, Byron and Trisha Tilly, Mandy Aspland, Dudley and Moira Cockcroft, Josephine and Duncan Green, Mary Heaton and Heather Bartle.

Reverends John Rogan, Arthur Moon (RIP), Peter Nunn, Ian Pusey, Douglas Jamieson, Stephen Race, Ann Turner, Ian Paul, Tim Roberts, Peter Hall, Greg Webb (RIP), Elwin

Cockett, Andrew Norman, Beth Maynard, Raewynne Whitely, Steve Proudlove, Helen Hodgson, Gerald Bray, Paul Woodbridge, Arani Sen, Debbi Turley, Richard Radley, Nigel Wright, John Long, John Ineson, Tracy Raistrick, Steve and Ali Walton, Mark and Leah Vasey-Saunders, Linda Maslen, Mike Royal, Theo Asare, George Jarvis, Cat Thatcher, Tim Harford, Mike Butterworth, Ann Mackenzie, Sam Corley, Bernhard Shunemann, David Foster, Tim Jones, Dave Male, Lisa Holmes, Magdalen Smith and Peter Mott.

Bishops John Pritchard, Nick Baines, Mark Tanner, Sarah Mullally, Philip North, Chris Edmundson, John Holbrook, John Flack and Jill Duff.

Dr Tim Keller, whose books and downloaded sermons have been a huge inspiration for this book.

Some other people who are mentioned in the main text of the book.

The music and lyrics of U2, Jethro Tull and Bruce Cockburn, the soundtrack to my life.

My editor, Mollie Barker, Donna Harris, Rachel Franklin, Becky Fawcett, Charlie Cuthbert and the rest of the team at Authentic Media.

And thank you to everyone else I have forgotten, because although I have over 600 friends on Facebook, I am not good at remembering names. But God loves you and me anyway . . . and he always remembers my name. He calls me by it.

Our Precious Lives

Why telling and hearing stories can save the church

Steve Morris

In a world of increasing social fragmentation and loneliness, *Our Precious Lives* demonstrates how listening to others can be transformational in creating a sense of belonging. Inspiring stories are grounded by practical ideas to put storytelling at the heart of the church, and questions in each chapter encourage us all to glimpse more of God, revel in our uniqueness and realize that we all have something valuable to offer as his followers.

Underpinned by practical pastoral experience, this is a book full of quirky and unexpected life stories that open us up afresh to the beauty of life and our God.

978-1-78893-079-6

Overflow

Learning from the inspirational resource church of Antioch in the book of Acts

Matthew Porter

Birthed out of The Belfrey, York's call to overflow with the presence and power of God into their locality and region with all the resources God gives, Matthew Porter shares stories of what they have been learning and how this may help the church to reach out in mission and see many come to Christ.

Overflow describes characteristics, structures and strategies that any community of Christ-followers desiring to reach out beyond themselves can adopt. Questions are included at the end of each chapter, with some for individual application and some to help start activating gifts in others.

Discover the God of overflow, who invites us to give away what he gives, and be encouraged to make steps to become a church of overflow, spilling out with the good news of Christ.

978-1-78893-125-0

A–Z of Prayer

Building strong foundations for daily conversations with God

Matthew Porter

A–Z of Prayer is an accessible introduction that gives practical guidance on how to develop a meaningful prayer life. It presents twenty-six aspects of prayer to help you grow in your relationship with God, explore new devotional styles and deepen your daily conversations with God.

Each topic has a few pages of introduction and insight, an action section for reflection and application and a prayer to help put the action point into practice. There are also references to allow further study.

978-1-78893-062-8

A-Z of Discipleship

Building strong foundations for a life of following Jesus

Matthew Porter

A–Z of Discipleship is an accessible introduction to the understanding and practice of the Christian faith. It presents twenty-six aspects of discipleship to help you grow in your relationship with God, connect with church and live as a follower of Christ in contemporary culture.

Each topic has a few pages of introduction and insight, an action section for reflection and application and a prayer to help put the action point into practice. There are also references to allow further study.

978-1-78078-456-4

Finding Our Voice

Unsung lives from the Bible resonating with stories from today

Jeannie Kendall

The Bible is full of stories of people facing issues that are still surprisingly relevant today. Within its pages, people have wrestled with problems such as living with depression, losing a child, overcoming shame, and searching for meaning. Yet these are not always the stories of the well-known heroes of faith, but those of people whose names are not even recorded.

Jeannie Kendall brings these unnamed people to vibrant life. Their experiences are then mirrored by a relevant testimony from someone dealing with a similar situation today.

Finding Our Voice masterfully connects the past with the present day, encouraging us to identify with the characters' stories, and giving us hope that, whatever the circumstances, we are all 'known to God'.

978-1-78893-037-6

God Conversations

Stories of how God speaks and what happens when we listen

Tania Harris

Stories of God talking to his people abound throughout the Bible, but we usually only get the highlights. We read: 'God said "Go to Egypt,"' and then, 'Mary and Joseph left for Egypt.' We're not told how God spoke, how they knew it was him, or how they decided to act on what they'd heard.

In *God Conversations*, international speaker and pastor Tania Harris shares insights from her own story of learning to hear God's voice. You'll get to eavesdrop on some contemporary conversations with God in the light of his communication with the ancients. Part memoir, part teaching, this unique and creative collection will help you to recognize God's voice when he speaks and what happens when you do.

978-1-78078-188-4

Infused with Life

Exploring God's gift of rest in a world of busyness

Andy Percey

In a stressful, task-orientated life, we know the importance of rest, but it is too often pushed out of our busy schedules.

Join Andy Percey as he reveals that rest is actually God's good gift to us, provided for us to experience a balance in our lives that isn't just about rest as recovery, but rest as harmony with our Creator and the world he has made.

By learning to practise life-giving rhythms of rest, we can be infused with the very best of the life God freely gives us.

978-1-78893-065-9